·CINCINNATI· CANDY

CINCINNATI

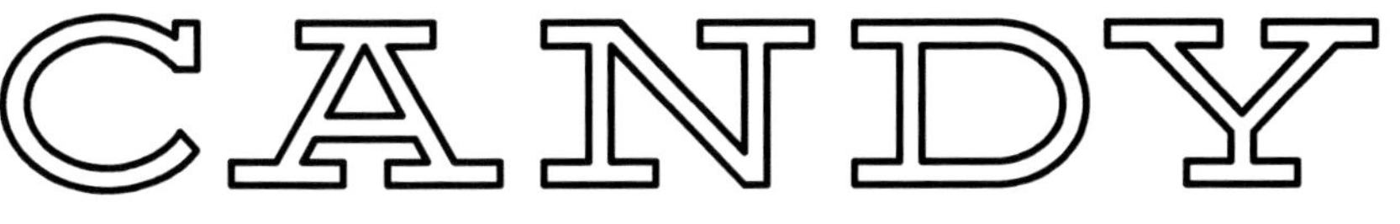

A Sweet History

DANN WOELLERT

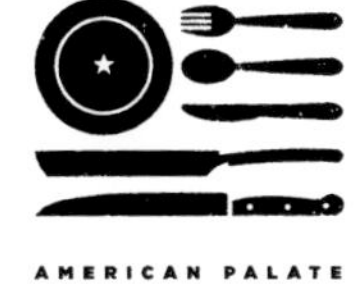

Published by American Palate
A Division of The History Press
Charleston, SC
www.historypress.net

Front cover, left to right: Doscher candy canes. *Jeremy Kramer*; Schneider's Sweet Shop. *Kenton County Public Library*; candy corn. *Author's collection*; Doscher Brothers. *Cindy Doscher*.

First published 2017

Manufactured in the United States

ISBN 9781467137959

Library of Congress Control Number: 2017948448

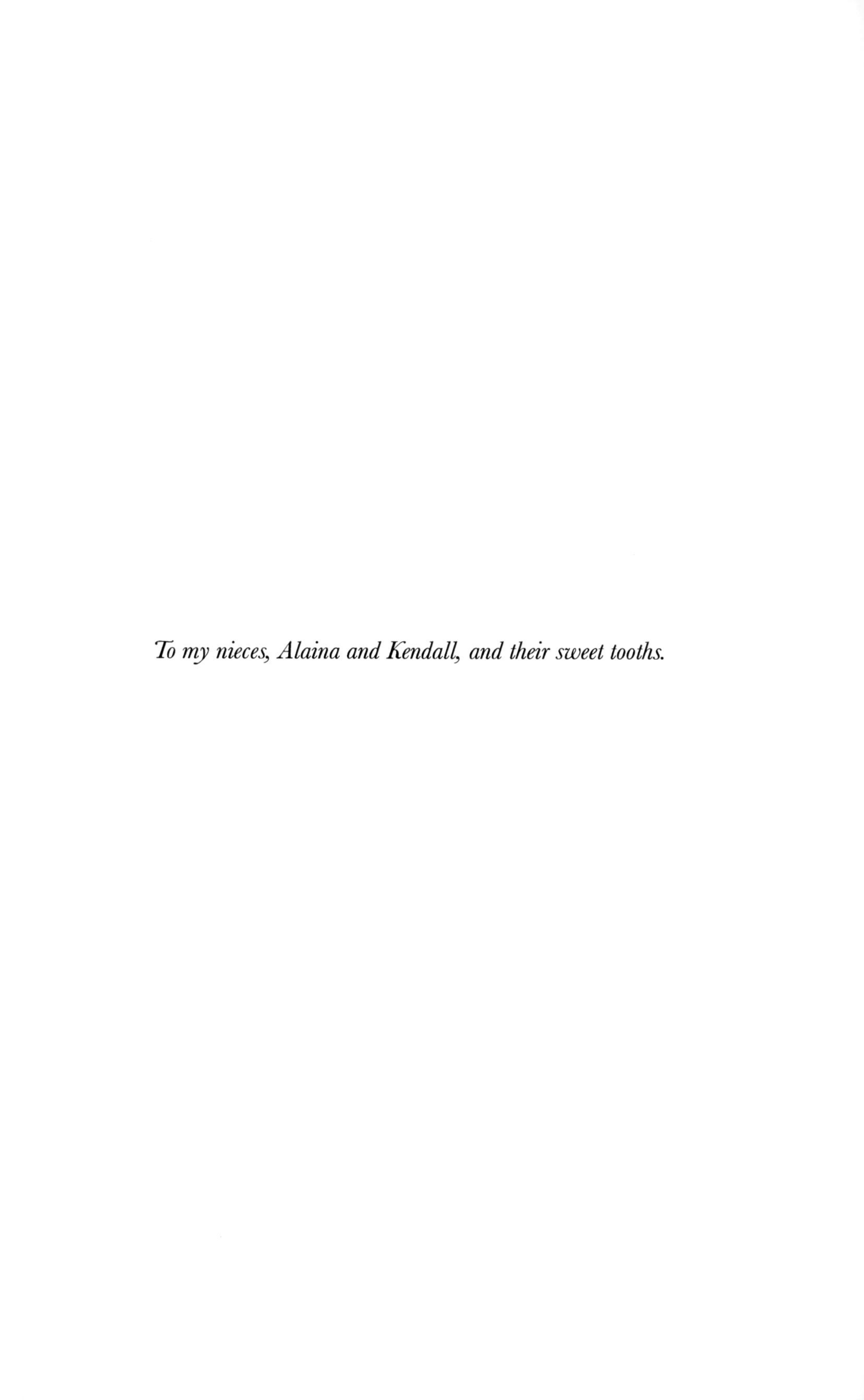

To my nieces, Alaina and Kendall, and their sweet tooths.

CONTENTS

PREFACE

The candy that was invented the year I was born is the Laffy Taffy. It was invented as a tie-in to the candy movie released the same year, *Willy Wonka and the Chocolate Factory*. What kid can forget the scene where the group first enters the candy factory room with all the edible plants and the chocolate river? My favorite line from the movie is delivered by the German mother who warns her son, "Augustus, save some room for later!" We should all take heed of that warning.

Like the character Augustus Gloop, we all have different aspects of candy that we flock to. There are aspects of a candy's gooiness, chewiness, crunchiness, saltiness, sweetness, sourness or bitterness. Recently, even savory flavors, like that of bacon and even fishiness or "umami," have been integrated into candy.

For me, the perfect candy is a combo of crunchy, gooey, sweet and chewy. And it also has to do with the degree of chewiness. Too chewy is off-putting—mildly chewy is better. The Goo Goo Cluster or the turtle candy are examples of this, with their crunchy nuts, chewy caramel and gooey filling. Maybe the universal appeal of crunchy texture is what makes chocolate-covered potato chips and pretzels so popular. The snack candy category integrating nuts, chips, pretzels and chocolate is a growth area for companies like Hershey's.

My top five favorite candies are anything toffee, like the Heath bar (crunchy, chewy), Goetz's bullseyes (chewy, gooey), Swedish fish (chewy, fruity), opera creams (gooey, creamy) and black licorice (chewy, bitter, salty). A close sixth is the Butterfinger bar and the related Chick-O-Sticks—ground roasted peanuts and candy extruded in a stick and dusted with coconut (crunchy, crispy, chewy, salty, peanut). I do like Almond Joy (born in 1946) and Kit Kat because of both having the crunchy aspect. I found my favorite flavor of Kit Kat in Japan in the form of the Green Tea Kit Kat, which can now be found locally at Jungle Jim's Markets. I do like Swedish fish and fruit slices, but I've never been a fan of gummy bears. Their chew is too polymeric and rubbery.

I'm not a huge fan either of dense taffy that takes more than a couple of chews to dissolve—like a Bit-o-Honey or a French Chew. I know that's Cincinnati fighting words, but I do like the new, smaller taffy—like French Chews that Doscher started making a few years ago.

Every Easter as a kid, I knew that there would be several opera creams in my Easter basket from Schneider's Sweet Shop in Dayton, Kentucky, right across the river from Cincinnati. My mother grew up in a baking family. Her family's bakery was only a few blocks from Schneider's "on the Avenue," on the border of Bellevue and Dayton, Kentucky. My mother loved these sweet confections, and her love was instilled in all of us at Easter. My dad's favorite is the turtle—the chewy, crunchy, caramely glob of deliciousness.

We also knew that my paternal grandmother would give us buttercreams in shapes of chicks, bunnies and ducks, probably made by the Kroger company. Grandma knew the legacy of buttercream candy manufacturing in Cincinnati in the early part of the twentieth century from companies like Goelitz, Nuss and Messer and developed a liking to that type of candy, passing it on to us.

My maternal grandfather ate Zero bars regularly. Now they're hard to come by. My brother-in-law is a huge fan of marshmallow circus peanuts, which I never developed a taste for. My sister is more a fan of hard candy than I am. I guess I'm too much a hedonist—I was always the one biting into the center of a Tootsie Pop, rather than waiting for it to dissolve. But I also do not like the flavors integrated into hard candy. The American Concord grape flavor is my least favorite candy flavor, but I do like a green apple Jolly Rancher.

During the snowy winters of my childhood in the 1970s, my next-door neighbors made snow candy. They poured hot maple syrup onto snow, letting it harden into weird shapes. My grandmother made potato fondant candy and butterscotch-enrobed Chinese noodles with peanuts. My niece and sister-in-law make them for Christmas and they're fantastic!

There are even preferred ways to eat candy. For example, 70 percent of people prefer to eat the ears off a chocolate bunny first. And who can forget the famous commercial with the owl asking how many licks it takes to get to the center of a Tootsie Pop?

There are many I would like to thank for their help in this history of the Cincinnati candy industry. Ron Case, son of George and Marilu Case, former owners of Mullane's, helped fill in the history of one of our oldest surviving confectioners. Warren and Jill Schimpff, of the Schimpff Candy Museum in Jefferson, Indiana, provided wonderful Cincinnati candy industry artifacts for photographing that they have wonderfully preserved in their Smithsonian-quality candy museum. Martha Becksmith Uhl, great-granddaughter of Cincinnati candy jobber Fred W. Becksmith, provided wonderful insight into the role of the jobber in the local industry and a great photo of her ancestor's beautiful candy truck. Greg Cohen of Lofty Pursuits in Tallahassee, Florida, who purchased the candy rolls of Mullane's, provided great industry information and contacts to the Mullane company history. I always have to thank the amazing staff at the Cincinnati Public Library downtown. We're lucky to have such a great library and such awesome staff. Sam Droganes, grandson of Soterios Droganes, provided great images and information about his Greek immigrant grandfather's candy business. Angela Westpfall of the Zion Illinois Library provided the image of Roscoe Rodda, inventor of the Marshmallow Peep. Bob Schneider was an asset in learning the true story of the opera cream in Cincinnati.

Gil Pietrzak of Carnegie Library of Pittsburgh provided the image of Ed Messer. Lisa Marine of the Wisconsin Historical Society provided the image of the Niehaus truck. Alice Ruzic Herfurt, Molly Herfurt Imhoff, Brian Herfurt and John Herfurt, descendants of Gerald Mullane, provided even more great images and information about the Mullane company. Jana Sanders Perry at the Jelly Belly Corporation in California provided images of the Goelitz family and connected me to the company archives to learn about the Goelitz time in Cincinnati. My uncle Jerry Ling, former owner of Ling's Pastry Shoppe and a former Kroger food scientist, provided assistance in decoding a legacy opera cream recipe and a background on stabilizers used in confections.

Chapter 1

CINCINNATI CANDYTOWN

Cincinnati is known for many things. It's well known that Cincinnati loves its chili. We're also a city of craft brewers. But is Cincinnati truly a candy city? We have all heard the history of Cincinnati's brewing industry or even the machine tool industry. But no one has produced a history of Cincinnati's candy industry. We know the Cincinnati beer barons, but few know the Cincinnati candy barons. These barons—names like Adolph Goelitz, John Mullane, Claus Doscher, Charles Eisen and Robert Putman—all contributed to our city's growth and development and gave back to their city. The 1850 census indicates that there were more confectioners than brewers in a city that would later become famous for its beer production.

The Queen City has been part of the great national candy story since the early days, and we have our native-born confections to prove it. Many have heard that our city gave the nation the opera cream and the French Chew, but there are more born-here stories than that. Many don't know that candy corn got its national start in Cincinnati or that the inventor of the Marshmallow Peep spent an interesting time in Cincinnati's candy industry—maybe even fueling his idea for the Peep in the Queen City. Prize packages were widely sold in Cincinnati half a century before Cracker Jack made the prize in a box a national icon. Cincinnati's H.D. Smith & Company produced the first bubble gum baseball cards in 1888. Then there were other favorite local candy creations like Johnson's Paul-I-Plop or Mullane's Woodland Goodies that have fallen out of memory.

In 1903, Judah Hart, manager of the Peter Echert Company, the largest at the time in Cincinnati, said, "The greatness of Cincinnati as a candy center is not realized by the home people." We've invented some beloved confections that the nation enjoys today. And our candy barons played a large role in the formation of Sweetest Day, the great merging of candy companies, as well as the formation of the National Confectioners Association (NCA) to stop the adulteration of candy with harmful ingredients.

In 1992, a rare 1850s daguerreotype of Cincinnati's oldest-known confectionery, Myers & Company, sold at auction in New York for $63,800. The roughly four- by five-inch image, taken outside the Myers & Company Confectioner's shop, was made by James Presley Ball, a noted black photographer, and shown at the October 1852 Ohio Mechanics Institute Exhibition. It's truly a rare glimpse into the beginning of a large industry.

What made early Cincinnati such a candy town? Well, it wasn't just the natives and their collective sweet tooth. With its Ohio River location, Cincinnati had a booming steamboat trade since the early 1800s. Steamboats arrived on a daily basis at the Public Landing in Cincinnati and grew to be the principal center for the industry, ranking above Pittsburgh, Louisville or St. Louis. The demand on these boats for sugar drop, hard candy, cakes, pastries and dried fruits was big business for Cincinnati confectioners. For convenience, most of the early candy factories were built near the Public Landing, south of Second Street, in what was called the River Bottoms. This is now the area of our baseball and football stadiums.

In 1841, there were twelve candy makers in Cincinnati, employing thirty-five people and producing $54,000 of product. A decade later, those same twelve factories employed more than eighty workers and were making more than $128,000 worth of candy. Charles Cist, author of *Cincinnati Miscellany*, in 1848 profiled the Harwood Candy Company on Fifth Street to illustrate the candy business. At the time, it employed twenty-four workers and made lozenges of every description and jujube pastes of various flavors. Think of these jujube pastes as the grandfather of Ju-Ju-Be candy and the jelly bean.

Early confectioners and candy makers made theatrical productions out of their store displays. An 1868 report on Christmas shopping reported a visit to Charles C. Leininger's Opera House Restaurant and Confectionery at 84 West Fourth Street:

> *The immense piles of fine candies of every color and style would remind one of a florist's bazaar. Here are huge heaps, in color like camelias, japonicas, violets and carnations. The sight is enough to ravish one with its exceeding*

> *beauty, to say nothing of its other temptations. Fancy and plain cakes, bon bons, mettoes, ice creams, water ices, pyramids of nougats and other good things can be found here in profusion.*

By 1900, Cincinnati ranked sixth in volume of candy produced, behind Chicago, New York, Boston, Philadelphia and St. Louis, employing 522 workers and making an estimated 31 million pounds of candy annually in Cincinnati. Cincinnati made as much candy as 162 other cities combined and consisted of nine large wholesale manufacturers and more than one hundred small candy makers, as well as more than five hundred confectioneries, not including bakeries. Cincinnati was also a large jobbing, or distribution, center for candy made both in the city and outside. Some of the larger manufacturers bought as much candy from outside the city as they made at their factories.

In 1927, it was said of the candy industry in Cincinnati:

> *There are nine concerns here manufacturing candy in a wholesale way, about ten fashionable confectioners making a high grade of goods for the local trade, and perhaps one hundred small candy stores making their own goods for sale over the counter. The wholesalers make about 31,500,000 pounds of candy annually, the larger confectioners perhaps 600,000 pounds and the smaller ones in 300,000 pounds.*
>
> *The total value of this product is about $1,700,000. About 700 persons and about $500,000 of capital are employed in the trade. The rank of the city in this time is about what it is in a general business way, say sixth or seventh perhaps.*
>
> *The wholesale branch of this trade is by far, of course, the more important. Staple goods chiefly are made and sold by salesmen throughout the country. The manufacturers here are jobbers also, and handle much candy in other cities. The business shows growth and increase and of late has been especially prosperous.*

There were a variety of candy makers in Cincinnati. Large factories downtown made wholesale candy to be distributed all over the country. They sold through a network of shop-to-shop middlemen called jobbers. These jobbers traveled the country selling to retailers, drugstores, lunch and sandwich shops and soda fountains. Then there were the smaller businesses that made confections on site for their candy retail shops. Some of these shops, especially those outside of downtown, might have also

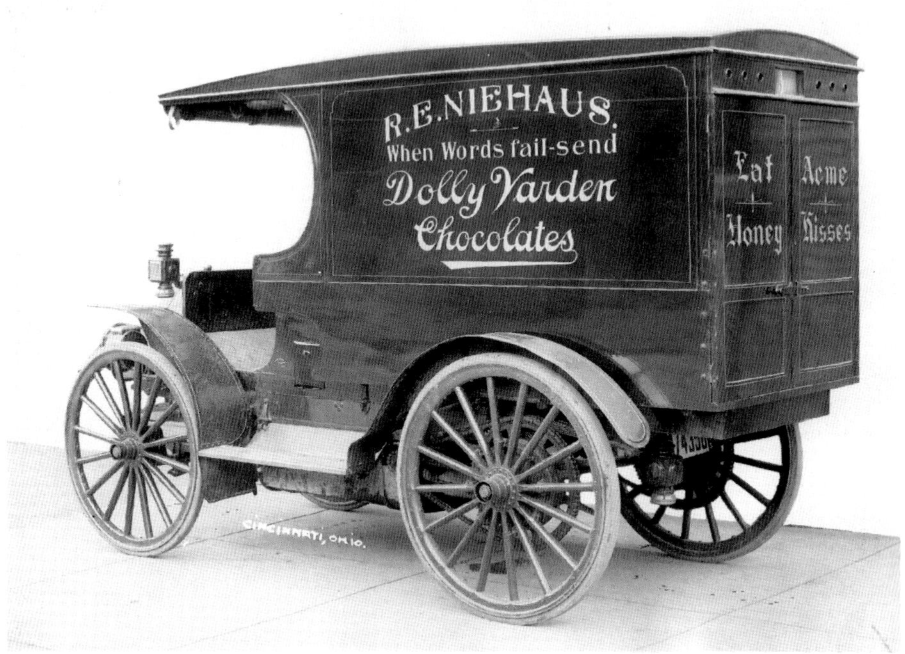

This 1913 Model M International harvester truck, owned by Cincinnati jobber Rudolph E. Niehaus, advertises locally made Dolly Varden Chocolates and Echert Company Honey Kisses. *Wisconsin Historical Society.*

carried toys, notions, stationery, cards and even fireworks. It seems even on the wholesale scale, a lot of large candy manufacturers also either supplied or manufactured and supplied fireworks along with their candy. At least three candy companies in Cincinnati that were founded before 1875 sold candy and fireworks together.

There were those like Meakins, which made chocolate only for its local retail stores or soda fountains. Even others made both confections and ice cream for their soda fountains and cafés, like Aglamesis, Graeter's and Cupid. There were some candy makers, like Dolly Varden Company, that were vertically integrated. They manufactured for the national market, had their own sales force and even owned their own branded retail stores.

Before the turn of the twentieth century, the Cincinnati candy industry, as one might imagine, was dominated by German immigrants. But in the early part of the twentieth century, a wave of new immigrants from the Balkans created a Greek dominance in the local and national candy industry.

Although we have some great confection creations like the French Chew and the opera cream, the Cincinnati candy industry never created its own candy bar. Candy bars were created for soldiers during World War I at the request of the American government with the intent of being an energy bar. After soldiers came back, the candy bar exploded, with nearly thirty thousand kinds of bars by 1920. The candy bar opened up the candy industry to a larger market: men. Bonbons were considered dainty and feminine. Candy bars were masculine and could be grabbed and chomped into, providing energy to a soldier or worker.

But the candy factories weren't all Willy Wonka fun and happiness. They were still pre-OSHA factories, and accidents did happen. The work was dangerous and hot. Child labor was employed illegally in many of Cincinnati's candy factories. A Mr. Moeller at Nuss Candy Company in the 1920s succumbed to the August heat and died of heat stroke. Workers made molten sugar in furnaces that had to be carried in large quantities and poured into molds. This provided the opportunity for lots of burns. Extruders and taffy pullers often pulled workers' clothes and limbs into their mechanisms, causing injuries. One girl, Maude Schambough, died from injuries after her hair was pulled into a candy machine at the Peter Echert Company and she was mangled.

Some of the names of candy would be considered extremely racist by today's perspective. Jymcrax, a candy made by the Peter Echert Company, derived from "Jimmy Crack Corn," a popular slave song used in the blackface minstrel shows of the mid- to late 1800s. "Jymcrax" was a slang term for worthless trinkets.

Most of the early candy manufacturing was manual, but most of it today is highly automated. The newspapers from the turn of the century into the 1930s advertised candy jobs. Calls for experienced chocolate dippers, runners, molders, packers and candy machine operators dotted the *Cincinnati Enquirer* want ads from the 1890s into the 1930s. These workers would

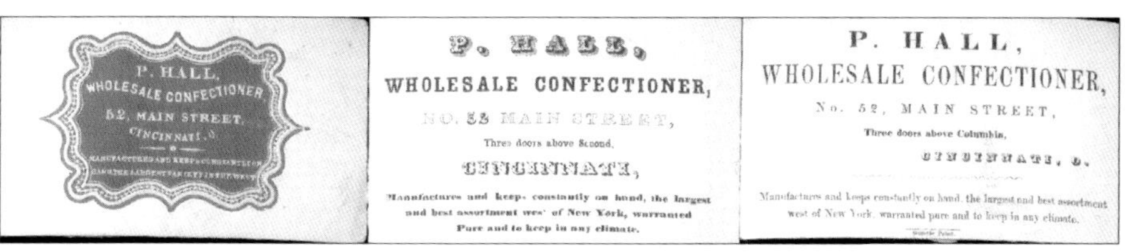

The 1850 calling cards of P. Hall, confectioner at 52 Main Street. *Schimpff Candy Museum.*

operate a variety of candy manufacturing equipment—hand-cranked drop candy molds, extruders, chocolate waterfalls, double boilers, nut grinders, marble tables and ball cream mixers.

Candy also paired well with other industries throughout its evolution in our city. As mentioned earlier, from the Civil War to the turn of the nineteenth century, more than a handful of Cincinnati candy companies supplied fireworks along with their wholesale candy trade. Additionally, for retail confectioners, candy and ice cream went along together seasonally. And before modern commercial refrigeration, several confectioners also supplied oysters to make the most of the ice they employed to cool ice cream. For a time, candy and cigars were supplied together, as many times they reached the same place—at a grocery, corner general store or sandwich shop.

The manufacturing methods have progressed, but popular flavors for candy have also changed dramatically over the last one hundred years. In 1890, Anna Martin Richardson published a recipe book in Cincinnati called *Homemade Candies and Other Good Things Sweet and Sour*. While seeming to be the Martha Stewart of her time, she also seemed to be very familiar with how large factories mass-produced candy, as she mentioned their methods in conjunction with her recipes. Perhaps she had worked in one of the great Cincinnati candy factories or at least taken a tour.

Richardson's recipes exhibited popular flavors at the time, of which most of us have never heard. Hoarhound candy, which is the extract of a leaf that is a member of the mint family, was very popular back then. Some say it has the flavor of a combination of mint, licorice and root beer. Another odd flavor was orris root caramels. Orris root smells like violets, which to me would be like chewing on an air freshener. Calamus root candy was another oddity. This root has a pungent aroma and a taste similar to a mixture of cinnamon, nutmeg and ginger, with a bitter aftertaste. Everton toffee was another popular candy. It was a type of lemon-flavored butterscotch created in England in the late 1700s. Another oddity in her book was carrot nougat.

With these wide variety of tastes, the candy market continues to grow and evolve in offerings and flavors. From the first native candy invented in the United States by Mary Spencer in 1803 in Massachusetts—the Gibraltar—we've come a long way. The U.S. candy market has grown to a size of about $35 billion in sales in 2015. America's most popular candy is the M&M, on which we spent $616 million in 2016. It was the first candy to be sent into outer space.

Candy sales are seasonal around the holidays, the largest being Easter, Valentine's Day, Halloween and Christmas. Candy companies today try to extend candies associated with particular holidays into others to expand their business: Peeps are not just for Easter anymore; they've made Halloween and Christmas Peeps. And there is now reindeer corn (candy corn) for Christmas.

Many candy stores in Cincinnati played to children and were placed near schools. Mullane's started near a schoolhouse on the West End in 1848. My own grandfather's school, Garfield Elementary in Cumminsville, had the Shockley Candy Store strategically across the street. I wonder how many jawbreakers, candy sticks or chewing gum he bought from the store on his way home from school. Brazell's Novelty and Candy store was across the street from the Salmon P. Chase School in Northside. The prize package and trading cards were developed by candy companies to form relationships with their young customers. Candy companies today still follow these marketing methods.

So, let's meet some of Cincinnati's candy barons and take a tour of their candy companies, learn what sweets they made and explore our city's tastes throughout the ages.

Chapter 2

THE EARLY CINCINNATI CANDY BARONS

THE E. MYERS CONFECTIONERY

The earliest known confectionery in Cincinnati comes with a great immigration story. Not surprisingly, it's a German one. Johann Meyer (1793–1875), also known as John Myers, or "Candy Myers," is credited as being the first German "sugar baker," or candy maker, in Cincinnati. Meyer was born in Eltingen, Wuertemburg, where his father, Joerg, and grandfather Hans-Joerg were simple farmers.

Johann's parents, Joerg and Barbara, were German Pietists and were persecuted by the Lutheran and Reform German majority. In 1804, the family of eight immigrated with a group of other Pietists to Baltimore to escape this mistreatment, as did thousands of others from their country. Conditions on their boat were horrible. Sickness plagued the boat, and Johann's father, a brother and two sisters died on the voyage and were buried at sea.

The remaining family members arrived in Baltimore, where all their possessions were stolen as they were leaving the ship. The ship captain demanded final payment of their voyage, or he would sell them all into indentured servitude, a common way for poor Pietists to pay for their voyage. So, to save his mother and siblings, Johann paid the ship captain for his entire family by indenturing himself to a German baker named Rapp for eight years. After his contract was up, Meyer enlisted in the War of 1812.

After this military service, he moved to Philadelphia, Pennsylvania, and worked for a baker there named Lauer. While working for Lauer, he became smitten with Lauer's daughter. They fell in love and married, and then Meyer spirited her away to Cincinnati in 1817, establishing his own confectionery. The Germans called them *conditorei*, and he was called a *zuckerbacker* or "sugar baker."

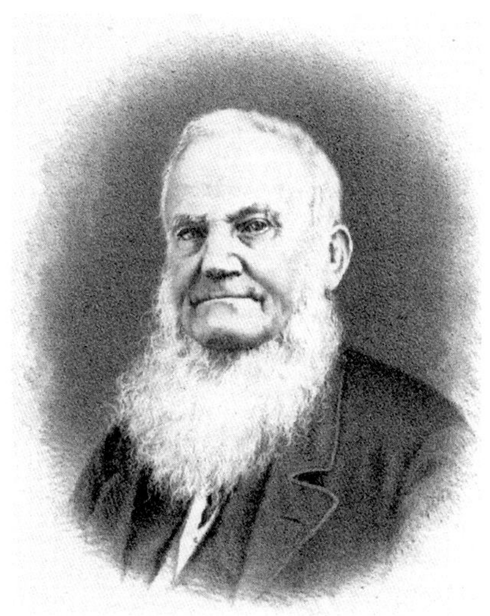

A portrait of Johann Meyer, Cincinnati's first confectioner. *Public Library of Cincinnati and Hamilton County.*

Meyer was able to marry his own daughter off well. Amanda Jane, in 1845, married Andrew Erckenbrecker, a Bavarian immigrant, who met her when he worked at Meyer's candy store. Erckenbrecker became a wealthy merchant and used some of his money to fund the creation of the Cincinnati Zoo and Botanical Gardens.

Johann Meyer had a golden opportunity to show off his talent on a national level. When General Lafayette, the famous aide of General George Washington in the Revolutionary War, was on his 1825 grand tour of America, Johann acquired the job of creating the dessert display for the grand ball held in his honor at the Cincinnati Hotel. Meyer created an elaborate six-foot-tall sugar pyramid with marzipan figurines showing scenes from Lafayette's experiences during the American Revolution. This sugar display really wowed the crowd at the ball and gave Meyer the reputation of "Confectioner of the West," solidifying his business for many years to come.

Gottlieb Myers joined Johann (John) in the 1830s, and by the time he had taken over the business in the 1840s, they sold candies, cakes and toys. Ownership then transferred to John F. Myers in 1844. Edward Myers had taken over the 40 Main Street Shop by the 1860s and operated it until 1881 with the help of his three sons. Edward Myers was also secretary of the Diehl Fireworks Company, for whom the company distributed fireworks. The 40 Main Street Myers Confectionery became a travel agency in 1881. The confectionery business transferred to George Myers and his sons at 165 Main Street.

During the Civil War, while the government was hoarding its coins, Myers Confectionery, like other businesses, issued its own Indian head private

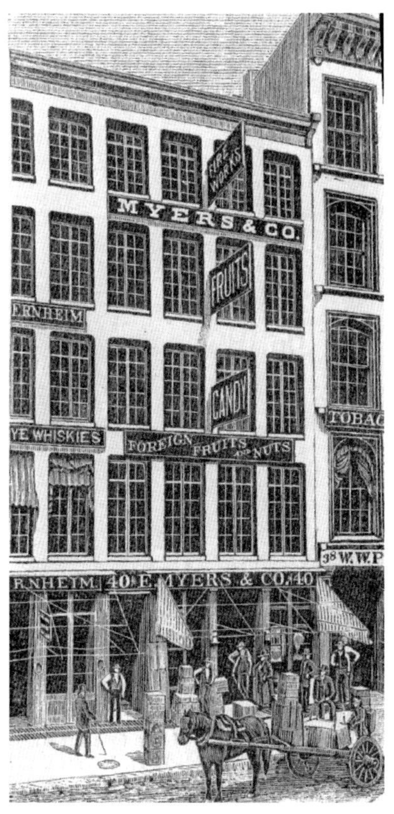

An 1875 lithograph of the Myers Confectionery at 40 Main Street. *Author's collection.*

tokens for business transactions, due to the scarcity of government-issued cents. Apparently, candy was valuable enough to mint its own coins.

The shop was one of several wholesale confectioneries crammed along the lower end of Main Street, with access to the Public Landing and the steamboat passengers. In addition to making candy, they also sold sardines, cove oysters, foreign fruits and nuts, and by 1859, they were following the trend of other Cincinnati candy companies by selling the fireworks of H.P. Diehl, who at the time was in Mount Adams. Other candy companies like A&J Doescher would also supply the fireworks of the Diehl company. The Myers Confectionery lasted for more than half a century, nearly reaching its seventy-fifth anniversary.

Reinhart & Newton

The Reinhart & Newton Candy Company is a legacy of the Johann Meyer confectionery. The business was founded by John Dietrich Reinhart (1842–1913), son of immigrants from Hesse, Germany. His parents, Dietrich and Margareth Muth Reinhart, immigrated to Franklin County, Indiana, where John was born in 1842. Moving to Cincinnati in 1844, John's father started a spice shop to support the family.

Finishing school at age fourteen, John started working for Johann Meyer. John Reinhart worked for Meyer a few years, learning the trade, and then transferred to the confectionery of another German immigrant, Charles Grundhoeffer at 651 Vine Street.

At the outbreak of the Civil War, like many other Germanic immigrants, John Reinhart volunteered to fight with the Union army, with the Fifth Ohio Infantry, and then transferred to the Kentucky Thirty-Ninth Regiment.

Upon leaving the army, John started his own confectionery in 1865 with his brothers Valentine and Conrad Reinhart. Valentine lasted one year and Conrad two. Needing another partner after his brothers deserted him, Reinhart brought on George D. Newton (1841–1912).

The company originally started out at a facility at 85 West Second Street, but that building was destroyed by an October 1886 fire. Like other candy companies at the time, Reinhart & Newton also sold fireworks, which were stored on the upper floors of their factory. During the blaze, the fireworks caused several explosions, contributing to the destruction of the building. After the fire, the company moved into a new building at 50 West Second Street. In the 1910s, they moved into a large factory at 210–14 Vine Street that employed more than two hundred people. But that building was also wrecked by fire in 1920, causing significant damage. Their last facility was at Third and Walnut Streets.

They made an early name for themselves locally by being awarded a medal at the 1870 Cincinnati Industrial Exposition for show of plain confectionery. Over the years, Reinhart & Newton also exhibited at the Municipal Food Shows at Chester Park and Pure Food Shows at the Cincinnati Zoo.

Their candy plant was outfitted with equipment to make pan-coated candies, jelly and cream, coconut and marshmallow products. Some of their earliest known products, referenced in 1911, were imitation pineapples slices and Maplettes, made with cane sugar and maple flavor.

In 1914, they had the following lineup of candies:

- Cinch, a molasses taffy
- U-Win, a butterscotch
- Sure Thin, orange and lemon taffy
- Lucky Butters, molasses butter rolls
- Yellow Possums, chocolate-covered marshmallows
- Pink Ovals, chocolate-covered marshmallows

Reinhart & Newton also made Phoenix brand Delmore Maples and Phoenix Maplettes. The packaging for Phoenix exhibited a bold iconography of a powerful bird rising from the flames. The brand was distributed through candy jobbers throughout the United States, Canada, Puerto Rico, South America, Cuba and Britain. They also made a line of candy called Pop's Cuties, which were soft cream centers fork-dipped in coconut cream. Another taffy candy they produced was called Base Hits and probably marketed to the Reds stadium and other sports parks. Cincinnati, is after all, a baseball town.

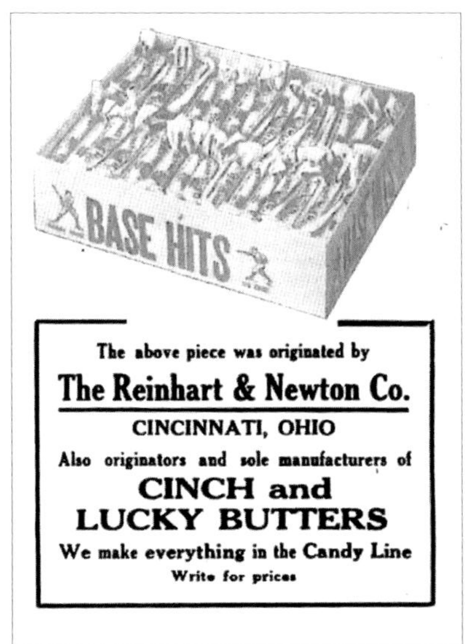

An ad shows the Base Hits candy of the Reinhart & Newton Company. *From the* International Confectioners Journal, *vol. 26 (1917).*

In 1921, Reinhart & Newton announced in the *International Confectioners Journal*, "We are now ready with our new caramel department. Send in your order for all kinds of caramels." They offered Cincinnati Cream Caramels, a candy similar to a bullseye. In 1922, they made an interesting product called Ranson's Eversweet Pencils, named after their new owner, R.H. Ranson, and made of pure fruit flavors in four colors: pink, green, violet and orange.

In 1924, Reinhart & Newton bought the Dolly Varden Candy Company in Cincinnati. The company lasted nearly sixty years in business. Reinhart and his family lived in Avondale and ran the business until his death in 1913, when the business was taken over by Richard H. Ranson. In 1920, the company was consolidated with the Headley Chocolate and Caramel business of Baltimore, Maryland, and the Lancaster Chocolate and Caramel Company of Lancaster, Pennsylvania, which had originally been founded by Milton S. Hershey in 1886 before he sold it and focused on chocolate. The three combined represented one of the largest candy companies in the world, with William C. Bidlack at the helm.

THE PETER ECHERT COMPANY

The Peter Echert Company has the second-oldest legacy of Cincinnati candy companies. The company was formed by Peter Echert and Jacob Buss in 1861 in Cincinnati but took over a candy business started in 1847 by a Robert Hedger. Hedger had learned the candy trade even earlier, in the early 1840s, from brothers Charles and Washington Thomas. The Thomas brothers owned a confectionery on the southwest corner of Twelfth and Walnut Streets in the early 1830s. Robert boarded with Charles Thomas and worked for their company.

By 1869, the Echert Company, composed of partners Peter Echert and Jacob Buss, then at 64 Walnut Street, was advertising itself as a dealer in pickles, oysters, sardines, canned fruit and fireworks in addition to candy. By 1875, the Echert Company was manufacturing a full line of stick candy, gumdrops, jujubes, rock candy, French cream bonbons, Christmas sugar toys and hearts, chocolate creams, caramels, lozenges and imperial and pan-coated candies. It also added party novelties to its lineup like Chinese lanterns, balloons, flags and sauces; jellies; catchups; maple sugar; cigars; and confectioners' tools and supplies. It certainly had a diversified business that would later focus only on candy as the city grew in population and demanded suppliers to focus on specific markets.

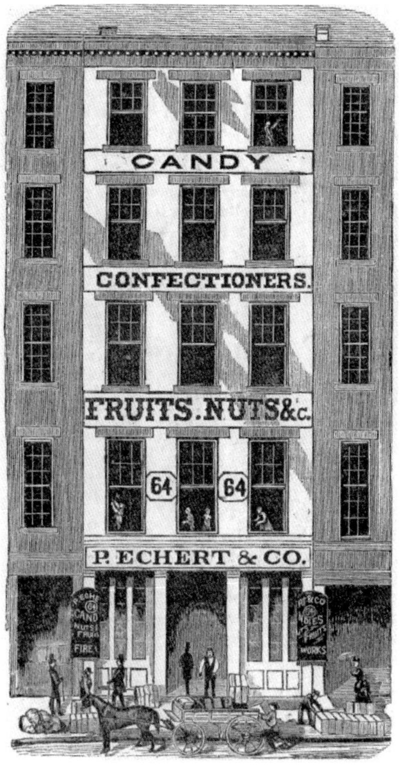

An 1873 lithograph of the Peter Echert Company. *Author's collection.*

By 1884, Echert was at 75–81 Walnut Street and had acquired a third partner, Mr. C.E. Brichett. It was soon to be incorporated in Ohio as the Peter Echert Company with Echert as president, Jacob Buss as vice-president, Brichett as secretary and Judah Hart and Lewis Englehart as directors. They had two five-story buildings, with four floors of candy making equipment, and employed between sixty and one hundred employees. Echert had two well-known brands, Acme and Honeycomb, and made lozenges, fine chocolates, handmade creams, decorated cordials, cream bonbons, panned goods like jelly beans and penny candy. It promoted the purity and wholesomeness of its candy at a time when others were adulterating or extending their candy with things like lime dust to lower costs.

Known as "Sweet Peter, the Candy Man," Peter Echert landed in Cincinnati in 1840 from the Kaiserlautern, Rheinpfalz, where he was born in 1832 to Heinrich and Elizabeth Echert. He attended the First English-German free school in Cincinnati until his fourteenth year. Starting work at a cigar factory, he then dove into the candy business, working at the Lamarche

Confectionery on Main Street between Ninth and Court for three years and then at the Matthias Demand's Confectionery. Finally, he partnered with Roger Hedger in 1850 until 1854. He went to Louisville, Kentucky, for a year to try his luck operating his own confectionery but soon was back at Hedger's, where he took over the business at 81 Walnut Street.

Peter married Catherine Von Ziefle and lived on Hopkins Street in the West End of Cincinnati. In the cramped quarters of the West End, Peter and Catherine lost three children, prompting a move up the hill, away from the polluted basin to Reading Road in Avondale near the Tollgate by 1880.

The candy business was good for Peter. He was a fan of world travel and made several transatlantic voyages to Europe; he had semi-retired from running the business by the 1890s. In 1897, he took his daughter, Laurie, on a yearlong European tour.

Peter was very active in the national candy scene, serving as vice-president of the National Confectioners Association and one of its founding members in 1884. He also served as director of the Atlas National Bank of Cincinnati and was very popular among the businessmen of Cincinnati.

In 1902, Peter was elected with a huge majority as a Republican Ohio state senator from Hamilton County's First District. Echert served with Nicholas Longworth III, the wealthy Cincinnati heir of Rookwood and the Longworth fortune, who would become U.S. Speaker of the House of Representatives. During his short term in the Senate, Peter, not surprisingly, chaired the committees on labor and municipal corporations, while also being an active member of committees on benevolent institutions, fish culture and game, manufacturers and commerce, penitentiary, sanitary laws and regulations and the banks and building and loan association. Unfortunately, Peter died of a lingering illness in 1903.

In 1902, the Peter Echert Company merged with the National Candy Company, along with *twelve* other companies. Echert continued to produce its Acme Brand of products, which included spicy jelly eggs, jawbreakers and marshmallow candies. It also produced a satin-finish hard candy known as Pinta-Pats.

Only two of Peter's four surviving sons were active in the business: Robert H. and Thomas P. Echert (1867–1937). Robert H. became involved in the management of the business after his father died and was president, and his son, Harry G., was a foreman at the factory up until 1922. Things were not so smooth under Robert's leadership. He was prosecuted in 1908 for employing ten kids on night shift in his factory.

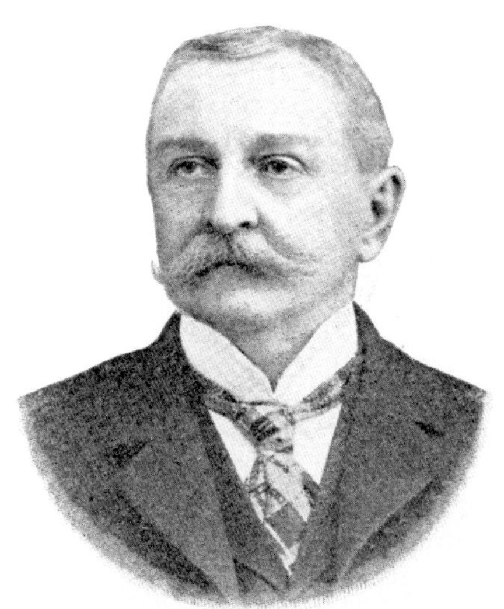

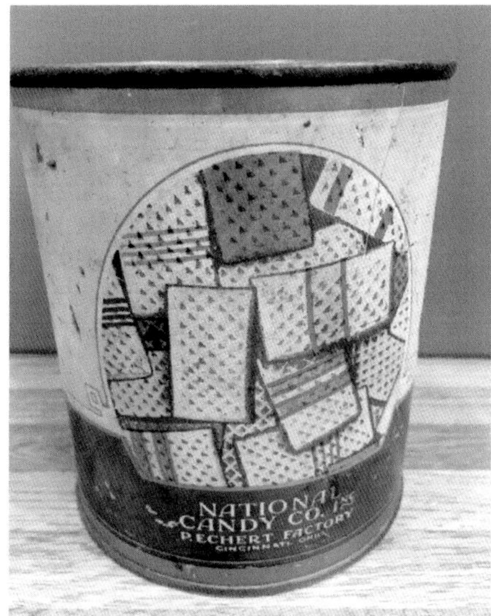

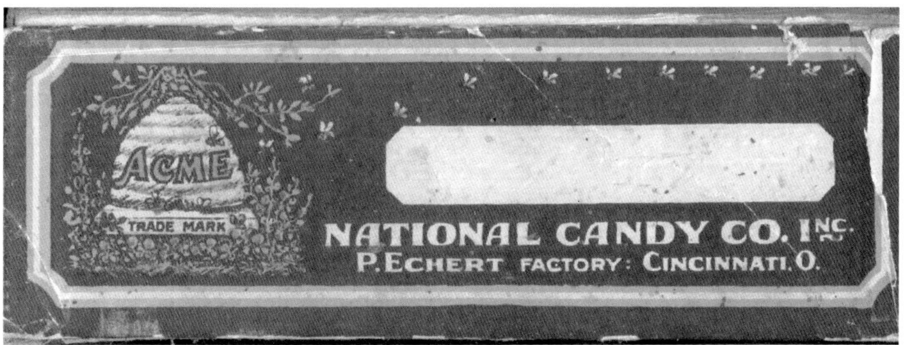

Top, left: A portrait of Peter Echert in 1902 during his term as Ohio state senator. *Public Library of Cincinnati and Hamilton County.*

Top, right: Under the National Candy Company, the Peter Echert Plant packaged satin-finish hard candies called Pinta-Pats in this tin. *Schimpff Candy Museum.*

Bottom: An image of a box of Acme spicy jelly eggs, made by Echert Company, after becoming the National Candy Company. *Schimpff Candy Museum.*

Robert was the only son who actually went into the confectionery business for himself, in addition to working with his father's company. In 1879, he opened up his own soda fountain, ice cream and confectionery shop on the 400 block of Madison Avenue in Covington, Kentucky. The business grew to a three-story building on the same block. His ice cream "saloon" was "furnished throughout with elegance and comfort, plate-glass show cases, marble-top tables, walnut fixtures, and a handsome soda fountain." He made ice cream, fine candies, confections and cakes, serving wholesale and retail throughout Covington, as well as catering, with an annual business of about $20,000 in 1884.

Thomas served as a corporal with Troop C of the Ohio National Guard in the Spanish-American War in Cuba. He retired from the candy business and moved to Santa Monica, California, in 1917 with his family to pursue his love of outdoors, hunting deer and bear in Arkansas and fishing and yachting in California.

Roscoe E. Rodda became general manager of the Peter Echert Company in 1902 but didn't stay very long. His very interesting story in the candy industry is told in a later chapter.

There were several father-and-son teams that worked at the Echert Company. Judah Hart started out with the Echert Company as a traveling salesman in 1866. He was considered nationally by his colleagues as a pioneer in the candy industry. One of his biggest contributions was the introduction of pails for candy into the industry. At his retirement in 1914, he related stories of how difficult it was to travel throughout the United States

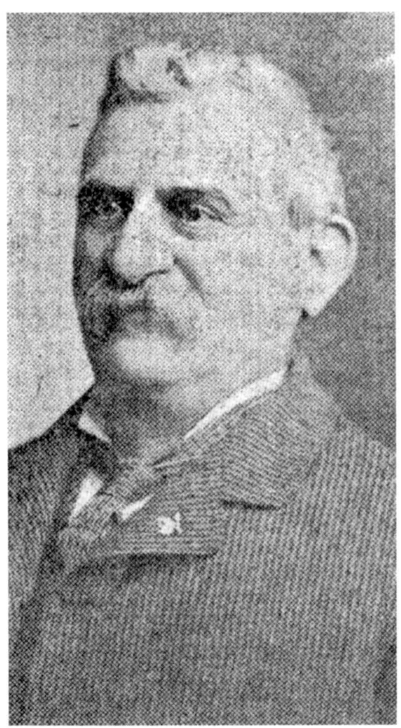

Right: Judah Hart, the dapper Cincinnati candy industry man, sporting his perpetual smile. *Public Library of Cincinnati and Hamilton County.*

Below: An ad for P. Echert's Jymcrax marshmallow candies. *From the* International Confectioners Journal, *vol. 24 (1915).*

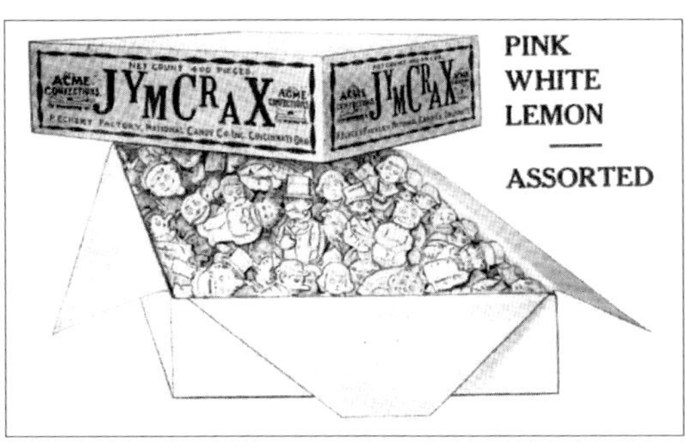

as a salesman in the 1860s. By 1902, when the company merged with the National Candy Company in St. Louis, he was manager of the factory. Hart was very active in the National Confectioners Association, serving on the executive board from 1898 to 1900, and retired from the Echert Company in April 1914. He brought his son, Charles D. Hart, into the company as a salesman. Before the everlasting gobstopper, Charles traveled to schools all around Ohio, giving free samples to schoolkids of Echert's All-Day Sucker, which was really a type of taffy on a stick.

The Cincinnati plant made a type of marshmallow candy called Jymcrax in the 1920s that came in shapes of recognizable cartoon and comic characters and sold for six per cent.

Oscar L. Graeser became manager upon Judah's retirement. Graeser started as a clerk for the company in 1887, and by 1920, he had become operations manager of the plant, serving as assistant manager behind Judah before his retirement. He was son of Louis Graeser, the first physical education teacher in the Cincinnati Public Schools and a member of the Cincinnati Turner Society, a Germanic sport and social club, like many of the other German candy manufacturers in Cincinnati.

Oscar's son, Carl Louis Graeser, was given credit for starting Sweetest Day during the early '30s while he was president of the National Confectioners Association and district manager of the National Candy Company in Cincinnati until 1937. But the story of Sweetest Day is a more involved one, to be told in another chapter.

Echert Joins the "Candy Trust": The Formation of the National Candy Company

In 1899, an idea among the largest candy companies in the East of forming a candy trust became news. The candy trust idea would eventually become the National Candy Company, a conglomerate of twenty-two firms. It was originally promoted by E.B. Walden, who had promoted a recently formed glucose company trust. Thirty firms in Chicago, Cincinnati, Baltimore, New York, Philadelphia, Pittsburgh, Boston, Detroit and Milwaukee were asked to become part of this trust, and a roadshow with the promoters visiting each city ensued.

In 1902, the promoter Edwin Corbin, representing a law firm with offices in New York and Chicago, and a New York trust company that accompanied him, representing the financial end of the deal, began a road show, wooing large candy manufacturers in big cities like St. Louis and Cincinnati. In early March 1902, they approached in St. Louis Blanke & Brothers, F.D. Seward Confectionery, O.H. Peckham Company, A.A. Walker Candy Company and Wenneker Morris.

Edwin Corbin outlined his plan to include all the large confectionery manufacturing plants in Detroit, St. Louis, Chicago, Milwaukee, Cincinnati, Kansas City and Omaha as a starter, with other cities to be added if these cities' big houses were included.

The two largest firms in Cincinnati, the Peter Echert Company and Reinhart & Newton, were asked to join the trust, but the latter declined. A total of fourteen firms joined, from St. Louis, Louisville, Buffalo, Detroit, Chicago, Indianapolis, Minneapolis and Grand Rapids. The conglomerate was incorporated in New Jersey on September 8, 1902.

There were four past NCA presidents on the first board of directors of the multimillion-dollar National Candy Company. The new conglomerate, erroneously dubbed the "Candy Trust," issued a total of a little over $8 million in stock, opening for business in October 1902.

Vincent L. Price was a vice-president and later president. He was the father of actor Vincent Price. Peter Echert of Cincinnati was also made vice-president. The corporate office was in Jersey City, and general offices were in St. Louis.

The same year, 1902, saw a colossus called the Corn Products Company absorb the stock of the largest glucose producers in the world, consuming in one deal such firms as the Glucose Sugar Refining Company, which less than ten years earlier had controlled 80 percent of the market. The capitalization of the firm was estimated at $80 million. The National Confectioners Association was alarmed at the influence of this new behemoth that they were placed under.

In order to compete, National Candy bought its own glucose manufacturing company, Clinton Industries in Iowa, in 1906, so it wouldn't have to deal with the strong arm of Corn Products Company. In 1946, the National Candy Company merged with Clinton Industries and became Clinton Industries.

Only a year after becoming part of the National Candy Company, the Echert Company did something that seemed like war to the other Cincinnati candy manufacturers:

> *In 1903 Echert sent out postcards to the trade in the Cincinnati market, offering a discount on staple candies, which was under the cost to other*

manufacturers. The deal was good for 50 days. This was seen by independent dealers as a "war of extinction" to drive them to fold into the National Candy Company or force them out of business. After the Cincinnati independents raised a stink about the practice, the Echert company went back to their old price scale.

Mr. Frank Pfaff, of Buhr, Pfaff and Co., one of the largest of the independent dealers said "When we heard of the cut in price made by the National Candy Company we immediately stopped selling the affected stock in this territory and sent it all to the stronghold of the corporation in the West, where we undersold them. We unloaded a lot of stock in the cities where they were getting the highest prices and still managed to make a profit on it. I understand today they have stopped cutting prices, but we intend to go ahead for a little while to see how they like it."

J.H. Hart, of the Echert factory, laughed off the whole matter. "We are not in business for our health and we are not cutting prices. Some days ago we were somewhat overcrowded with certain stock and wanted to unload. Wishing to give our customers the benefit we cut the price in this locality. This lasted not more than 48 hours. We are perfectly friendly with all our competitors and are not cutting prices. In fact, in most cases we are charging more for the same article than the others."

Candy hit its high point nationally in the 1920s, when thousands of new and different candy bars came on the scene. Although candy bars were typical on the East Coast, sugar, milk and corn syrup were readily available in the Midwest and, combined with the booming economy, made St. Louis, the headquarters of the National Candy Company, an excellent place for candy companies to thrive. National Candy's biggest seller was the Bobcat Bar, although it was also known for the Hippo Bar, a block of peanuts.

Candy making was a labor-intensive operation, and the high temperatures needed for cooking the sugar made the factories extremely hot. For this reason, large-scale candy production was primarily seasonal, with factories closing down in the warm summer months. But as competition increased during the 1920s, manufacturers found it necessary to work more months of the year.

The National Candy Company survived the Depression and war years, outselling its largest local competition, the Jack Rabbit Candy Company. As the longest-running wholesale manufacturer of candy in St. Louis, the company became attractive to those looking to expand their own operations.

The Chase Candy Company of Missouri was one of the corporations that saw the advantages of the nationally recognized National Candy Company. In 1948, Chase purchased the company from Clinton Industries. Chase continued to sell the well-known National Candy brands, while adding its own items, including the popular Cherry Mash. The Echert operation of the National Candy Company lasted in Cincinnati until 1948, probably a casualty of the Chase purchase. Chase was bought out in 1953, and the headquarters of National Candy moved to Chicago, Illinois.

MITCHELL & WHITELAW

This firm was established in 1872 by William Mitchell and Francis M. Whitelaw at 70 Walnut Street in a six-story factory with a basement. The Whitelaw family had come to Cincinnati from Canada in the 1840s. The factory made all types of plain and ornamental American and French confections, as well as prize boxes. It also dealt in foreign fruits, nuts and fireworks (as agents of the Oriental Gunpowder Company).

It primarily manufactured the brand Angelic Sweets, improved stick candy with fruit flavors. Its print advertisements in the *Cincinnati Enquirer* indicated the two biggest concerns with candy manufactured at the time: its purity and its accurate weight, as candy was sold by the pound. It advertised that its stick candy was made from only the best crushed sugar, not from glucose or grape sugar or other adulterations. It also proclaimed that it was full weight and was shipped in a twenty-five-pound patented metal half bushel.

In the 1890s, Mitchell & Whitelaw employed inventive ways to peddle its candy. In an effort to cut out the candy jobbing middleman and sell directly to the consumer, the company tried to engage boys to sell for it, advertising candy stores for boys:

> *Wanted 100,000 boys—Active intelligent boys, who can count money, are making from $0.50 to $1 a day, after school, at home, among their playmates. Each one a complete store, with large signs, circulars, to distribute, etc, and over 450 articles of Fancy Candies, to retail at 1 cents each. Money doubled in a few days. "It's lots of fun." Sent by express on receipt of $2. Full description and list of articles included by receipt of 3 cent stamp.*

The ad showed the types of candy Mitchell & Whitelaw provided: rubber chewing gum (not chicle based, like many others), cream chocolate drops, bullseyes, long nine molasses candy sticks, assorted stick candy, Greek fig paste, peerless butterscotch, Arabian gum, jawbreakers and sugar-cured hams.

One member of the firm, Herman Kuchenbuch, would go on to form his own candy business in Indiana. He started at an older Cincinnati candy company, Austin and Smith, in 1864. Then, from 1878 to 1887, he worked for Mitchell & Whitelaw, becoming its foreman and learning the art of stick candy manufacturing. During that time, he also served two years as president of the Cincinnati Confectioners' Union. After his stint with Mitchell & Whitelaw, he moved in 1888 to Richmond, Indiana, starting his own candy company at 169 Fort Wayne Avenue. It was here that Kuchenbuch invented a regional stick candy called the Ferre Stick that became very popular.

Francis Whitelaw took over the business from Mitchell in 1884 and continued into the early 1900s.

H.D. Smith & Company

In 1856, in a small store at 8 East Second Street, Alvin Austin and Lorin N. Smith opened a candy store and began making candy. The business quickly grew to a regional supply and was moved to a larger location at 56 and 58 Main Street, near where the original Myers Confectionery started. The company operated at the new location until 1877, when Austin retired and the name was changed to the H.D. Smith & Company.

When Harry D. Smith took over the company, offices were moved to 206–10 Main Street, and in the 1890s, the company employed thirty men and forty-five women.

H.D. Smith products were featured in the "Commercial Supplement" to *Leslie's*, dated October 27, 1888:

> *Prominent among our Cincinnati industries is to be found the well and favorably known house of HD Smith & Co., manufacturers of confectionery and chewing-gum, making a specialty of the latter. Their goods are known and sold from Maine to California. Among their large variety, the brands "Red Riding Hood," "Crystal Palace," "Beauty," "Cough," "Excelsior," and "Ylang Ylang" are the most prominent, and which the trade at large*

are familiar with. A novel production of theirs this season is the St. Louis and Detroit Champion Baseball Gum—a piece of gum with a perfect lithograph picture of one of the champion nine of the National League or American Association on each piece. The pictures were made to order in Germany, and are wonders in their way. Their "Beauty" gum (with mirror attached) commands a large sale the country over. H.D. Smith & Co. believe in and make only pure goods, and at all times are alive to the wants of the trade in their line.

A mystery about baseball cards was solved recently from this advertisement. The cards described here that came with the Baseball Gum that H.D. Smith made were referred to as "Scrapps tobacoo cards." Rather than being an actual brand, "Scrapps tobacoo cards" was a catch-all term for all die-cut paper cards meant to be glued into Victorian scrapbooks, a popular hobby at the time. The H.D. Smith & Company gum cards, likely issued in early 1888, are probably the earliest baseball gum cards ever issued in America.

H.D. Smith offered a wide variety of exotic chewing gums. The "Cough" brand gum was a patented medicinal gum it offered in the 1880s and 1890s. It advertised its "Big Long Chewing Gum" on trade cards, including one in the form of a rooster that proclaimed, "I'm Crowing for Smith's Big Long Chewing Gum—it's the best paraffine gum made—try it and be convinced." H.D. Smith's "Red Riding Hood" gum was advertised as "Popular and Delicious" on ceiling fan pulls, intended to be installed in Victorian-era candy stores and groceries. The Ylang Ylang gum used the essence from a flower of a tree native to Indonesia, Malaysia and the Philippines. Its flavor is described as rich and deep with notes of custard and bright with hints of jasmine. Ylang ylang essence is still used in perfumes like Chanel No. 5 and is thought to be an aphrodisiac and help reduce high blood pressure.

H.D. Smith was part of the American Association of Chewing Gum Manufacturers. In 1897, the association lobbied Congress against the duty on gum chicle, used in manufacturing. Its argument was that the small amount of revenue the government gained was out of proportion to the sum paid by each gum manufacturer and its effect on their profits. In 1899, flamboyant chewing gum baron William White formed the $9 million American Chicle Company, nicknamed the "Chicle Trust," of six top chewing gum companies. One of the six companies was nearby Kiss-Me Gum Company of Louisville, Kentucky. The formation of this large conglomeration of chewing gum companies is probably what forced H.D. Smith out of the chewing gum market.

Chicle is a natural gum that is harvested from trees. It was used in chewing gum until about the 1960s, when it was replaced by butadiene-based natural rubber, which is cheaper to make. The Mayans and Aztecs of South America chewed chicle to curb hunger and keep teeth clean and used it for fillings.

H.D. Smith also created candy toys to market to children. One advertised in 1890 showed a candy gum marble game called Phen-Hunch. The product is simultaneously a candy and a game and could be played and then eaten. It's not clear if children actually played the games, but the candies mimicked the shapes of other common toys. This is probably something that today would be frowned on because of child safety issues.

Fueled by a strong business, the company moved into a five-story brick building, making a capital investment in new candy making equipment. The factory employed between seventy-five and one hundred skilled candy workers, in addition to supporting eight traveling salesmen constantly on the road. In addition to making candy and an extensive line of chewing gums, H.D. Smith also supplied foreign fruits and fireworks, being the exclusive agent for the mining and sporting powder of King's Western Powder Company in King's Mills, Ohio.

The King's company that supplied the powder to H.D. Smith was owned by Joseph Warren King and his nephew, Ahimaaz King. Joseph had purchased the Austin & Carleton powder mill on the Little Miami River in 1855 and expanded it as the Miami Powder Company. King sold the Miami Powder Company in 1877 to build the Great Western Powder Works, with the company town of Kings Mills at a more favorable hydropower location at a deep valley of the Little Miami River. King's became the Peters Cartridge Factory in 1885, when King died and his son-in-law, Gershom Peters, a Baptist preacher, took over. This building still stands near the Loveland entrance to the Little Miami Bike Trail.

In addition to games and trading cards, H.D. Smith saw the market for (and later added) prize packages, which amounted in 1882 to more than $100,000 annually in sales, one of the largest in the United States. In the early 1900s, Harry D. Smith brought on his cousin, Fred A. Smith, as a partner, who came into the candy business from frames and carpets. The company stayed in business until the mid-1920s.

P. Huber

Another business that supplied fireworks in addition to candy was the Philip Huber Company. This business, specializing in stick candy, was formed in 1868 by Phillip Huber and Francis B. Meyer. It's not known if Francis Meyer was related to the family of Johann Meyer, Cincinnati's first confectioner. Meyer died in 1882, and then Huber took over full control of the business. In addition to candy and fireworks, it supplied exotic fruit and nuts. The majority of its business was wholesale to the Tristate region of Ohio, Indiana and Kentucky.

The George Ast Candy Company

George Ast (1872–1923) started the George Ast Company around the turn of the century. It manufactured the St. Clair brand of hard candies, which included assorted fruit tablets. Part of its St. Clair hard candy line were the very popular hoarhound drops, made with hoarhound tea. It was also the exclusive dealer for the cough drops of the Bower Candy Company of Atlanta, Georgia, in the early 1910s. By 1915, George Ast was located at 929 Main Street in Cincinnati.

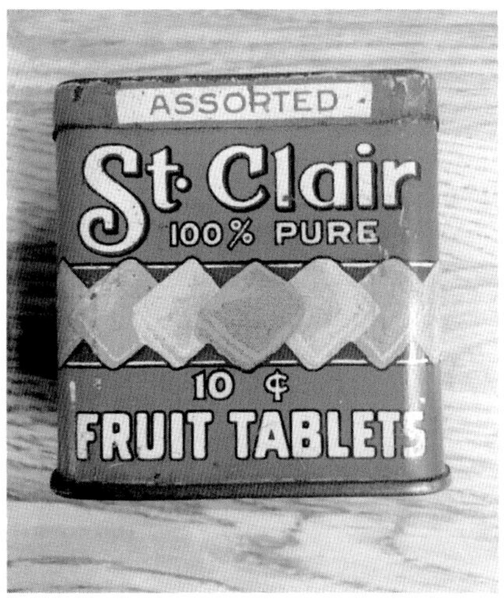

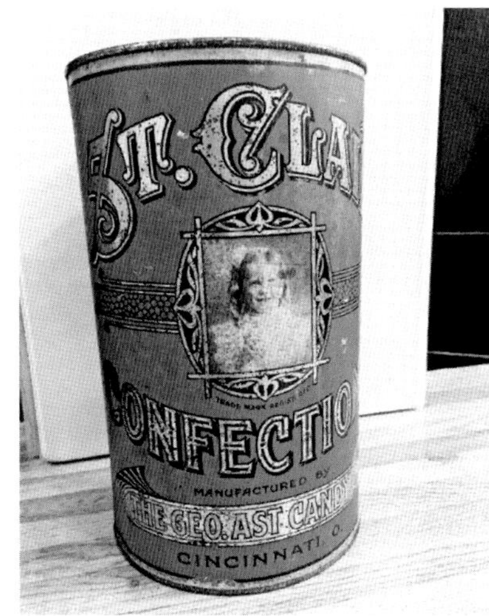

Left: A small tin of St. Clair fruit tablets from the George Ast Company. *Schimpff Candy Museum.*

Right: A large tin of St. Clair candy from the George Ast Company. *Schimpff Candy Museum.*

George and his wife, Catherine, with their two sons, Frank and Charles, and three daughters, Helen, Dorothy and Marion, lived at Prospect Place in Avondale. George Ast was involved in the North Cincinnati Improvement Association, sort of the business association for the Clifton area and Avondale neighborhoods. He was also very involved in the local candy associations, holding office in the Ohio Confectioner's Association and Commercial Jobbing Confectioners' Association.

Like with the Mullane Company family, after the founder passed on, George's children squabbled over the business. After George died in 1923, his sons Frank G. Ast and Charles Ast took over as president and secretary, respectively. In 1940, their sister Mrs. Marion Ast Marks sued her brothers after they refused to buy her out, alleging that they had been giving themselves ridiculously large salaries; she demanded an accounting. This family squabbling is probably what led to the company's demise.

Chapter 3

THE FORMATION OF THE NATIONAL CONFECTIONERS ASSOCIATION

Cincinnati's candy barons led the formation of a national organization made up of manufacturers that would become the National Confectioners Association. Today, it is one of the oldest trade organizations in the world. Its original intent was to put limits on how low manufacturers priced their candy. But what became more important was building public confidence in candy by cracking down on manufacturers that used hazardous substances and adulterants to stretch their goods. It became sort of a public relations organization for the candy industry.

In January 1884, a large group of candy manufacturers from Ohio, Kentucky, Indiana and Michigan came to Cincinnati, at the call from the Cincinnati Confectioners Association, to set a list of prices on the leading staples for the jobbing and retail candy trades. Manufacturers from other states—including Illinois, Missouri, Iowa, Tennessee and West Virginia—promised their cooperation by letter.

Calling itself the National Candy Manufacturers Association of the United States, it circulated the resulting price schedule among other confectioners that did not attend the meeting, asking them to join the organization at a ten-dollar fee. The executive committee wanted everyone to understand that the only way to break up cutthroat prices prevailing among candy manufacturers was through concerted action and thorough organization. Then, in February, a group of confectioners from Chicago called for a convention there on April 23 to form the National Confectioners Association. A total of seventy-four representatives attended and sixty-nine member companies banded together to form the organization. New York had the largest membership with thirteen companies, followed by Chicago (eleven), Philadelphia (eight) and Cincinnati (eight).

Cincinnati sent one of the largest group of attendees to the convention. Present were Charles and John Reinhart of Reinhart & Newton, Albert Doescher of A&J Doescher, Peter Echert and Jacob Buss of Peter Echert Company, Joseph Buhr of Buhr & Wendt, H.D. Smith of H.D. Smith & Company and John Doscher of Doscher Brothers. The only remaining firm from those in attendance is Doscher Brothers. At that time, Doscher Brothers had a large factory at 9–15 West Canal Street, now Central Parkway.

Members of the convention enjoyed a hearty dinner of Blue Point oysters, mock turtle soup (which the Cincinnati contingent must have requested), Kennebec salmon, sweetbreads, calf's head in tomato sauce, turkey in aspic and lobster, among other delicacies of the day.

In 1884, the news media broke a story about confectioners in New York using marble dust or "terra alba" to extend their candy. Marble dust hardened in the stomach like plaster of Paris and caused a number of ailments. So, by creating laws within the National Confectioners Association requiring manufacturers to use more expensive (and less harmful) ingredients, they were in effect killing two birds with one stone—price fixing and product quality. The Cincinnati Confectioners Association would continue creating laws regulating adulteration of candy. In 1915, it stopped the use of talcum powder to polish chocolate Easter eggs, which was a standard practice at the time.

Adulteration was not the only public perception the candy industry had to face. Along with the temperance movement gaining steam came claims that candy was distracting proper little girls from reading their schoolbooks. A candy temperance league was formed for "controlling this particular vice as essential to the progress of our country as the suppression of whiskey is where men are concerned."

Cincinnati provided several presidents of the organization that led lobbying for the industry with the government. Reinhart was vice-president in 1905, while Frank Pfaff was on the executive committee. Judah Hart was a member of the executive committee from 1898 to 1900. When members came to conventions in Cincinnati, they were entertained at local institutions like Coney Island and the zoo. Charles Eisen, president of the Dolly Varden Chocolate Company, served as president of a related industrial organization, the Cincinnati Manufacturing Confectioners Association, in 1917.

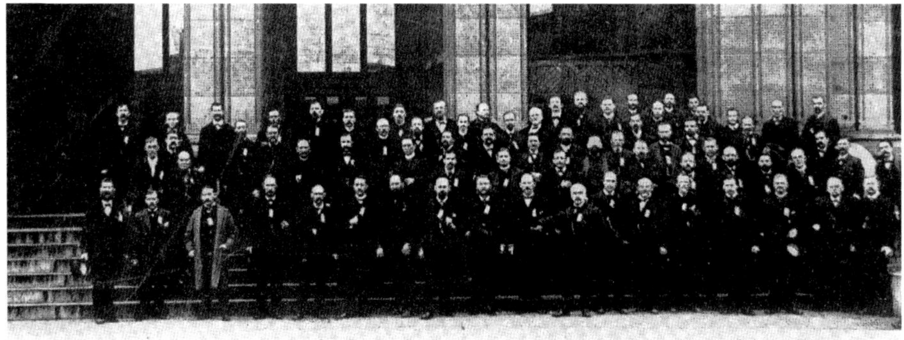

The 1884 Inaugural NCA Convention photo in Chicago with eight Cincinnati candy barons. *Public Library of Cincinnati and Hamilton County.*

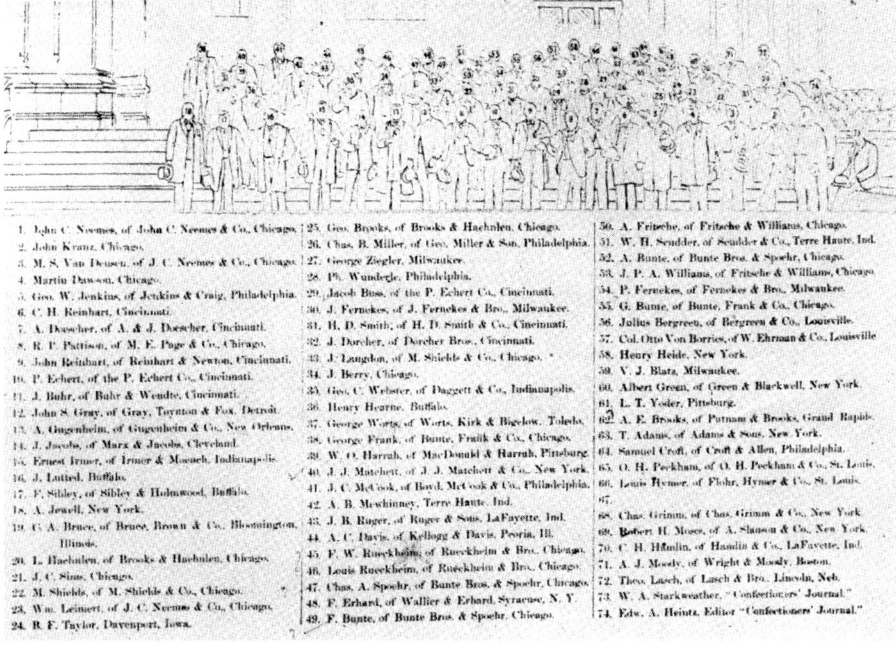

The key showing the eight Cincinnati candy barons at the 1884 NCA Convention, nos. 6, 7, 9, 10, 11, 29, 31 and 32. *Public Library of Cincinnati and Hamilton County.*

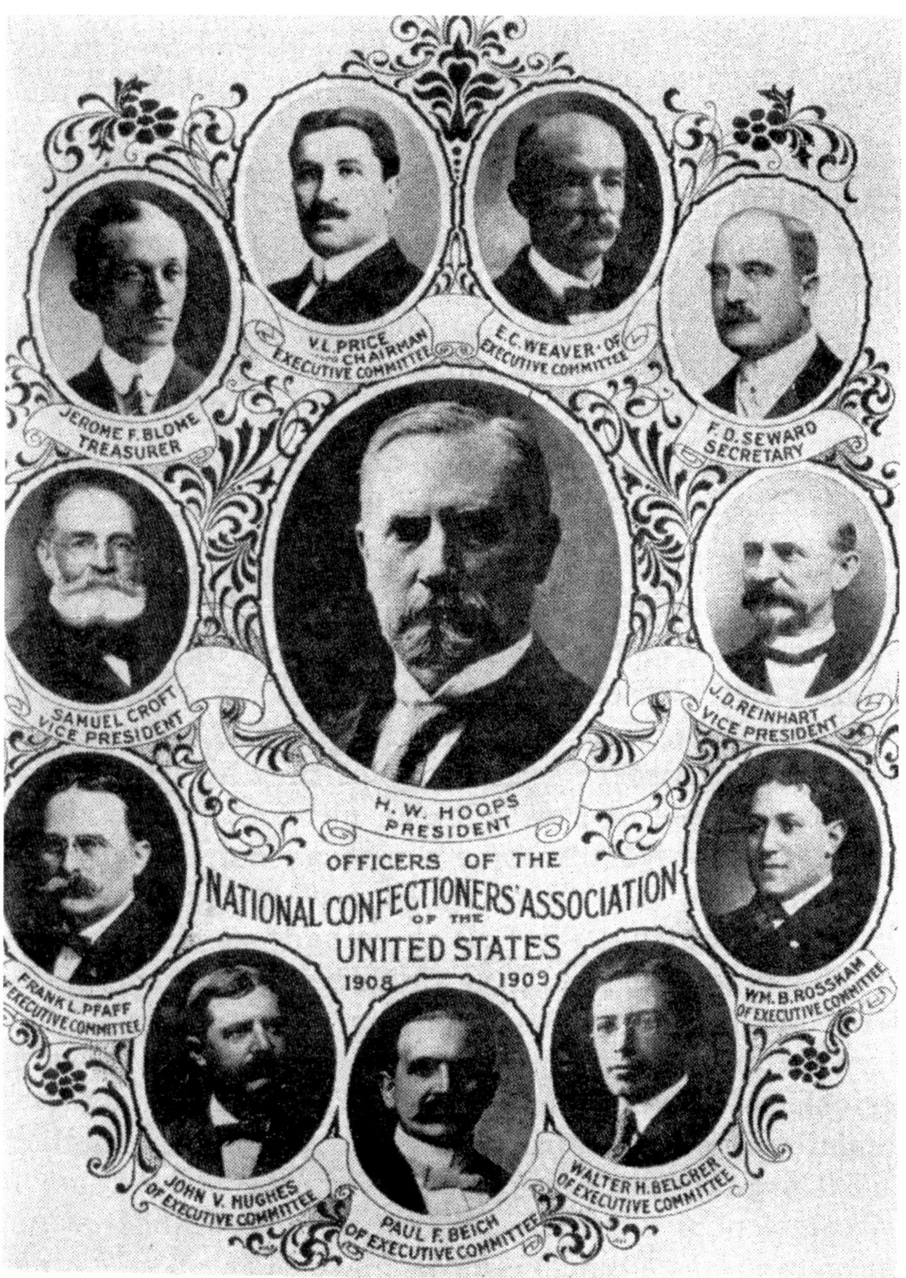

The 1905 board of the NCA shows two Cincinnati candy barons, Reinhart and Pfaff. *Public Library of Cincinnati and Hamilton County.*

The NCA used its power to lobby against legislation that would hurt the candy industry. One example of this came in May 1921. Hubert B. Fuller, a Cleveland, Ohio lawyer who was special counsel of the NCA, led a special hearing with the Internal Revenue Service (IRS) in support of repealing the manufacture excise tax on candy.

The tax had been imposed on candy during World War I as a way to ration sugar as an emergency war measure. However, as the NCA argued, that emergency had passed, and there was no excise tax on cookies, fancy crackers or other things that compete with candy like toys and novelties. This created an unfair disadvantage to the whole industry.

The repeal of the wartime excise tax on soda fountains had already been proposed by the secretary of the treasury. With this repeal, another unfair disadvantage would be looming over the candy industry. Vincent L. Price, president of the National Candy Company, testified at the hearing. Some of his speech had a bit of anti-Greek sentiment, as when he claimed that the Greek makers of candy in the United States kept no record of their transactions—by not paying the excise tax, they were cheating the system and creating an unfair advantage in the wholesale candy manufacturing industry.

The National Confectioners Association exists today and annually hosts the National Candy Show in Chicago, as well as the Candy Hall of Fame, of which at least one local candy maker, Richard Ross of Galerie, is an inductee. It continues to help the industry share trends and best practices among manufacturers.

Chapter 4

THE DOSCHER CANDY COMPANY

CINCINNATI'S OLDEST CONFECTIONERY

The story of Doscher's, Cincinnati's oldest continually operating candy company, starts with the tale of Johann Heinrich Doescher. Johann Heinrich was the father of Claus Doescher, the founder of the Cincinnati company. At the age of seventeen, in the 1830s, Johann Heinrich Doescher bravely came to New York City to partner with a Mr. Havemeyer and a John Spreckels at the Havemeyer Sugar Bakery, a sugar refining operation on Vandam Street in what was then Greenwich Village, now SoHo. Havemeyer's father and uncle had come to New York from Buckeberg, Germany, founding the sugar refinery in the early 1800s. "John Spreckels" was Adolph Claus Johann Spreckels. Spreckels had followed his childhood sweetheart, Anna Christina Mangels, from Lamstadt, Hanover, to New York City. J.H. Doescher only stayed a few years, returning to Germany, where he married Margaret Steffens and had sons Melchior, Claus, Albert and Johann.

J.H. Doescher left what would become a huge American sugar market behind. "Mr. Havemeyer" was none other than American sugar baron Fredrick C. Havemeyer, who in 1856 moved the sugar refining business to a waterfront lot in Williamsburg, Brooklyn, and created a sugar empire that eventually became Domino Sugar in 1900. After the move to Brooklyn, Spreckels moved his family to San Francisco, California, first operating a brewery and then, in 1867, his own sugar refinery at Eighth and Brannon Streets, calling it the California Sugar Refinery and, later, the Spreckels Sugar Company. He eventually came to dominate the Hawaiian sugar trade

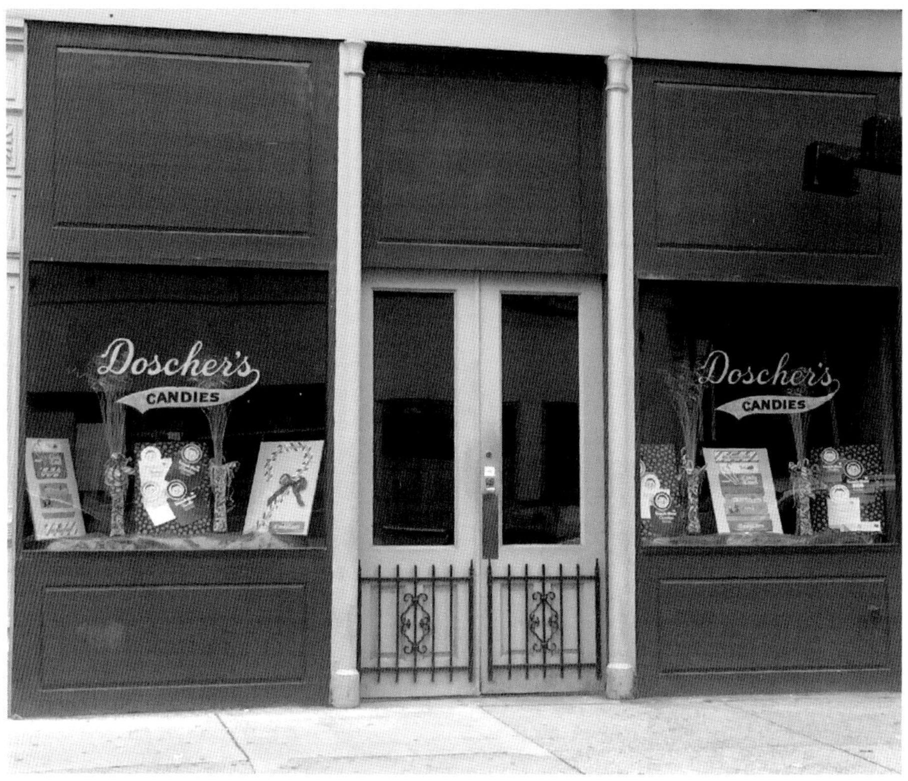

Doscher candy canes and French Chews have been made at this 24 West Court Street factory since 1946. *Author's collection.*

on the West Coast and then butted heads with former partner Havemeyer as their businesses dueled it out in the U.S. sugar trade.

Another interesting story surrounds John Spreckels's son, Adolph Spreckels, and the term "Sugar Daddy." His considerably younger wife, Alma de Bretteville Spreckels, a former artist's nude model and socialite, used the term for him as a pet name. The couple met after she had modeled for the Dewey Monument in Union Square in San Francisco as the image of Nike, the Goddess of Victory.

Johann Heinrich's experience must have inspired his brothers to strike out on their own in America, too. By 1850, brothers Albert and Johann had headed west to the California Gold Rush, digging to find their fortune, oddly enough, at a mine in El Dorado County called the Cincinnati Mine. They came to San Francisco, California, from Germany by way of South America. Albert moved to Cincinnati and married Gesina Pape in Cincinnati in 1856 at the German United Evangelical Church at Elm Street between Fifteenth and Liberty Streets, opposite the orphanage. His brother John would marry Catherina Rapp in 1865, narrowly escaping conscription in the U.S. Union army during the Civil War. John and Catherine Doescher would live at Walnut Street in Over-the-Rhine, raising five children, none of whom went into the candy business.

In 1865, just as the Civil War was ending, Claus Doescher (1846–1883) and his brother John (1848–1932) came to Cincinnati from Grossenhain, Germany, near Dresden, in what was then the Kingdom of Hanover, now Lower Saxony. They came to work with the two gold mining uncles, Albert and Johann, who had, since moving to Cincinnati, started the A&J Doescher Sugar and Candy Company at 52 and 54 Twelfth Street at the corner of Jackson Street in the Over-the-Rhine section of Cincinnati. Albert had come first, listed in the 1857 *Cincinnati Williams Directory* as a confectioner.

Another brother, Heinrich Doescher (1855–1907), followed in 1870, no doubt urged by positive letters sent back home from his older brother Claus. And to round it out, two more cousins joined the three brothers, another John and Albert, sons of another of Claus's uncles, Melchior Doescher. Like many immigrant families in Over-the-Rhine, the four nephews—Claus, John, Albert and John—packed into their Uncle John and Aunt Gesina's house at 34 Jackson Street, with five other cousins. They were all one big happy German-immigrant candy making family. Eleven people crammed into one apartment wasn't uncommon then in the Tenth Ward of Over-the-Rhine.

No reclamation on Fruit. Bills payable in Cincinnati or New York Exchange. All Claims to be made within Five days after receipt of goods.
TELEPHONE 2497.
A. & J. DOESCHER,
WHOLESALE CONFECTIONERS,
AGENTS FOR THE DIEHL FIRE WORKS CO.
(MANUFACTURING BY STEAM POWER.)
PENNY GOODS A SPECIALTY.
Terms Net Cash.
Nos. 52 & 54 TWELFTH STREET, Corner Jackson Street.
Cincinnati, O., June 12 1888
Sold to Wood and Hand assignee Weber Bros Co
6 Empty Sugar Bbls N 90
Paid Albert J. Doescher

An 1888 invoice from the A&J Doescher Company of Cincinnati. *Cindy Doscher.*

A&J Doescher specialized in wholesale penny candy, which it proudly advertised as made by steam power. And like the other wholesale candy manufacturers in Cincinnati, it also distributed fireworks for the Diehl Fireworks Company. As a sugar manufacturer, there is evidence that the company supplied to some of the local breweries, as one of its agents was the local Weber Brewing Company in Over-the-Rhine. Albert and John ran a tight ship with their business, offering no credit to buyers and requiring cash payment within five days of shipment.

Albert Doescher died in 1877, and his two sons, Albert and John, took over the business. In 1887, the brothers erected a large factory building at Jackson Street for $25,000, which they borrowed in loans. Their sales weren't able to finance the building and other expenses, given the economic depression occurring at that time. So, in February 1892, A&J Doescher went into receivership after thirty-five years in business.

After working for his uncles for several years and learning the business, Claus said goodbye to them in 1871. With his two brothers John and Henry, they embarked on their own candy making venture on Fifth Street between Broadway and Sycamore. By 1893, they had opened a candy store at 152 West Fifth Street, and their four-story factory was at 9 and 15 West Central Parkway on the Ohio & Erie Canal. The first Doscher candy store on Fifth Street conveniently stood next to a dentist's office.

Claus met and married Sophia Koenemann (1846–1916) in about 1876 and started his own family. He and Sophia raised sons John and Harry Doscher and a daughter, Minnie Doscher Meyer (1879–1979), who lived to be one hundred. It must have been confusing with all the Johns and Henrys in the family! They all lived together with Sophia's sister, Lena Koenemann; Claus's two brothers; and, for a time, their cousin Gesina, who thought it would be more fun to clerk at her cousins' confectionery than at her father and uncles'.

With respect to their uncles, who were also still making candy at the time, they dropped the *e* from their name to eliminate confusion between the two companies. The Cincinnati candy market was big enough for both A&J Doescher and Doscher Brothers, at least for the first few decades after Claus and his brothers started their business. It would be the large investment in the new factory that caused A&J Doescher to go out of business.

One of the first products Doscher Brothers made was caramel popcorn, which it called Popcorn Fritters. It was sort of a flat version of the popcorn ball, similar to a rice cake, that was popular at the time. Doscher sold this product to a new local baseball team called the Cincinnati Redlegs, who

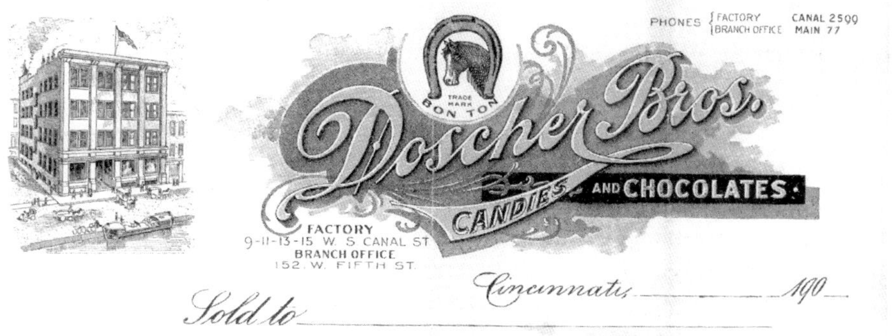

The letterhead from a 1905 invoice of Doscher Brothers, showing the factory and BonTon candy logo. *Marilyn Doscher Johnson.*

played at a park then called the Palace of the Fans. This made the Doscher company one of the first concessioners in American baseball, two decades before Cracker Jack was introduced at the 1894 Chicago World's Fair. We should be singing "Buy me some peanuts and Doscher Popcorn Fritters" at the seventh-inning stretch here in Cincinnati. But then that doesn't have as much of a ring to it. Doscher's Popcorn Fritters were also sold on the grounds of the local amusement parks Chester Park and Coney Island and all the riverboats, like the *Island Queen*, which transported people there from Kentucky across the Ohio River.

Luckily, there was a local machine supplier, Kingery Manufacturing Company, that supplied both the Faultless Popcorn Popper and the Eureka Corn Fritter machines to Doscher. With the Faultless fritter model, one man with two helpers could turn out at least two thousand fritters an hour. Doscher even offered a testimonial for the company in its 1901 *Equipment* brochure: "Your corn popper we bought of you two months ago [August 1898] we find same to be labor saving, and we could not do without same, as we find it does again as much work as the old style popper, and with less expense." Two other Cincinnati wholesale candy manufacturers were making candied popcorn as well and offered their testimonials in the same company brochure: the H.D. Smith & Company and Sauerstein and Brown. The Kingery Company would later become the Gold Medal Products Company, which still supplies the Kingery Popcorn Popper brand, as well as the premier cotton candy machines.

These large popcorn poppers and the corn fritter machines were on the fourth floor of the Doscher candy factory on Central Parkway, which was the canal at the time. The factory was convenient to flatboats, which could transport large amounts of sugar and corn syrup to its doorstep. A streetcar bridge right across the canal in front of the factory made it easy for workers to commute to work.

With a name like Claus on staff, it's no surprise that Doscher Brothers started making candy canes in 1871, the first year it was in business. The family were very familiar with all the stick candy that was made by the other large confectioners in Cincinnati, so the candy cane was an interesting new novelty to Cincinnati.

The reference to the first candy cane in America came in 1847 in Wooster, Ohio, when a German immigrant tailor named August Imgard (1828–1904) decorated his Christmas tree, another new novelty in America, with candy canes. But the candy cane didn't see its red stripe, at least as documented in Christmas cards, until after 1900. Before then, candy canes were white only. There's no indication that the original 1871 Doscher candy canes didn't have their red stripe.

In 1896, the Doschers decided to capitalize on the new Turkish taffy craze that was taking the south of France by storm and developed their recipe for the French Chew. It is described as a candy that's something between nougat and taffy. It was originally sold in big pieces that were broken up in the candy stores and sold by the pound. The advertising slogan was "Freeze It, Crack It, Smack It." After it became popular in Cincinnati—and dental bills went up—it was made into a long bar and wrapped in the now recognizable wrapper with the cartoon freckled boy licking his lips. Originally, the mascot was a tropical-looking Polynesian woman. The French Chew would have competed locally with the largely popular Mullane taffies.

The Doschers also made several other products at their candy factory, including chewing gum, molded maple sugar candies, molded chocolate candies, bonbons, a product called Grandpa Corn Toast and a line of chocolate candies called BonTon, whose logo was a horsehead in the center of a horseshoe. The Doscher family still has in their possession the many chocolate candy molds used over the century. One particularly unique candy they made in the 1920s was called the Glad Hands Candy Sucker, a hand-shaped sucker on a stick. They also made beautifully hand-painted chocolate eggs at Easter. At the height of its manufacturing, Doscher made about nine different types of candies.

A recipe for Doscher's cordial cherries from about 1905 includes an ingredient that might indicate why many early candy factories also supplied fireworks. Doscher used a very high-quality chocolate for all its candies. It used a mix of African bitter chocolate beans for its dark chocolate and a mix made from Java and Ceylon beans for its lighter chocolate. For this high-value chocolate, it wanted to ensure its shelf stability, so it added one specific preservative to the manufacturing process: saltpeter, or sodium nitrate. Saltpeter had been used as a preservative for centuries before the advent of commercial refrigeration. In addition to its use as such, it is also a primary component of gunpowder, explosives and fireworks. So the saltpeter used as a preservative could be stored in the same area as the fireworks that these candy manufacturers stored and distributed.

Apparently, Doscher candy was so good and so highly valued that it was a regular target for thieves in Cincinnati. The *Cincinnati Enquirer* reported break-ins at the Doscher factory in 1883 and 1894, during which several lots of chewing gum were taken.

Employee group photos from the early 1900s into the 1920s show that the company employed about fifty factory workers, nearly evenly split between men and women. Today, the focus is on candy canes and the French Chew. Doscher is very proud to claim that it is one of the oldest manufacturers of candy canes in the country.

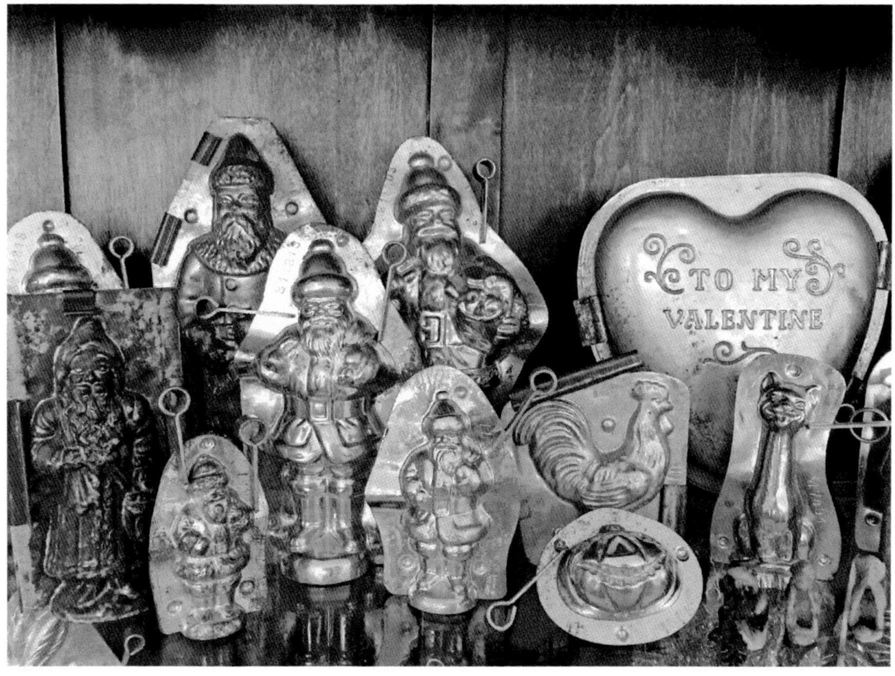

Doscher's used hundreds of chocolate molds like these pre-1900 examples. *Marilyn Doscher Johnson.*

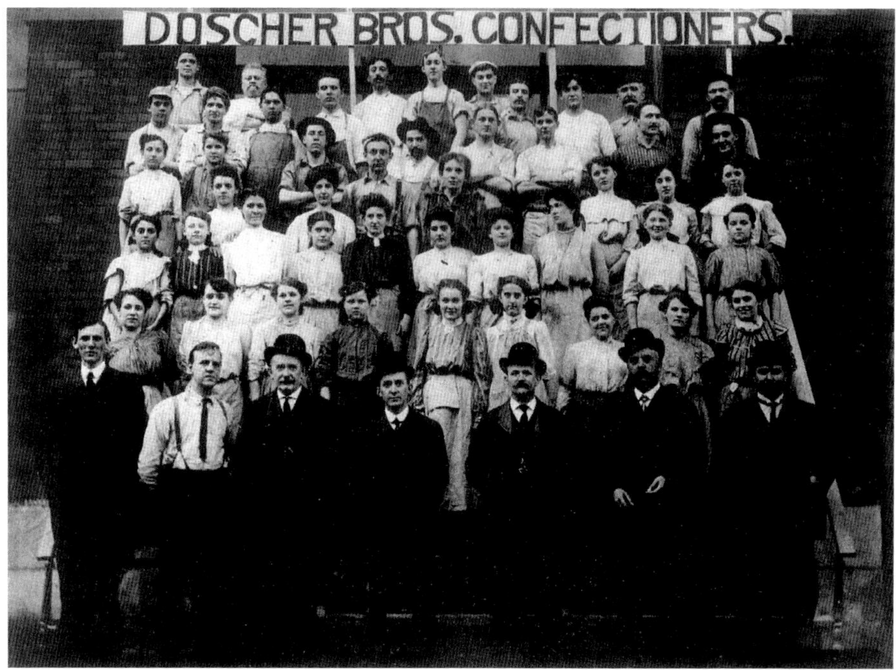

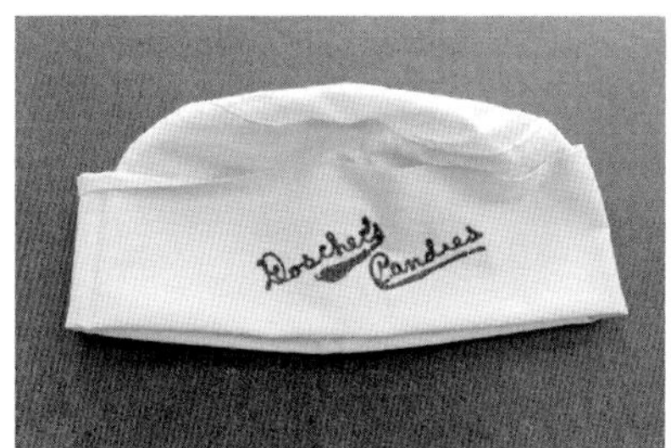

Above: A photo from the early 1900s of the employees of Doscher's. *Cindy Doscher.*

Left: Workers wore white hats, as shown here, embroidered with a red "Doscher Brothers." *Marilyn Doscher Johnson.*

John Doscher (1848–1932) took over the company after Claus's death in 1883 and quietly married his brother's wife, Sophia, eight years later. Sophia's sons John (1877–1941) and Harry (1883–1939) became partners in the business. By 1900, they had moved into a large red pressed brick house in Avondale at 3416 Harvey Avenue, which they bought from Julius Rothschild for $11,000. Julius moved to New York with his brothers David and Louis to move their furniture and billiard business. They became loan sharks, and Julius and David were both convicted of fraud and imprisoned at the infamous Sing Sing. John and Sophia; her sons John and Harry and their families; and Sophia's sister, Lena Koenemann, all lived together in the beautiful eight-room home. Lena worked as a clerk at the Doscher store and never married.

The Doschers didn't forget their surrounding community, and the business regularly donated to the German Old Folks Home in Cincinnati. Sophia Doscher was a very active member of the Woman's Club of St. John's Lutheran Church in Mount Auburn, serving on committees for various charity events. The Doscher men were members of the North Cincinnati Turnverein, a very influential German sport and social club in Corryville on Short Vine. They were also founding members and attendees of the first National Confectioners Association Conference in Chicago in 1884. Harry Doscher was elected vice-president of the Ohio Confectioners' Club at its convention in Cleveland in 1918.

A 1916 advertisement for chocolate and cream dippers and packagers at the Doscher factory at 9 Canal Street, now Central Parkway, showed their need for skilled candy workers. The same jobs were also listed in the same paper for the Reinhart & Newton and William C. Johnson companies, so there was quite a competitive market in Cincinnati.

By 1921, it had become clear to the Doscher family that the wholesale business was more profitable, and they decided to exit retail. They leased their store at 152 West Fifth Street, which they had operated for fifty years, to Clarence Poole.

From then on, Harry Doscher traveled around the region in a horse-drawn wagon and, later, a new truck, delivering candy in bulk to their wholesalers. Delivery by horse-drawn wagon was a dangerous business. During a delivery to a customer in Hamilton, Ohio, in 1924, he, his mules and the wagon were hit by a streetcar on High Street.

Starting with the death in February 1932 of John Doscher, brother of Claus, a series of hard times fell on the Doscher family. Claus's sons, Harry and John, passed away in 1939 and 1941, and Harry's wife, Elsie Doscher, took over the business. The Doschers had put all their money into the only bank in Cincinnati that folded during the Depression, so they lost their savings and cash flow for the business. Determined not to lose the business, Elsie became the strong matriarch, graduating from the University of Cincinnati as the first woman with a degree in finance. She held the business together and remained the strong force behind it into her old age. Her candy legacy was adding new flavors of chocolate and strawberry French Chews. She ran the business herself while her son, Harry II, obtained a University of Cincinnati business degree and served two years in the army. He would join her in the business in 1953. It was Elsie who moved the business to 24 West Court Street in 1946, where it has been ever since.

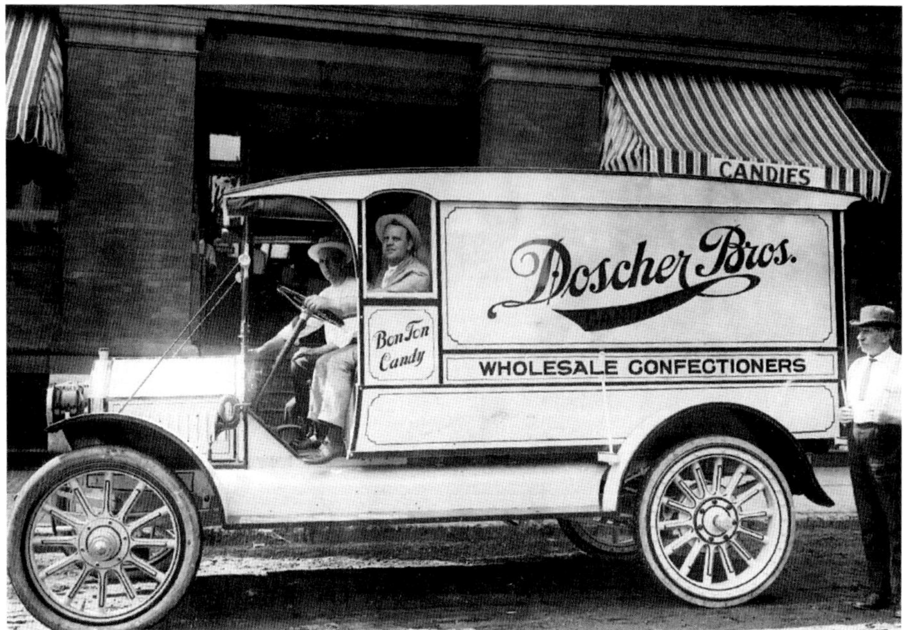

This 1920s image of the Doscher delivery truck shows, *from left to right*, Harry II, Harry Sr. and John Doscher. *Cindy Doscher.*

For Doscher, the candy cane making usually starts in early October. During peak times, twenty-five batches of ninety-pound candy canes are manufactured per day in a way that is nearly the same as it was in 1871. This amounts to about 2 million total candy canes per Christmas season. Also, during this time, the factory and even the apartments upstairs are fragrant with the smell of peppermint oil used in the candy. The renters of the apartments above the Court Street factory reminisce about smelling peppermint wafting up into their apartments during the holiday candy cane making process. And there was always a supply of warm candy cane pieces to be had from mistakes.

The candy cane process begins with the loading of a one-hundred-pound sack of sugar into a large copper kettle, where it is joined with water and corn syrup. After the three ingredients are cooked and cooled to the proper consistency, a now ninety-pound glob of molten candy is plopped onto a cooling table. There, one candy maker and two aides begin forming the candy canes into their final shape. The batch is divided into two portions. One will become the red stripe. The other will have calcium carbonate added to prevent the red from bleeding into the white. The white portion is placed on a wheel and spun until it becomes white and translucent. During the spinning is when the pungent peppermint oil is added. It's probably this spinning that gives the Doscher candy canes their signature crunch and chewiness.

After spinning, the red and white layers are fed at the same time into a machine that rolls them together. After they are twisted together, thin sticks of striped candy emerge from the rolling machine, and they are bent into hooked candy canes while they are still warm.

Doscher's customers are mostly wholesalers in Ohio, Kentucky and Indiana. But the company also has several large Cincinnati retailers like Kroger. In the past, it sold to other Cincinnati department stores, like Van Leunen's and Swallen's.

Harry Doscher II was a one-man show until his son, Harry III, joined in the late 1990s. Harry Doscher II made the candy, did the accounting, hired the helpers, marketed the product, negotiated with brokers and did everything else required by the business.

Harry Doscher III wanted to update the manufacturing from the old taffy-pulling machines and copper kettles his great-grandfather had used nearly a century before. But after much deliberation, the Doschers decided in 2004 to sell the four-generation family business to Greg Clark, who continues to use the old Doscher family recipes and original equipment. Greg Clark has a candy legacy, too—his father was a partner in the Marpro Marshmallow Products Company. Marpro makes the local Yum Yum marshmallow cones popular at swim clubs and candy shops all across the country.

Clark released several new products after taking over the company. The first was small individually wrapped French Chew Minis with new tropical flavors like Lemon Chill, Key Lime and Island Orange, as well as gourmet flavors like Sea Salt Caramel, Chocolate Raspberry, Cappuccino and Butterscotch. In 2016, Doscher released Peppermint Dust, for use in cake and confection decoration. This product is the result of reutilizing the throwoff of broken and off-spec candy canes. So not only are Doscher's candy canes one of the oldest candy cane products in the United States, it also may be the only no-waste candy cane product.

Chip Nielsen became partner in the Doscher business in 2015. Nielsen was formerly with Al Neyer, a real estate developer. He brought his wife, Robin Nielsen, and daughter, Amy, and her husband, Kevin Gilligan, into the business as additional partners.

In December 2016, Doscher's collaborated with Braxton Brewery of Covington, Kentucky, to create Claus Peppermint Sweet Stout, an imperial stout named after Claus Doscher, the company founder. The Braxton Brewery's website said of this collaborative product, "The beer is dark brown in color, with hints of red from the Doscher's peppermint added to the brew. No peeking, but if you're nosey, you'll get scents of milk chocolate and creamy sweetness with subtle mint. The flavor is primarily chocolate and as the beer warms, peppermint becomes prominent."

Braxton showed the brew with a Doscher Peppermint Dust–rimmed pint glass, opening up the confection to a new market of rimming boozy cocktails.

In 2011, Harry Doscher, great-grandson of founder Claus Doscher, bought the Señor Murphy Candymaker in Santa Fe, New Mexico. Señor Murphy is another family business founded in 1971, one hundred years after his great-grandfather founded Doscher Brothers. Señor Murphy's has two locations and a plant in Santa Fe and two in Albuquerque. Harry didn't take any candy making heirlooms with him, but he did take his grandfather's 1869 Ohio-made, wooden-framed, iron-clad wheel velocipede bicycle known as a "bone shaker." He now makes candies with local New Mexican ingredients, like pinon toffee and chile-flavored chocolates. Señor Murphy's most popular candy is the Twin Peaks, two roasted almonds on a patty of caramel that's then dipped in dark chocolate.

The latest news of the Doscher business is a planned 2017 move into a historic 1820s homestead in the village of Newtown, east of Cincinnati. The new 1.7-acre site will give the company and its ten employees an 8,300-square-foot kitchen, where they will offer product demonstrations and continue the legacy of the nearly 150-year-old business.

Chapter 5

MULLANE'S

MADE WITH LOVING CARE FOR MORE THAN 140 YEARS

For more than 140 years, Mullane's delighted Cincinnati and the American sweet tooth with its candy. It's a strong testimonial when a candy company lasts more than a century and through several owners even after the founding family sells the business.

Mullane's was one of the few female-owned companies before the Civil War. Irish immigrants William and Mary Fitzpatrick Mullane founded the company in 1848 on Valentine's Day, according to family legend. Catering to the sweet tooth of children, they started a small candy store at Mound Street in the West End of downtown Cincinnati, near the schoolhouse. William worked for the Robert Clark Printing Company but died tragically in 1863, leaving a young family. The candy store became Mary's sole support for her and her three sons: Will Jr., Charles and John. As the business grew, she moved to a larger store at the corner of Court and Baymiller Streets on the West End of Cincinnati.

By the mid-1870s, Will Jr. and Charles had both died, and John was left to help his mother carry on the business. To bring some expertise into the business, John left Cincinnati in the 1870s to apprentice in Quebec, Canada, under the famed confectioner William McWilliams. John came back in 1876 with a wealth of knowledge, as well as something else: a new French Canadian wife. He had met and married Harriet Giroux on the Isle of Orleans, in the St. Lawrence River, north of Quebec City. Together, they had three sons: Harvey Paul, Arthur Gerald "Jerry" and Charles Giroux—all of whom became involved in the business.

Harriet died in 1891, and eight years later, John remarried Mary Cahill, with whom he had one daughter, Alicia. John Mullane built a new factory at Central Avenue in 1892. Then, in 1895, he opened a large store at Number Four Ladies Square on Fourth Street between Race and Vine, a busy shopping area of Cincinnati. A large bulb-lit, heart-shaped sign hung from that building, enticing customers in for a confection or a soda fountain concoction.

The Fourth Street store was long and narrow, with one side featuring the marble-topped soda fountain and an overflowing candy counter opposite. A small back room with tables was separated by an ornate Victorian screen for customers who wanted a more private setting than the soda counter.

The Mullane's soda fountain served more than thirty flavors of ice cream sodas, with house-made syrups, from the standard to the bizarre (such as beef tea syrup). Sodas with syrups indicating Cincinnati's early wine industry were on the menu—a Catawba syrup and an Ives Seedling Syrup. A forgotten syrup called Nesselrode was also on the menu, which was a popular Victorian-era drink and confection containing Maraschino cherries, candied pineapple, crushed Marrons (hazelnuts) and rum flavoring. The syrup is named after Count Karl Nesselrode, who was a Russian diplomat from 1815 to 1855.

Mullane's taffy was a popular candy at the Cincinnati movie houses and vaudeville theaters. A ten-cent slug of Mullane taffy didn't make it through many shows. In the Mullane recipe book by John Mullane, the following description shows how truly these candies were "made with loving care" and with quality ingredients:

> *To make these Taffies and to keep them up to the high standard that has always been maintained it is essential that only the best and purest materials be used. Only the finest flavors and essential oils and the sweetest creamery butter are to be used.*
>
> *It is even more important that the batch be cooked to exactly the right degree as too high a test will spoil the effect of the finest materials. If any leeway is to be allowed it is better to have the test too low rather than too high, as the greatest fault will then be stickiness and poor keeping quality.*
>
> *It is our aim to have these taffies cooked just high enough to stand up well and low enough to soften quickly in the mouth. If cooked too high, these goods will be brittled and will stick to the teeth unpleasantly.*

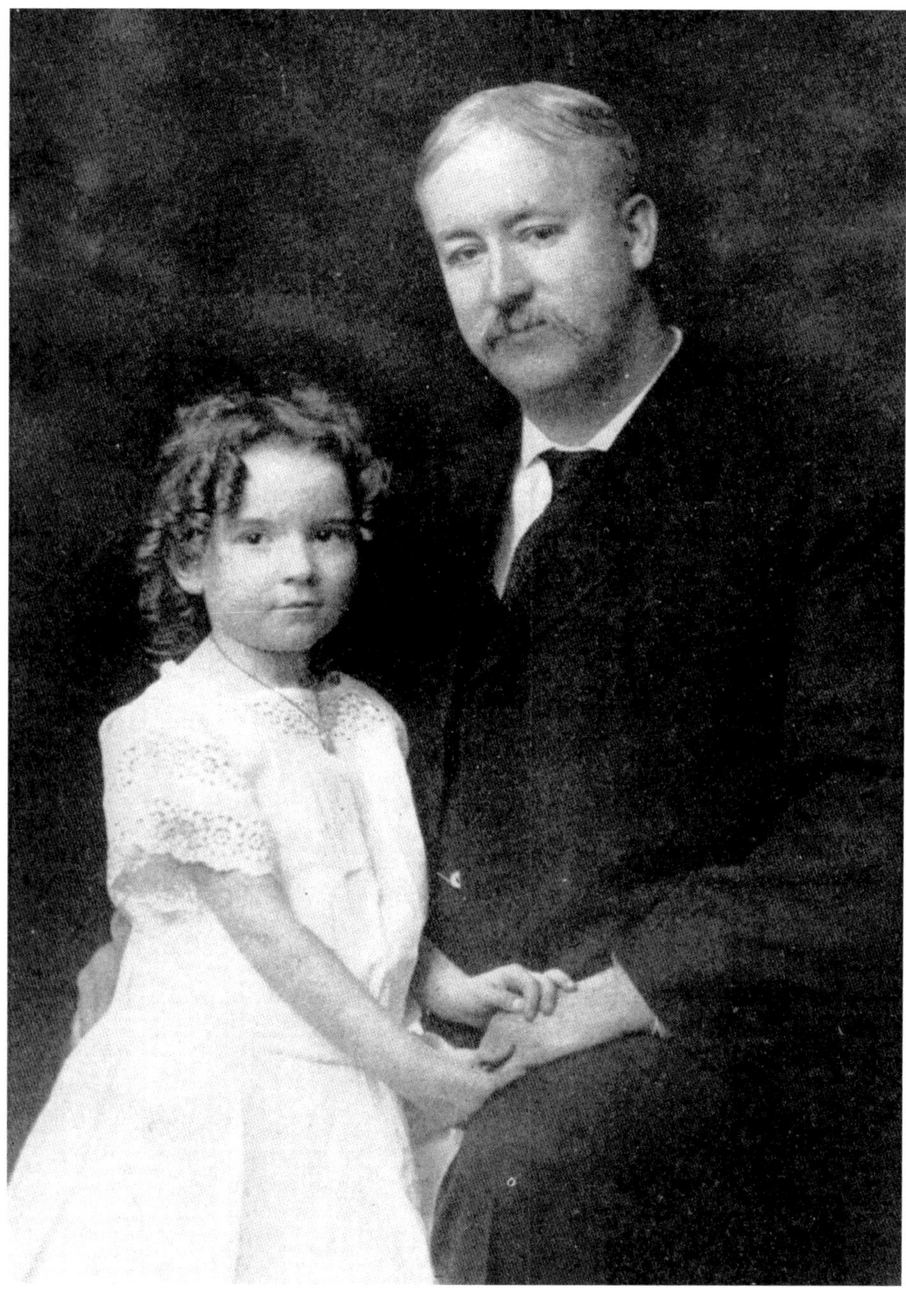

John Mullane and his daughter, Alicia. *Public Library of Cincinnati and Hamilton County.*

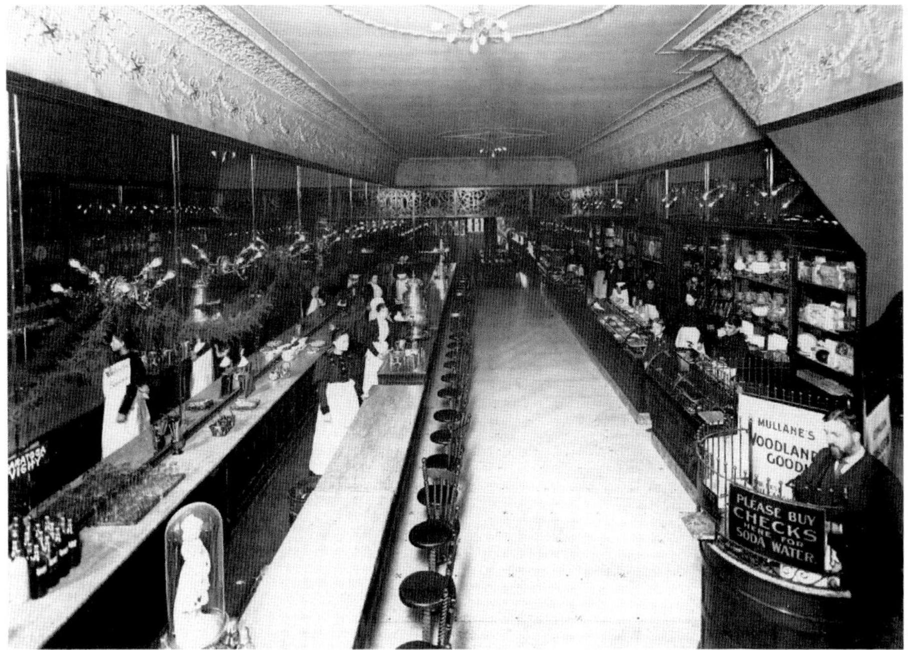

Above: The 1895 interior of the Fourth Street Mullane's store. *Molly Erhart Imhoff.*

Opposite, top: The majestic entrance to the Fourth Street store, shown here in 1895, allowed for fantastic displays of Mullane's candy. *Molly Erhart Imhoff.*

Opposite, bottom: A page from the 1918 candy catalogue showing the extensive taffy flavors. *Ron Case.*

Dental health was an important consideration to the Mullanes with their taffies. Taffyettes and kisses were introduced in the 1950s and marketed for safety: "It's bite sized now—no more denture trouble."

By the 1950s, the standard taffy flavors were molasses, vanilla, peppermint, anise, licorice, nectar, coconut and cinnamon.

One of the earliest candies that Mullane's was known for were its nectar drops. These were pink round-shaped hard candies with a combination of vanilla and almond flavors. The drops are described as tasting like pound cakes. Mullane's also served the flavor at its fountains in the form of Cincinnati's original nectar soda, which every local fountain imitated.

Mullane's invested in hundreds of candy dies, with specialized shapes for all the holidays. It even had a die with an axe for President's Day. Its Easter candies were also extensive, and it used a large assortment of chocolate bunny molds, including a rare leapfrog pair.

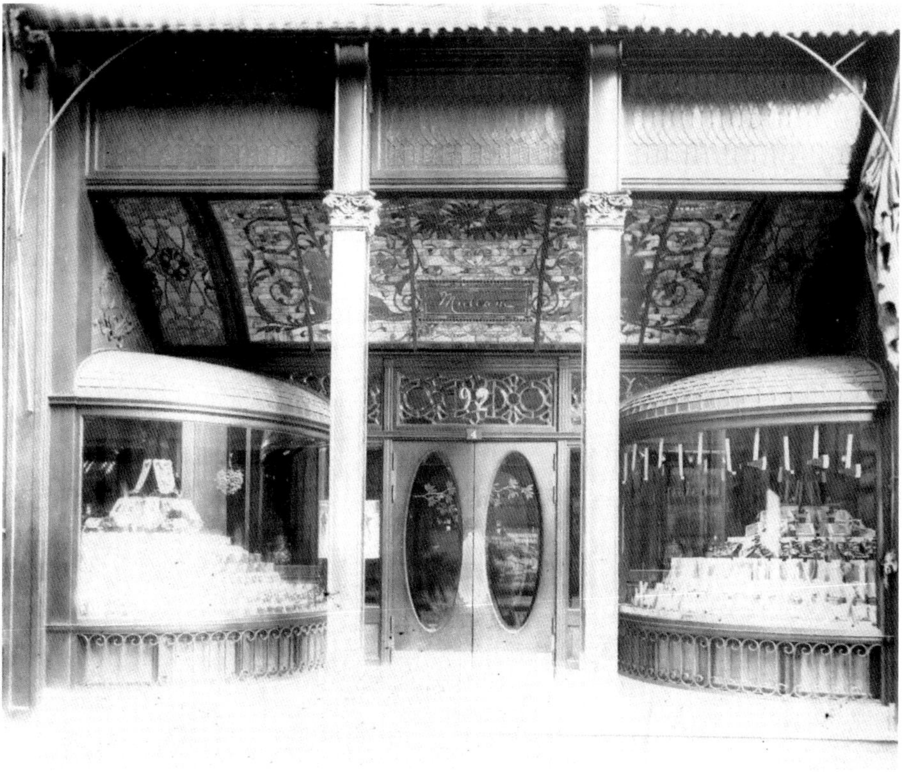

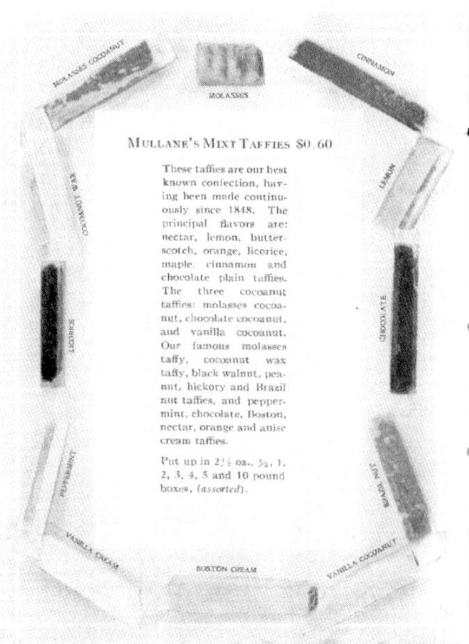

MULLANE'S MIXT TAFFIES $0.60

These taffies are our best known confection, having been made continuously since 1848. The principal flavors are: nectar, lemon, butterscotch, orange, licorice, maple, cinnamon and chocolate plain taffies. The three cocoanut taffies: molasses cocoanut, chocolate cocoanut, and vanilla cocoanut. Our famous molasses taffy, cocoanut wax taffy, black walnut, peanut, hickory and Brazil nut taffies, and peppermint, chocolate, Boston, nectar, orange and anise cream taffies.

Put up in 2½ oz., ½, 1, 2, 3, 4, 5 and 10 pound boxes, *(assorted)*.

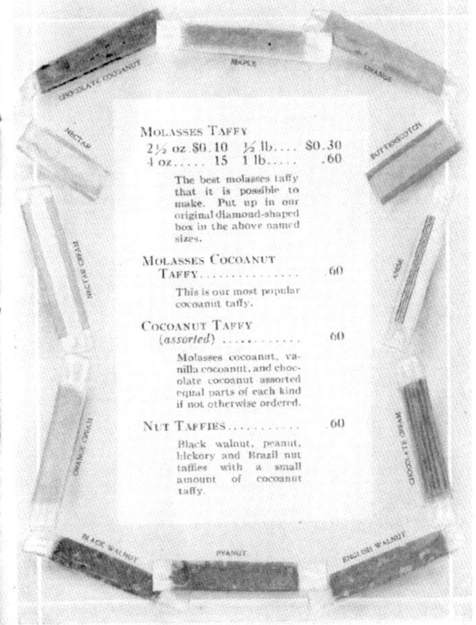

MOLASSES TAFFY
2½ oz. $0.10 ½ lb.... $0.30
4 oz..... 15 1 lb..... .60

The best molasses taffy that it is possible to make. Put up in our original diamond-shaped box in the above named sizes.

MOLASSES COCOANUT TAFFY.............. 60

This is our most popular cocoanut taffy.

COCOANUT TAFFY *(assorted)* 60

Molasses cocoanut, vanilla cocoanut, and chocolate cocoanut assorted equal parts of each kind if not otherwise ordered.

NUT TAFFIES........... 60

Black walnut, peanut, hickory and Brazil nut taffies with a small amount of cocoanut taffy.

Mullane's became known for a confection called Woodland Goodies, which were nut brittle–like clusters. A twenty-dollar gold piece was given to the winner of a naming contest held by John Mullane in the late 1880s. The brand was the idea of Mrs. Virginia Howell of Covington, Kentucky, who was chosen out of thousands of entrants. Woodland Goodies were mixtures of nine types of nuts, encased in an amber candy cluster. The nut varieties were pecans, English walnuts, black walnuts, hickory nuts, Brazil nuts, peanuts, almonds, pignolias (pine nuts) and filberts (hazelnuts). An assortment of clusters came in a round gold metal tin to keep them fresh.

A 1918 candy catalogue shows the wide variety of candies the company produced. No other Cincinnati candy company sold such an extensive line of fine candies. It produced more than sixty types of chocolate bonbons, twelve flavors of caramels, more than fifty types of chocolates, fifty types of floral wafers, hard and soft gumdrops, eight varieties of hard candies, candied popcorn, more than forty types of fine reception candies, salted nuts, special candies (which included marzipan fruits and vegetables), taffies and Woodland Goodies.

The high quality of the ingredients is really what set Mullane's apart from other candy makers. It used real oil of Bergamot orange in its butterscotch taffy. It specified New Orleans molasses for its taffies. For its marzipan, it ground Catania almonds from Sicily. In its licorice flavors it used Dulce de Corioliano licorice. It even hand-shaved San Blas coconuts from Panama for its candies. It would be Mullane's loyalty to these high-end ingredients that would later make it uncompetitive and force it into bankruptcy.

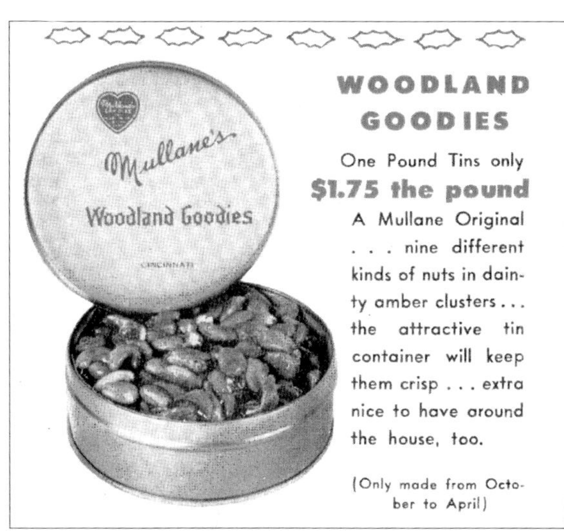

An advertisement for Mullane's Woodland Goodies. *Ron Case.*

"the Cases" . . formerly of Radio
Take pleasure in Announcing this Welcome to Cincinnatians

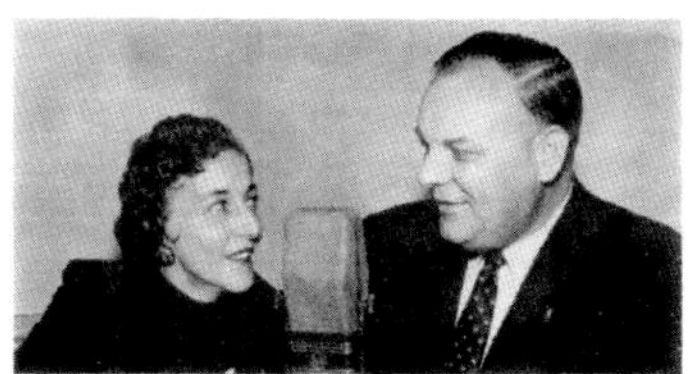

Please visit us soon in our New Shop
MULLANE TAFFY CO.
4705 Montgomery Road
JE 1-7887 **Cincinnati 12, Ohio**
"We Ship Anywhere In The World"
Mullane Taffy is a welcome gift for any occasion. Special attention to your Remembrance and Christmas Lists.
Charge Accounts Invited **JE 1-7887**

MARILU & GEORGE CASE
of
THE MULLANE TAFFY CO.
4705 Montgomery Rd.

Invite you to come in and bring this with you to participate in the drawing for **15 TWO POUND BOXES OF DELICIOUS MULLANE CANDY** of your choice.

We will be pleased to open your charge account for your convenience when you visit us, or phone.

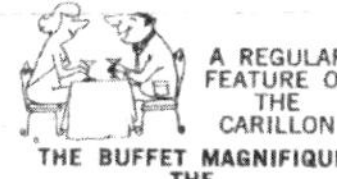

A REGULAR FEATURE OF THE CARILLON
THE BUFFET MAGNIFIQUE
THE
THE Carillon
WAS DESIGNED FOR GUESTS ON MODIFIED-AMERICAN PLAN
OUR PLAN FOR OUR TWO WINNING COUPLES!

The announcement in 1958 of the Cases buying Mullane's. *Ron Case.*

John Mullane died in 1910, leaving his three sons, wife and daughter to take over the business, now representing the third generation of the Mullane family. But family sibling trouble was soon to come.

In 1935, a family squabble split the company into the Mary Mullane Taffy Company and the John Mullane Company. Charlotte Cahill, who was John Mullane's sister-in-law and treasurer of the company; her sister, John Mullane's widow, Mary Cahill Mullane; and the children of John Mullane—Charles, Harvey and Alica Mullane Cahill—sued their brother Gerald Mullane. Gerald got the Mary Mullane Taffy Company, and his other siblings got the John Mullane Company.

The Mullanes were connected to three separate and unrelated Cahill families of Cincinnati. John's second wife was Mary Cahill. Mary Cahill's sister, Charlotte Cahill, was secretary of the Mullane company. John Mullane's son Gerald married Alice Cahill. And his daughter, Alicia, married and later divorced Lawrence Cahill.

In 1958, WSAI radio personalities George and Marilu Case tossed in their microphones and bought the Mary Mullane Taffy Company from Sandy Shepherd. As George Case put it, "Sandy Shepherd came to our home and practically gave us the candy company. We paid it off in monthly installments in eight months." At the time, Mullane's had a store in the old Palace Theatre building at 20 East Sixth Street.

With the purchase of the company came an old portrait of the founder, Mary Mullane, that hung in the various stores. Apparently, it was imposing and the object of many jokes for the later generations. In a June 25, 1956 *Cincinnati Enquirer* article, Ruth Cahill gazes proudly at the portrait of her great-aunt during an interview. It was Mary Mullane's push that built the pull-taffy business more than one hundred years ago. "But something's wrong," mused Miss Cahill, who managed the Mullane Taffy store at 20 East Sixth Street. She studied the canvas. "Ah! I've got it!" she finally exulted. "She needs lipstick!" And with that, she applied some of her own to her ancestor's face. Ron Case, son of George and Marilu, had the portrait in his house for a while, until they sold it with the house.

The owners of the Palace Theatre weren't cooperative in coming up with a good lease for the Cases, so within the period of a few weeks, they moved the company to Norwood and a new home at 4705 Montgomery Avenue, three doors down from Norwood City Hall. This gave them an expanded 1,600 square feet of space, nearly three times larger than the downtown space.

The John Mullane Company still existed, with a candy facility at 318 Longworth Street and a restaurant downtown. In 1963, the struggling John Mullane Company approached the Cases to make candy for them, but nothing materialized. Then the Cases learned that the John Mullane Company was going into bankruptcy and was for sale. The Cases made the highest bid at the auction and took over the company on October 14, 1963. After more

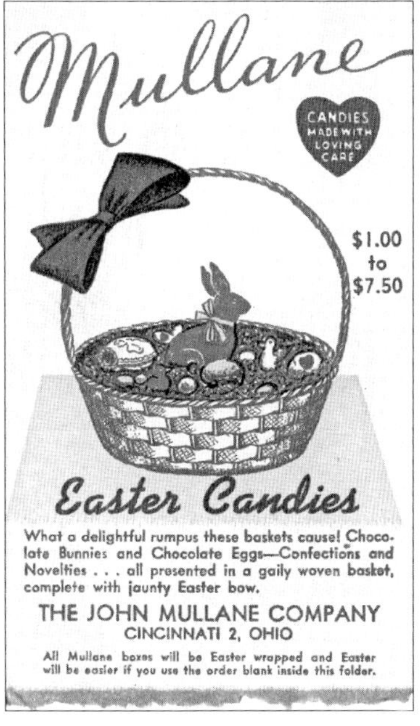

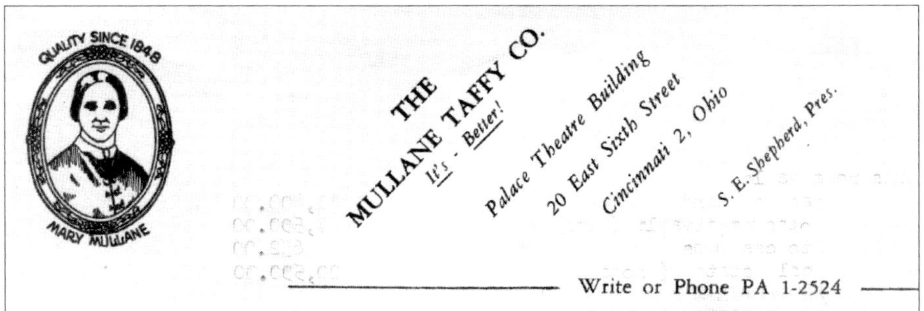

Top: An ad for Mullane's Easter candy under the Cases' ownership. *Ron Case.*

Bottom: The logo and letterhead of the Mary Mullane Taffy Company from 1958. The logo of Mary Mullane is based on a portrait of her that the Cases inherited with the company. *Ron Case.*

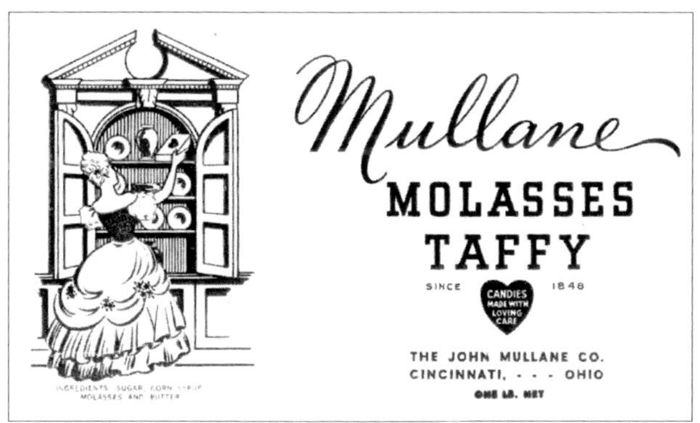

The box cover art for Mullane's taffy. *Ron Case.*

than three decades, the Cases were able to reunite what the Mullane family had torn apart.

The Longworth street factory had to be abandoned to make way for urban renewal and the new Cincinnati Convention Center. So, machinery, facilities and equipment were moved from downtown to 4108 Spring Grove Avenue, near Northside. The new facility was four thousand square feet, to allow for manufacture, storage and cold room facilities, with easy access to Interstate 75.

In 1960, the Cases branded and packaged a large foot-long flat taffy they called Daffy Taffy, with a freckled boy as the mascot, but were quickly sued by a company in California that had already trademarked the name.

During the years of ownership, George Case ran a candy booth at Lesourdesville Lake Park, in Middletown, Ohio, north of Cincinnati. He would drive up every morning after loading up the day's candy inventory from the Norwood plant, work the stand and drive home at night. After only a year, they decided that although it was good for promotion and exposure, it wasn't worth the time and effort.

In 1983, George Case sold Mullane Taffy to the Prince brothers. They bought it specifically to sell taffy to Kings Island Amusement Park. But that lasted only a few years, and then the Princes threw in the towel. The Mullane's name dropped from the candy world after nearly 140 years. One brother, Robert Prince, made quite a name for himself as a cake decorator for the BonBonerie in the O'Bryonville neighborhood of Cincinnati after shutting down Mullane's.

Ron Case, son of George and Marilu, sold the old Mullane bronze drop candy dies to Greg Cohen of Tallahassee, Florida, who uses them in his candy shop to demonstrate antique candy making methods. So the Mullane dies may continue to make vintage candy for decades to come.

ORIGIN OF NECTAR FLAVOR

New Orleans claims that it invented the nectar soda. The man given credit for inventing the nectar flavor was a druggist, I.L. Lyons, who immigrated to New Orleans from South Carolina after the Civil War and started selling the syrup to a chain of soda fountains called Katz and Besthoff, or K&B, in New Orleans. The topic of nectar soda history has been presented many times at the Southern Food and Beverage Museum in New Orleans, where presenters claim that until recently, the nectar soda flavor was lost, as well as that it's only known in the Crescent City.

In Cincinnati, we've been serving the nectar soda continually since John Mullane introduced it in the late 1870s at his soda fountain and made it into a hard drop candy. It's been available locally since Mullane's went out of business at Graeter's and Aglamesis Ice Cream Parlors. And it's never been purchased as a premade syrup like it was in New Orleans—every Cincinnati ice cream parlor that served it made its nectar in house. It may not be as well known as black raspberry chip ice cream, but it's been sipped in Cincinnati continuously for more than 140 years.

Mullane had trained from 1875 to 1876 near Quebec City at the French confectionery of William McWilliams, which was established in 1857. Here he learned all the recipes that he would bring back to Cincinnati, including the nectar soda.

Although it sounds more like a fruit drink, nectar actually tastes more of pound cake. Early marketers even recommended changing its name for that reason.

So as much as New Orleans foodies would like to think the nectar soda is a southern invention, it's actually not a Louisiana thing, nor even a South Carolina thing, where its inventor originated. It's actually a recipe that originated among the French Acadians.

The Acadians were a group of French colonists who originally settled in Nova Scotia, New Brunswick, Prince Edward Island and in the Gaspe Peninsula, among other parts of eastern Quebec. During the French and Indian War, 1755–68, they were expelled from Canada to the American colonies, including South Carolina, where several ships landed in 1755.

Acadians later immigrated to southern Louisiana, including New Orleans, and became known as the Cajuns. Mullane's made nectar candy and sodas from the time John Mullane came back from his training on the Isle of Orleans in eastern Quebec. What the New Orleans nectar and the Mullane's nectar have in common is the Acadian background.

Mullane's used bitter almond extract for the nectar soda, not sweet almond, which is typically used in marzipan, nougat and French macaroons. The difference is that bitter almond is an essential oil, whereas sweet almond is a fixed oil or carrier oil. Essential oils can evaporate but are the essence of the plant from which they are derived. They are what is generally used for flavor and aroma.

And why the pink color for nectar? The sweet almond tree (*amygdalus*) is different from the bitter almond tree (*amara*). The bitter almond tree has pink blossoms, while the sweet almond tree has white blossoms.

Chapter 6

PROMINENT CINCINNATI CHOCOLATE COMPANIES

Dolly Varden Brings the Chocolate-Covered Cherry to Cincy

January 3 is National Chocolate-Covered Cherry Day. It may be a lesser-known food holiday, but it is a recognized holiday by the National Confectioners Association, and the confection has American origins in Cincinnati's Over-the-Rhine. They are also called cherry cordials because at one time they included cherry liqueurs like kirsch inside.

A chocolate company called Dolly Varden, founded in 1900 in Cincinnati's Over-the-Rhine by Jewish entrepreneur Isaac Weinreich (1878–1945), is credited for bringing the chocolate-covered cherry to the American market. Dolly Varden was a character from the Charles Dickens novel *Barnaby Rudge*. She was a locksmith's daughter and known for her flowered hat and dress, which gave its name to a popular women's outfit of the nineteenth century. Her character was well known in America and thus a brilliant name for a chocolate company. The company motto was "When Words Fail—Send Dolly Varden Chocolates."

Weinreich was the son of Bavarian immigrant David Weinreich, who was a cattle dealer and butcher. He would become involved with the Montgomery County, Ohio Democrats and chairman of the Democratic convention in Dayton in 1894. He also became a sports promotor, particularly of amateur baseball, and after selling the company, he moved with his family to Hollywood, California, where he died in 1945.

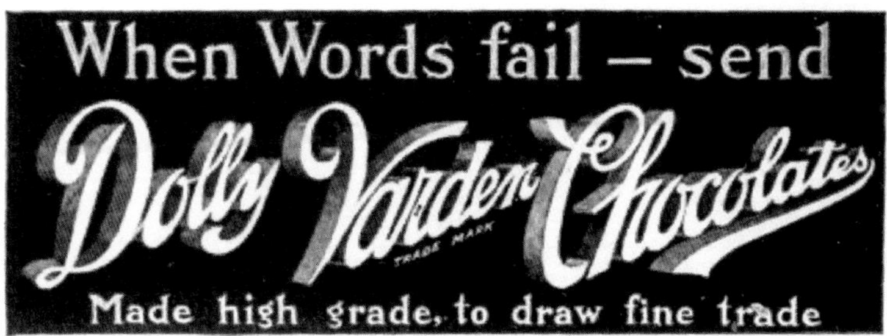

There's always a lingering memory of that perfect blending—of a delicious freshness—when one thinks of Dolly Varden Chocolates. And then the desire for more. Each first sale makes a regular customer.

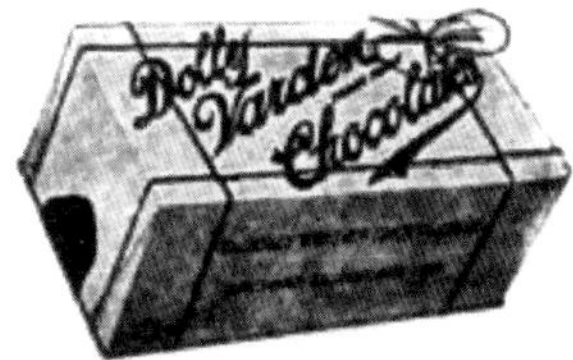

THE DOLLY VARDEN CHOCOLATE CO., Cincinnati, O.

An ad for Dolly Varden Chocolates, with its slogan, "When Words Fail—Send Dolly Varden Chocolates." *Public Library of Cincinnati and Hamilton County.*

Isaac's brother, Elias, owned a cigar manufacturing company in Dayton, Ohio, where Isaac grew up with his other siblings. Apparently, cigars and chocolate went together well in retail at the time. Dolly Varden chocolates were advertised as a good companion gift or a free box with purchase of cigar brands like Knauf's cigars in Sheboygan, Wisconsin, or Litman's in Coffeyville, Kansas. Perhaps Isaac and Elias worked together in retailing their chocolates and cigars.

The company had humble beginnings. Starting as a small retail store, Weinreich first patented a medicinal cough drop called "Checkers" in 1901 that he sold at the store on Vine Street. When they added eleven flavors of soft-centered chocolates, including the chocolate-covered cherry, their business grew, requiring two Over-the-Rhine moves to Fourteenth and Plum and then Canal and Walnut Streets. Finally, in 1919, they built a five-story factory on the West End at Laurel Street that employed four hundred workers and sat next to the Dolly Varden Movie Theatre. Coveted positions for women in Cincinnati were chocolate and bonbon dippers, who could make good money for the times. Beginning wages at the factory in 1914 were four dollars per week.

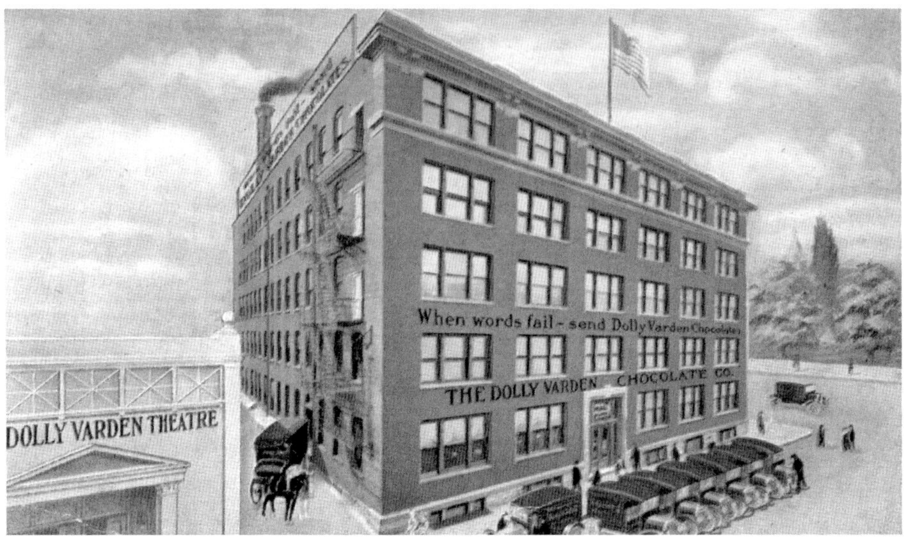

Above: A postcard of the large Dolly Varden Factory on Laurel Street. *Schimpff Candy Museum.*

Below: A 1910s glass slide used in a magic lantern projector in a movie theater advertises Dolly Varden. *Schimpff Candy Museum.*

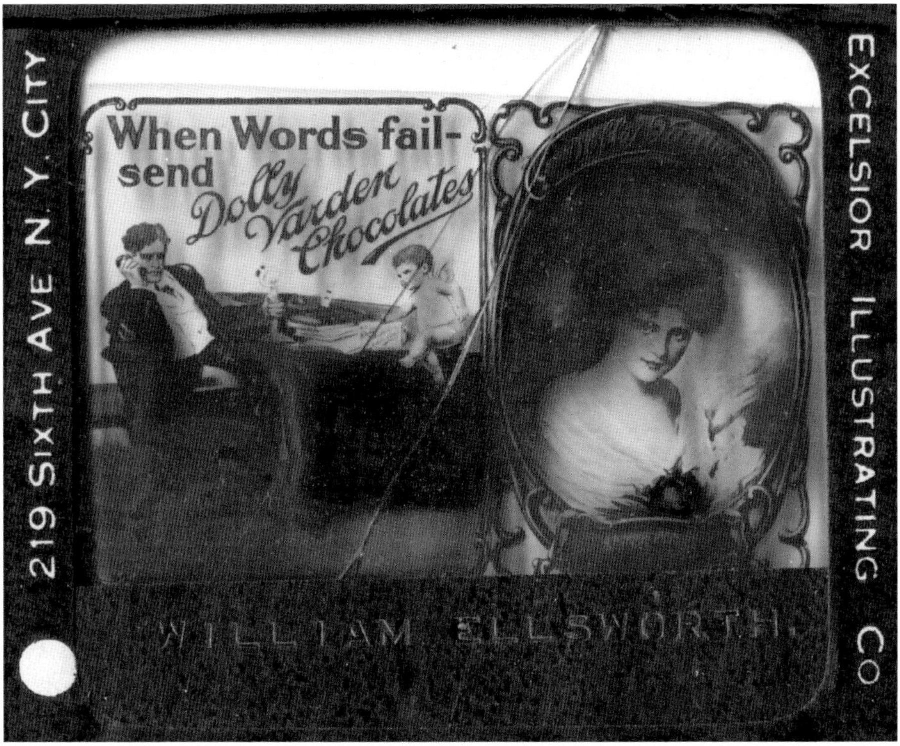

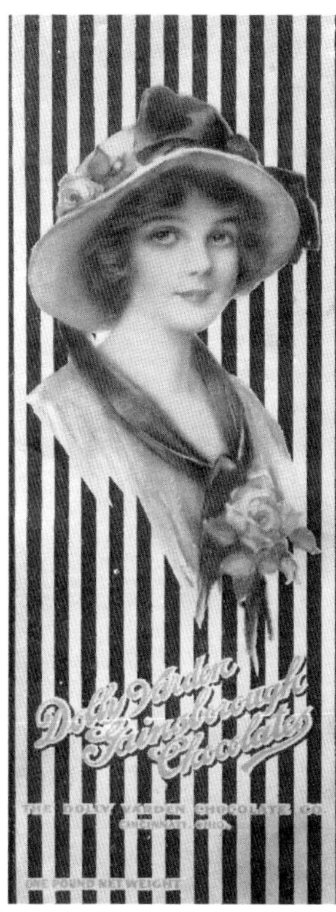

A 1910s Dolly Varden Chocolate box, featuring a pretty girl in a flowery hat. *Author's collection.*

In 1917, the National Confectioners Association put together a roll of honor among the member companies' employees. This recognized those within the industry who had answered the call to arms for World War I. Six brave Dolly Varden employees made this roll: Charles Lind, Wallace Smith, Frank Hutchinson, Eldridge Davies, Charles Zuefle and Paul Groene. Another Cincinnatian, Puritan Chocolate Company employee Second Lieutenant E.F. Dalton, also made the roll of honor

From about 1910, the company sponsored the Dolly Varden Candy Kids, a local baseball team in the Queen City league that boasted undefeated seasons in 1914 and 1917, playing other teams like Cincinnati Milling Machine and Andrew's Steel, according to a 1916 *International Confectioners* article. It also sponsored an adult league, the Dolly Varden Candy Makers, which played in the Brendamour M&M league and played local teams like Wurlitzer Piano and the Henderson Lithography Company.

By the 1920s, Dolly Varden chocolates had become a national brand, and a sister division in St. Louis, Missouri, was formed. Charles Eisen, son of Baden immigrants, became president in 1905 and believed in large advertising budgets. As a result, a lot of store signs and elaborately decorated Dolly Varden candy boxes can still be found by antique buyers. The Dolly Varden fortune allowed him to build a mansion in College Hill on Hamilton and Belmont Avenues, designed by Cincinnati architect Samuel Hanniford. Eisen retired from the company, becoming a famous piano player with the Cincinnati Symphony.

In 1923, Dolly Varden registered the brand names Rosemary and Dusky Lasses. In the 1920s, many candy companies, particularly chocolate companies, used the images of Gibson Girls and other pretty girls on their candy boxes. And Dolly Varden followed that trend with its packaging.

In 1922, Newell H. Hargrave (1880–1967), after buying an interest in the company, succeeded Eisen as general manager of the company. A native Cincinnatian and former track star at Yale, he had shifted industries from lumber to chocolate. He had previously been with the Kirkpatrick Lumber Company and was president of the Cincinnati Lumbermen's Club. He would later sell Dolly Varden to the Reinhart & Newton Company in 1924. It was closed shortly thereafter when both companies were merged into a conglomerate of several other candy companies.

Today, the three main brands of cherry cordials on the market are Cella's, Brochs and Queen Anne. Cella's is the oldest, established in 1865, but it only started mass-producing chocolate-covered cherries in 1929. Broch's started making chocolate-covered cherries in 1930. Finally, Queen Anne was founded in 1921 but didn't start making the cherry treats until 1948. The oldest record of Dolly Varden making chocolate-covered cherries is 1917, but there is reference to it making them as early as the founding in 1900. Whatever the date, although Dolly Varden didn't invent the chocolate-covered cherry, it did bring it to the American market.

THE PURITAN CHOCOLATE COMPANY

The Puritan Chocolate Company was founded in 1900 by Clifford L. Fowler, president; Malcolm A. McDonnel, secretary and treasurer; and Louis V. Arrico. By 1921, the company had reached $750,000 in sales and had just relocated to a six-story factory with basement, at 109–17 West Central Parkway. The new plant was eighty by ninety-six feet, with a full line of manufacturing equipment to make high-quality chocolate candies and marzipan fruits. This was the third move the company made in its eleven-year existence.

The company logo was a silhouette of a Pilgrim woman spinning yarn, and the tagline was "Puritan Chocolates—the Perfect Gift." They placed a variety of ads around the various holidays, all of which showed a curtseying female Pilgrim and a bowing male Pilgrim. A 1925 ad on Sweetest Day proclaimed, "Men be glad that Candy Day gives you more chance to remember the woman whose happiness depends on your thoughtfulness. Puritan, with the center she likes, with thicker, richer, smoother coatings, the finest she *ever* tasted is the pinnacle of thoughtfulness, '*The Perfect Gift*.'"

One of Puritan's sales targets were YMCA canteens all over the country. It advertised a free thirty-day trial starter package for YMCAs. The package consisted of a handsome "fumed oak" display cabinet with a twenty-five-dollar assortment of Puritan chocolates and other five- and ten-cent candies from other prominent national companies.

In 1920, its extensive chocolate lineup consisted of three lines: Preference Chocolates, which included cherry cordials, nut nougats, cream Brazils, milk almonds, filbert clusters and vanilla creams; Squirrel Chocolates, which integrated nuts with maple walnut creams, filbert clusters, peanut brittle, cream nut nougats, Brazil nuts and grenoble nuts; and finally, the Puritan Maid assortment, which included creams, caramels and hard centers.

Puritan advertised a chocolate-covered grenoble walnut. The grenoble walnut is a specific type of walnut grown in the Isere River Vally in the Rhone-Alps. The fresh water of the river gives the characteristic freshness and fineness to the nut. It's the only nut in the world to receive the French quality symbol AOC, which protects the product name and guarantees the link to its geographic origin.

In addition to candies, Puritan ventured out into the peripheral industry of soda fountains by offering a Marshmallow Crème product, advertised as "a spread for cakes, crackers, and a topping for ice cream, fruits, salads, etc." It also offered a product called Velvet Whip specifically for soda fountains that could be used as an ice cream topper or diluted with simple syrup or water.

In 1926, it opened a retail confectionery store called, not surprisingly, the Puritan Store. It was proclaimed "the finest of its kind west of New York." It featured a display of Puritan chocolates, and the site had a retail candy kitchen to produce specialty confections just for the store. A counter served the house-made French Pot ice cream with new "Frigidaire Iceless Equipment."

Puritan sponsored candy booths at the annual Protestant Orphan Home banquet at Burnet and Melish Avenues in Cincinnati to fund a much-needed new heating system: "There will be plenty of sweets at the Orphans' Feast Sunday at the General Protestant Orphan Home, Burnet and Melish Avenues. Eleven candy booths will be operated. Other candy booth Chairmen include Ralph Kleine, Clifford Fowler, Louis Arrico, Jacob Huber, Frank C. Ast, Robert Gorman, Rolo C. Crandall, Charles P. Tuch, and Fred J. Morr."

By 1950, the Puritan company had become the E.W. McDonnall Company and was making the brand of Arrico's Liquid Cream Chocolates, made by Louigi Vincento Arrico (none other than Louis Arrico, former executive of Puritan, playing on his Italian immigrant ancestry). His mother had been a candy maker in 1878 at 173 West Third Street. In April 1951, 190 boxes of Puritan's coconut, chocolate and opera cream eggs were seized and destroyed for having filthy substances—in the form of insects or rodent hair. This may have been a component of their eventual demise as a company.

WILLIAM C. JOHNSON COMPANY

The William C. Johnson Company was the only known candy company in Cincinnati to do celebrity co-marketing. In the 1930s, the company offered a five-cent doughnut-shaped confection called the Paul-I-Plop. It was named after Paul Whiteman, who was bandleader of the Whiteman Orchestra, a popular big-band group that played in Cincinnati at places like the Sinton Hotel and in other cities. The packaging had a print of Whiteman's caricature. The candy itself was a delicious combination of chocolate, caramel and coconut. Whiteman, a sweets aficionado, was most definitely a fan of his namesake confection.

The candy plant was at Plum and Laurel Streets in Cincinnati's West End. Johnson was known for its Shakespeare Chocolate Assortment, which consisted of Penochias Mex, orange sours, raspberry fruit creams, Ting-a-Lings, Italian pecos royale, almond rolls, colleens, figaros, cream walnuts, dipped Brazils, prunelias and Valencia buds.

It also had an assortment called Verigud, which included pecans in cream, nut nougats, apricot jellies, sour lemon creams, sour orange creams, pineapple creams, vanilla hand rolls, raspberry hand rolls and cream caramels. Another candy it sold were Bungalow Marshmallows, which were heavily chocolate-coated confectioners' marshmallows. The company closed in 1936.

BUHR & PFAFF

Buhr & Pfaff was a manufacturer of wholesale confections. Started in 1874 by partners Joseph Buhr (1844–1934) and Peter R. Wendt, it was located at 217 Walnut Street. The factory and office eventually occupied five separate buildings at the northeast corner of Second and Race Streets in Cincinnati's candy manufacturing district. Two of its lines were the New Era Brand of Princess Coconut Clusters and New Era Brand Butterscotch.

Frank L. Pfaff started working for the company in his early teens in 1872, becoming a traveling salesman for the company at age sixteen in 1874. In 1885, he was admitted as a third partner and was responsible for its great success. He was very involved in the National Confectioners Association, serving on its board in the early 1900s, as well as the Cincinnati Manufacturing Confectioners' Association.

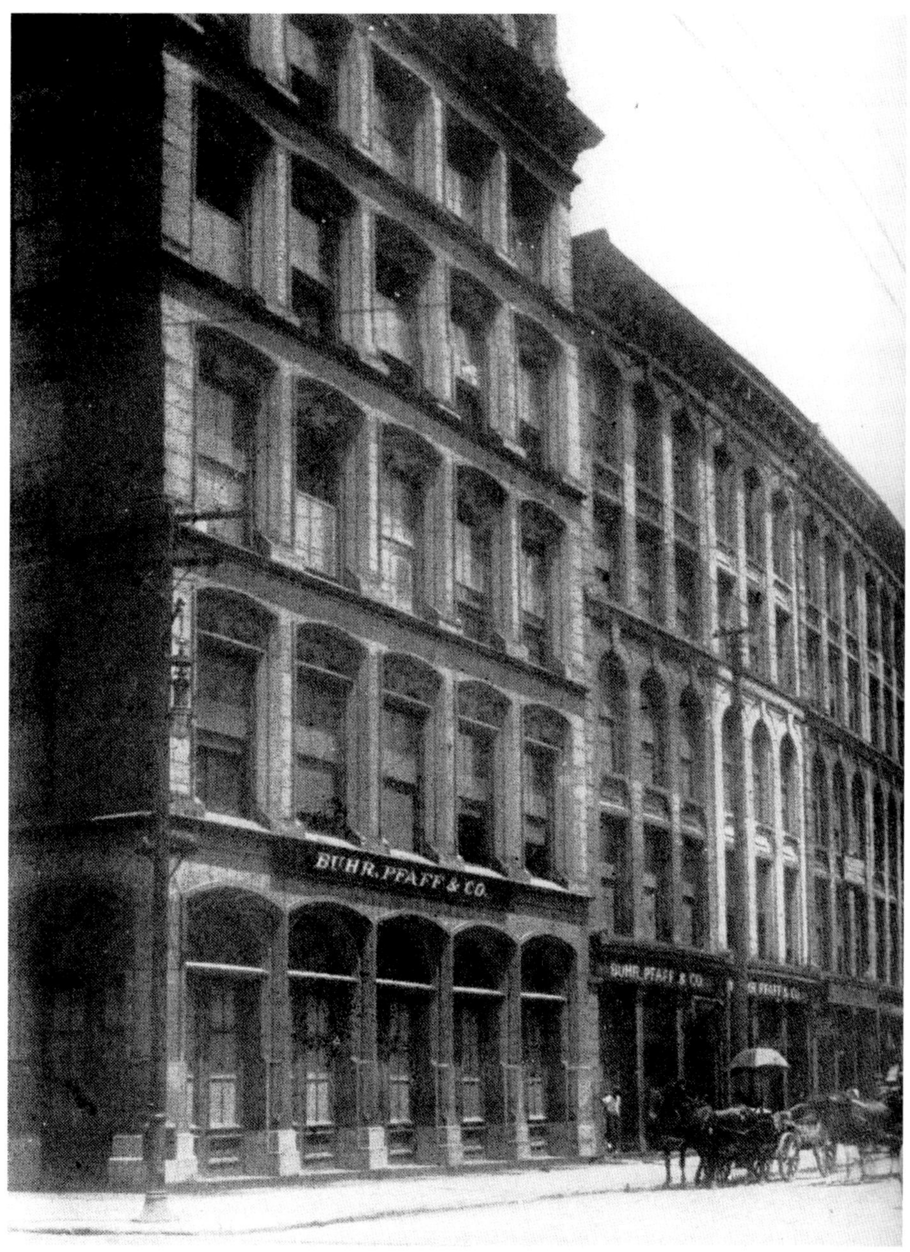

The Buhr & Pfaff candy company factory in 1914. *Public Library of Cincinnati and Hamilton County.*

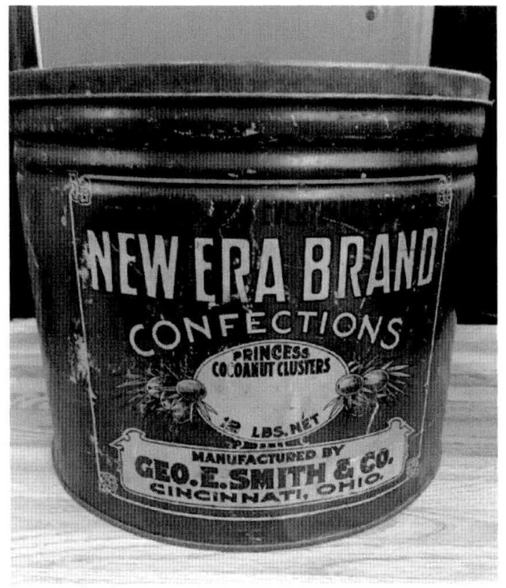

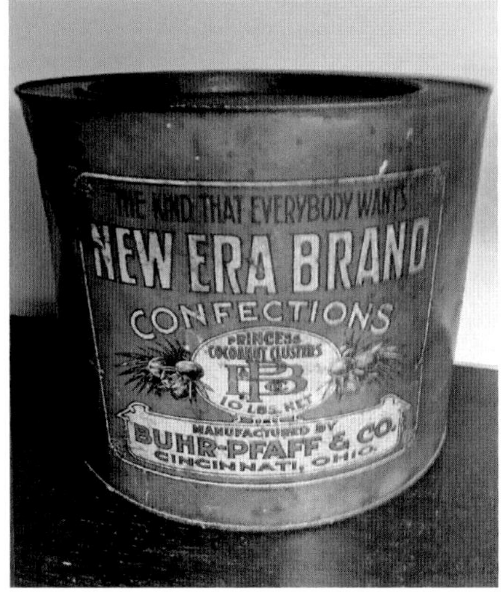

The Coconut Clusters wholesale candy tins of George Smith, *left*, and its predecessor, Buhr-Pfaff, *right*. *Schimpff Candy Museum and the author.*

Starting in 1897 with the death of Peter Wendt, there was a series of management changes. In 1905, Joseph Buhr retired, and Frank admitted his brother, Fred G. Pfaff, and Joseph Buhr's son, George J. Buhr, as partners in the company. Fred Pfaff became the plant superintendent.

In 1902, Buhr & Pfaff was asked to become part of the National Candy Company, but like the Reinhart & Newton Company, it declined. In 1903, it bought property and erected a five-story brick warehouse on Sycamore and Third Street. It had turned an older property in 1900 at the corner of Second and Race Streets into its candy factory, where it made stick candy, chocolate bonbons and chocolate-coated peanuts.

Before retirement, Pfaff complained about a new Ohio employment law that affected his Christmas holiday business. In 1913, the Ohio state legislature passed a law making it illegal for girls to work at night. Of his reasons for retiring, Pfaff said, "My retirement is due to two causes. In the first place I am in such a position that I can afford to retire. In the second place, the Socialistic laws which have been enacted in Ohio impel me to retire."

Pfaff retired from the business in 1914, passing it on to his son, Fred G. Pfaff; George C. Buhr, son of the founder; and George E. Smith. After retirement, Pfaff became vice-mayor of Cincinnati, no doubt fighting the evils of "socialistic labor laws."

The firm was one of the larger Cincinnati candy companies, employing between 225 and 250 people in its factories, which produced a line of candies known as the New Era brand. This brand would be taken over in 1922 by Frank Pfaff's son-in-law, George E. Smith, when he started the George E. Smith Company.

THE MEAKIN CANDY COMPANY

One family chocolate company had very artistic beginnings. In 1863, the Meakin family, headed by Lewis Henry and Sarah Keats, came to Cincinnati via Montreal, Canada, from Stratford-upon-Avon, England, where Lewis was a pottery manufacturer. In 1883, son Charles J. Meakin became a molder of chocolate instead of clay, opening his first confectionery shop on Baymiller Street in the West End and setting up his two sisters, Sarah and Nellie, to work in the shop while he pursued his main career of painting and decorating. By 1886, Charles saw that the confectionery business was so profitable and busy that he abandoned his other career.

With the help of his sisters, he built the business into five large stores in downtown Cincinnati, each with a large soda fountain. The stores were at 517 Race Street at Opera Place, 15 East Sixth Street near Vine, 529 Main Street and 831 Main Street and 1002–4 Baymiller Street. The Meakins made all their own fine candy and ice cream used in all their stores, making opera creams and fantastic panorama eggs at Easter. Charles involved one of his sons, Charles James, a World War I veteran, in the candy business.

A 1910 article in the *American Pure Food and Health Journal* featured the Meakin company as a model confectionery:

> *In the early eighties a little candy store was opened in the West End. In external appearance, it was not much of a store, but inside of it were perfect cleanliness and delicious sweetmeats calculated to tempt the appetites of the Gods of Olympus away from their fabled Ambrosia. A little sign, hanging above the door of the little store told passersby that this was "MEAKINS." And that candies were here for sale. It was in those days that the now famous "Old Original English Taffy" was first introduced to the American market. Never since has anything to equal it been produced and today it is the favorite confection of thousands.*
>
> *From the very beginning, the Meakin company has been noted for the absolute purity and high quality of all materials entering into its products,*

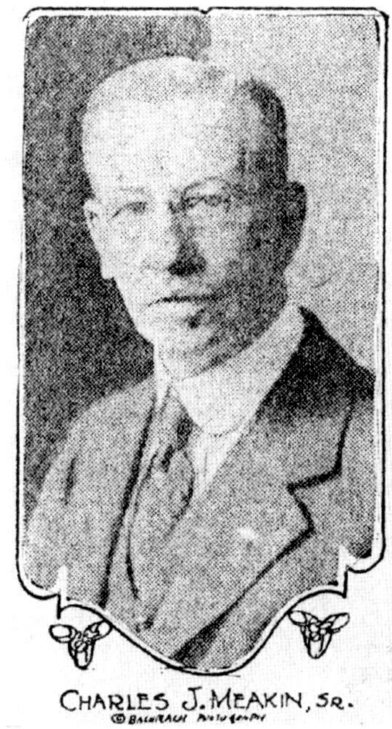

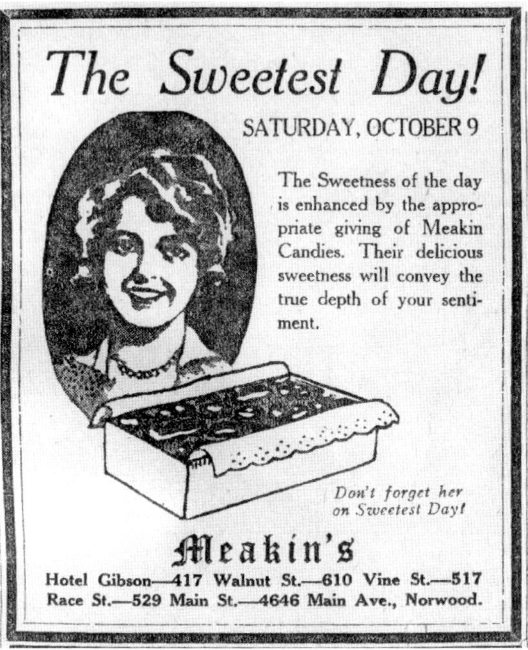

Left: Charles J. Meakin, owner of the Meakin Candy Company. *Public Library of Cincinnati and Hamilton County.*

Right: A Meakin newspaper ad from 1919. *Public Library of Cincinnati and Hamilton County.*

> *as well as for the perfect cleanliness of its methods of manufacture and the faultless sanitation of every place in which its candy is made or sold. The United States pure food laws are more than complied with.*

The slogan used in advertisements was "Meakins Candies Can Stand the Test." At that time, it employed forty people at the factory on Main Street near Sixth and manufactured one hundred distinct varieties of candy. In 1922, Charles expanded even further by buying another large factory at 610 Vine Street, near the Main Street factory. The company stayed in business into the 1950s.

Another brother, Lewis Henry Meakin Jr., became a famous American landscape painter after attending school at the Cincinnati Art Academy, and he later taught there with another famous local artist, Frank Duvenek. Sadly, there are no known paintings from him of Cincinnati candy factory workers, but his landscape paintings did hang in several of the Meakin candy stores.

Chapter 7

THE GOELITZ COMPANY AND THE BIRTH OF CANDY CORN

Candy corn is embedded in Cincinnati's candy history. It's one of the most iconic American Halloween candies. But you can now find it in other forms at other holidays like at Christmas as reindeer corn in green, red and white; at Easter as bunny corn in pastels; and even on Valentine's Day as cupid corn in red, pink and white. The newest version is a Fourth of July variation called freedom corn, colored red, white and blue.

Although George Renninger, an employee of the Philadelphia company Wunderle, probably created the chewy kernels in the 1880s, Cincinnati-based Goelitz Confectionery Company was the first to commercially produce candy corn in 1898. The tricolored niblets—yellow, orange and white—soon became a Goelitz specialty, leading the company to crown itself "the king of the candy corn field." The candy was released at a time when America was largely an agrarian economy.

Why was it produced in three colors—white, yellow and orange? It was an impression of reality. If you look at a cross section of a real kernel of corn, you can see that where it attaches to the husk it is light, and then it gets more yellow until at the end it's a darker yellow.

There is a long legacy in French and German confectionery of marzipan fruits and vegetables. Cincinnati confectioners like Mullane's, which based its offerings on French confectionery, supplied these marzipan treats.

Around the turn of the century, a new process of making a candy called buttercream was adopted that used sugar, marshmallow, corn syrup and fondant. This was basically the fast-food version of marzipan candy, the

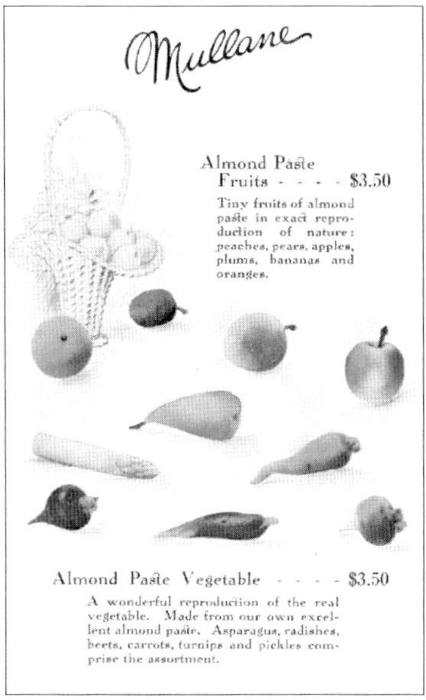

This page from the Mullane's 1905 candy catalogue shows its marzipan fruit offerings. *Ron Case.*

cheaper way to make molded sugar fruits and vegetables. Marzipan is made of almond paste and is a lot more expensive than sugar and the other ingredients in buttercream candy.

Buttercream candies, of which candy corn is a type, are made by cooking sugar, water and corn syrup; adding fondant for texture and marshmallow for softness; and then pouring the molten mixture into large buckets forty-five pounds at a time. Candy corn used to be made painstakingly by manually pouring three colored layers into molds. Now the process of making candy corn is highly automated.

Like their marzipan versions, buttercream veggie-shaped candy was popular, and the Goelitz Candy Company made other veggie shapes for a while.

THE GOELITZ COMPANY

The company that became the Jelly Belly Corporation was founded by two immigrant brothers from the Harz Mountain region of Germany. Gustav and Albert Goelitz were born to Adolph and Augusta Domyer Goelitz in Osterode am Harz, at the southern edge of the Kingdom of Hanover, now part of the federal state of Lower Saxony. While in Hanover, Gustav Goelitz had been in merchandising and later worked as a traveling salesman for a business house.

They came to the United States shortly after the Civil War and settled in Illinois with an uncle, George, who had immigrated earlier and settled in the town of Waterloo, Illinois. In Belleville, Gustav Goelitz put his business skills to use as a salesman for William Theodor, a German-born baker and candy maker. Over the next two years, Goelitz learned to make candy and lived with Theodor and his family above their business on Main Street. He also integrated into the thriving German American community in southern Illinois.

The brothers went into business in 1869 in Belleville, making and selling candy. Elder brother Gustav, who was twenty-four at the time, made the candy in the back room of their store and handled retail sales up front. Albert, who was twenty-one, sold their candy in neighboring towns, traveling tirelessly in a horse-drawn wagon.

In 1884, the Goelitz brothers employed two full-time salesmen. One traveled via the growing regional rail network, delivering samples throughout southern Illinois, while the second continued the wagon deliveries begun by Albert in 1869. They employed five additional men to manufacture and sell their products, which included stick candies, caramels and figurines and flowers for trimming cakes. The company also participated in a thriving wholesale trade in fruit and nuts, crackers and "fancy groceries." Gustav Goelitz candies were well known throughout southern Illinois, and the business soon outgrew its Belleville location.

The brothers focused on their wholesale business and continued to expand, while Gustav Goelitz's family continued to grow as well. By 1891, his family included Hermann, Johanna, Helena, Armin and twins Frieda and Karl. Older siblings Adolph and Gustav Jr. worked in the St. Louis business and learned the art of candy making, as well as the business skills necessary to run the family firm.

The business prospered, and the two brothers married and raised families. Gustav's sons eventually joined the business. By about 1890, the business had moved into a handsome brick building on Main Street in St. Louis. But the candy company was hard hit by the depression that gripped the country a few years later, as well as by the infamous Panic of 1893. Economic turmoil, combined with labor unrest, hurt the previously successful confectionery, and the brothers were forced to sell the business in order to satisfy debts. Gustav Goelitz was apparently shattered by the loss, and he died in 1901 when he was only fifty-five years old. Albert, on the other hand, lived to be eighty and worked until his death as a traveling candy salesman, selling another company's products.

By 1898, with the panic behind them, Gustav's sons decided to restart the family business. This is where the Goelitz story comes to Cincinnati. Adolph Goelitz moved to Cincinnati in 1898 to take advantage of existing distribution networks for raw materials and finished products. They started at 220 Main Street and in 1904 moved to 16 and 18 East Second Street.

In the spring of 1900, Adolph partnered with a seasoned candy industry salesman, Rudolph Boger, forming the Boger & Goelitz Company. Boger had owned his own company, the Miller & Boger Cracker and Confectionery

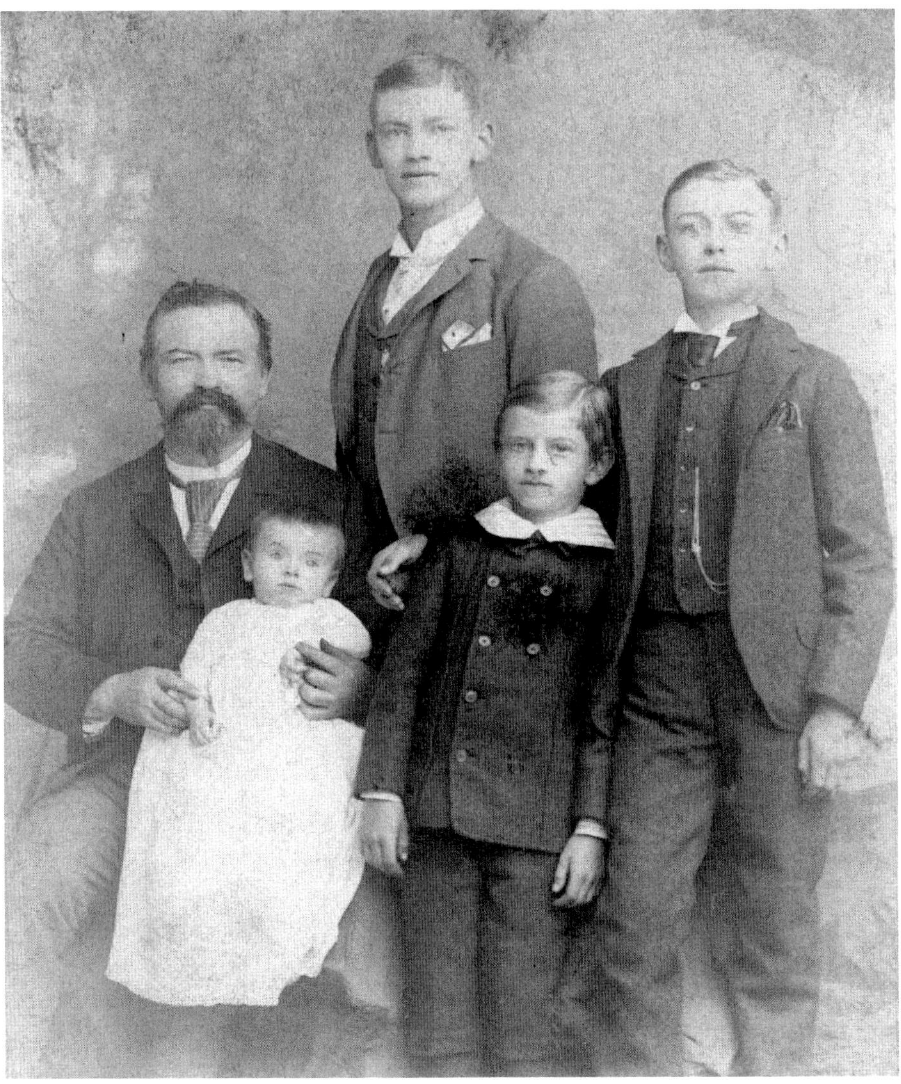

Gustav Goelitz poses with his four sons, Adolph, Gustav Jr., Herman and Armin. Adolph moved the company to Cincinnati. *Jelly Belly Corporation.*

Company in Quincy, Illinois, until it was destroyed by fire in 1889. He then moved his family to Cincinnati in 1890 to be central to his East Coast territory as a traveling salesman for O.H. Peckham Company, one of the largest wholesale confectioners of St. Louis, and would later become president of the National Candy Company. Sadly, Boger died only a few months after partnering with Goelitz, in August 1900, at the early age of thirty-seven.

Boger's widow, Mary Wessels Boger, sold her part of the business to Goelitz and moved back to their original hometown, Quincy, Illinois.

Adolph Goelitz was then joined by his friend and former Belleville neighbor, William H. Kelley. They hired Kelley's cousin and Goelitz's future brother-in-law, Edward F. Kelley, as their bookkeeper in 1901. Adolph Goelitz was quickly joined by his brothers Gustav Jr. and Herman. They reorganized under the name Goelitz Confectionery Company and began making buttercream candies, candy corn in particular. Candy corn was also called "buttercreams" and "mellocremes." In 1904, they opened a plant at 55 South Desplaines, Illinois, and began manufacturing there, too.

At the time, buttercreams were a relatively new style of candy. The Goelitz Confectionery Company did not invent candy corn, but it found success by adapting to changes in candy production and following trends within the industry. The Jelly Belly company estimates that its candy corn recipe was formulated in Cincinnati sometime between 1898 and 1900. Candy corn became extremely popular, and it remains a seasonal favorite. It ensured the continued stability of the family business. Even today, Jelly Belly claims that it continues to make candy corn using the Goelitz Confectionery Company's original Cincinnati recipe. Given changes in the production of corn syrup over time, however, there have likely been some variations in the original recipe.

The Kelley and Goelitz families became more closely tied when Goelitz accountant Edward Francis Kelley (1872–1960) married Adolph's sister, Joanna Goelitz (1882–1971), in Cincinnati on June 18, 1902. The couple settled into a home at 3106 Durrell Avenue in Walnut Hills. Kelley had been involved with his family's shoe store in Reading, Pennsylvania, but now his ties were deep in the candy industry, as noted in the *Reading Times* on June 23, 1902. The leadership of the Herman Goelitz Company in California that would become the Jelly Belly Corporation would pass on through Joanna and Edward Kelley's line, first with their son, William Henry Kelley (1903–1962), born in Cincinnati, and then his son, Bill Kelley, who took over in 1965, retiring in 2005. He was inducted into the Candy Hall of Fame in 2005.

This second start for the Goelitz candy empire was a good one, and it was fueled by its signature product: candy corn. The candy industry in the United States was growing overall, and by 1912, Goelitz Confectionery had so much business that it had to turn down new orders. In order to expand production, the company moved to North Chicago, Illinois, a factory town with low land costs and easy access to railroads.

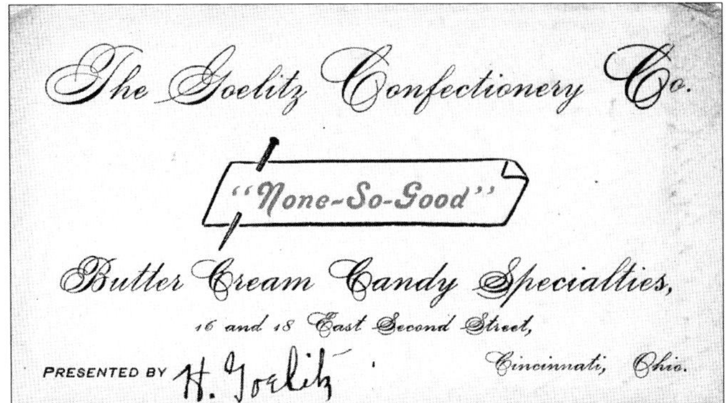
The Goelitz Confectionery Co.

"None-So-Good"

Butter Cream Candy Specialties,

16 and 18 East Second Street,

PRESENTED BY H. Goelitz Cincinnati, Ohio.

The 1905 Cincinnati business card of Herman Goelitz. *Jelly Belly Corporation.*

While in Cincinnati, the Goelitz family lived in the Hyde Park neighborhood on the north side of Erie between Shaw and Paxton. Adolph Goelitz was also involved as an executive of the Hyde Park Lumber Company, which still exists today. Helen Goelitz, Adolph and Herman's mother, and their younger sisters lived at the corner of Griest Avenue and Delta Avenues, at the corner of what was then known as St. John's Park and the end of the streetcar line from downtown Cincinnati.

Adolph and Herman's father, Gustav Goelitz, had been a member of the Turnverein in Belleville, Illinois, a German sport and social club that had started in Cincinnati in 1848 by refugees of the failed revolution. The Turners were a very connected group throughout the country, and many of the early Cincinnati candy manufacturers were also Turners—the Graesers, Oscar and his son, Louis, of the Peter Echert Company, as well as the Doschers. Perhaps the Goelitz men had met the Cincinnati candy manufacturers while competing at Turnfests throughout the country in the 1880s and 1890s, the height of the organization nationally.

While licorice, chocolates and peppermints were also available, buttercreams kept the business growing for the next five decades. Candy corn was the single best seller of the buttercream line of candies.

In the early decades of Goelitz Confectionery Company, the candy business was mainly seasonal. From March through Thanksgiving, the number of employees would double to thirty workers in preparation for the big autumn candy season.

The factory was generally hot, particularly through those midwestern summers. Air conditioning had not become prevalent, and even electric fans were not much in use. In the kitchen, where more heat was generated, the men often removed their white shirts in an attempt to stay cool while they cooked up as many as fifty batches of candy per day. They inhaled and their

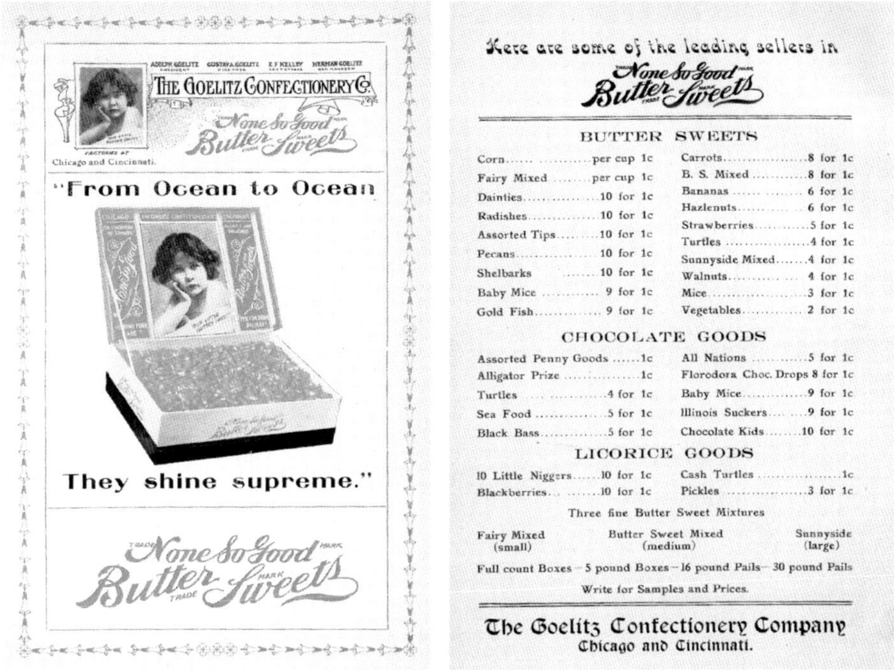

Left: A 1905 Goelitz "None So Good" brand Butter Sweet Corn ad from its time in Cincinnati. *Chicago History Museum.*

Right: The extensive list of Goelitz candies made in Cincinnati. *Chicago History Museum.*

clothes were littered with the starch used in the buttercream molds to aid in the candy removal once cooled. The typical worker put in six days, ten hours per day. For that effort, the average salary in 1900 was $5.22 per week. By 1917, the weekly salary had risen to $11.18.

During the slower summer months of the early 1900s, the Goelitz and Kelley families loved traveling together in their new automobiles for fishing trips in northern Wisconsin.

Large kettles were used for cooking sugar, water and corn syrup into slurry. The buttercream recipe required whipping in fondant for smooth texture and marshmallow for a soft bite. The hot candy was then poured into "runners," handheld buckets, each one holding forty-five pounds.

Men working as "stringers" would walk backward pouring the steaming candy into trays of cornstarch imprinted with kernel-shaped molds. For candy corn, three passes were needed for the orange, white and yellow colors—a strenuous job by any standard.

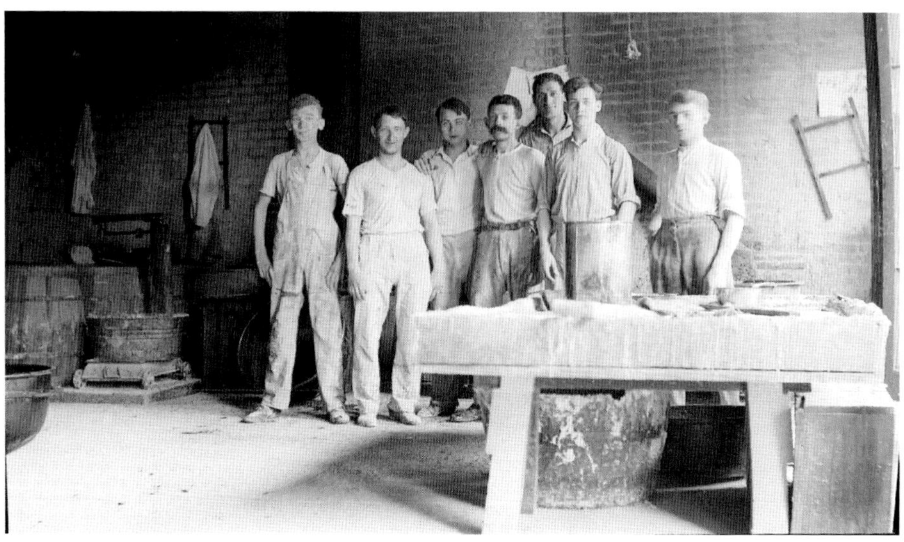

These "candy stringers" at the Cincinnati Goelitz plant poured molten buttercream into starched molds to make candy corn. *Jelly Belly Corporation.*

In the Cincinnati plant, workers were instructed and spoke to one another in German. Adolph Goelitz reportedly refused to stop speaking German in public despite his family's wishes, even during the anti-German sentiment leading up to World War I. The average number of workers in the Cincinnati plant was about fifteen. And although they made candy corn, the majority of candy made in the Cincinnati plant were the mallowcreme candies.

Finally, customer orders had to be filled and shipped. Originally, wooden buckets, tubs and cartons were used to pack the candy. Labels were affixed with paste that the workers made themselves. Wagons delivered the orders to customers in the area, while railroad cars handled the longer distances. Still, shipping candy very long distances was not attempted because of perishability.

Adolph attended the Atlantic City National Confectioners Association in June 1908 with local candy company owners Frank Pfaff and J.D. Reinhart. It would be his last hurrah with his Cincinnati candy baron buddies. On July 1, 1908, during the slow candy period, Adolph Goelitz moved the Cincinnati plant operations to Chicago and merged with its branch there, leaving the Queen City behind. They had been operating a plant in Chicago since 1904.

In October, the Cincinnati Confectioner's Club gave Goelitz a banquet in celebration of his time in Cincinnati at the Zoo Clubhouse. Frank Pfaff was the keynote speaker, and all of Adolph's buddies from the candy industry were there to give him a final goodbye: Oscar Graeser from Peter Echert Company, Isaac Weinreich of Dolly Varden, Harry Doscher, the Smiths and the Reinharts.

The Goelitz family were not forgotten after their exit from Cincinnati. In fact, Helen Goelitz, Adolph's mother, stayed in Cincinnati at their Hyde Park home on Delta Avenue at the corner of Griest Avenue with her youngest three daughters. It was easier to keep them circulating in Cincinnati society for a mate than ship them off to a new social scene in Illinois. They had certainly left an impression on the Cincinnati social scene, as in September 1918, the wedding of younger daughter Freda Goelitz to Emerson Wales Walker, a U.S. Army recruit, was announced in the *Cincinnati Enquirer*. The Helen Goelitz house was at the edge of what was then St. John's Park, which was where the streetcar from downtown Cincinnati ended.

After World War I, Herman Goelitz took copies of the family recipes and moved to Oakland, California, where in 1922 he founded the Herman Goelitz Candy Company. Because the two companies distributed to different regions of the country, Herman Goelitz and his descendants were not in competition with descendants of Adolph Goelitz and the Kelleys, headquartered in Chicago. Each of the candy manufacturers weathered the Great Depression, a very difficult era for candy makers, when credit

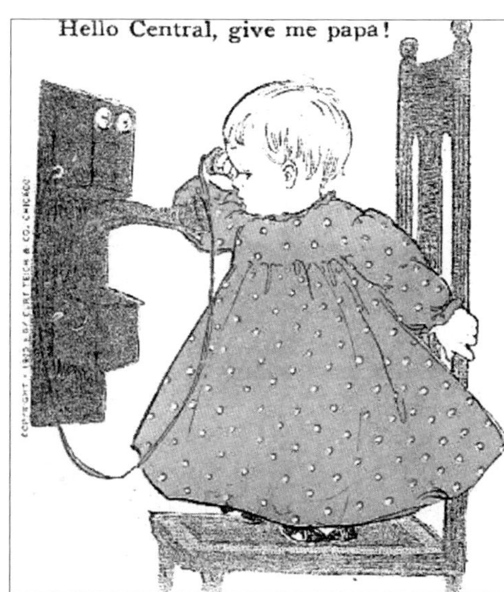

A 1905 Goelitz Christmas postcard reads, "Bring me Some Butter Sweet Corn—Hang up the Babies' Stockings, Fill them full of 'Corn.'" *Cincinnati Views.*

restrictions affected most manufacturing firms. Both companies experienced a boom during World War II.

Most chocolate candy was reserved for service members. However, non-chocolate products such as the Goelitz companies' specialties, buttercreams and jellybeans, experienced a resurgence in popularity as they fulfilled Americans' desire for candy.

The two firms merged as the Jelly Belly Candy Company in 2001. Herman Goelitz's grandson Herm Rowland still runs the Jelly Belly company and likes to visit the Schimpffs at their candy museum in Jeffersonville, Indiana, when he visits Louisville, Kentucky, for the Kentucky Derby.

NUSS COMPANY

After the Goelitz Company left Cincinnati, a big opportunity existed for another company to take over its production of candy corn. That company was the Nuss Candy Company. George H. Nuss got his start with the Goelitz Company in Cincinnati, where he learned the business of making buttercream candy. With a name like Nuss, which is German for "nut," it's no surprise that he became involved in the trade that was quickly replacing the almond paste marzipan candy industry in America. George was born in Pennsylvania to Adam and Mary Nuss, immigrants from Hesse-Darmstadt, Germany, but was a native of Baltimore, Maryland, where he got his start at an oyster house. Oddly enough, many early confectioners who made candy and ice cream also distributed oysters to make the most of the ice they had on hand.

Nuss moved from Maryland to Chicago, where he was a traveling salesman for a confectioner, probably Goelitz. After learning the trade, he left Goelitz in 1909, after it moved manufacturing out of Cincinnati, and started his own company. The Nuss company began production of Butter Cream Corn, which sold in boxes, pails and "snappy novelty packages."

His company became a prominent manufacturer of buttercream candies, taking over where Goelitz left off. In addition to making its version of candy corn, Nuss made a seasonal line of Thanksgiving and Christmas buttercream candy mixtures.

Nuss was a bit of an inventor and patented a machine called a starch buck with Charles F. Heckel of Newport, Kentucky, which removed starch from candy. Starch was used as a non-stick device in candy molds, which was part of the process in buttercream and candy corn manufacturing.

A Remarkable Seller and Repeater

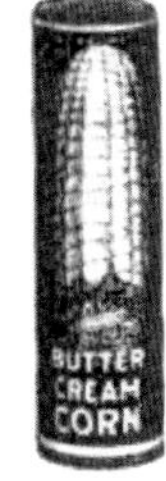

NUSS' BUTTER CREAM CORN

Sold in pails, boxes and in snappy, typical, novelty packages for

Christmas and New Years'

These novelties also make attractive window displays

This beautiful
5c PACKAGE
is sure going big.
48 BOXES TO THE
CASE.

We are specializing in

Butter Cream Christmas Mixtures

Write for particulars

The Nuss Confectionery Co.

311-317 West Third Street CINCINNATI, OHIO

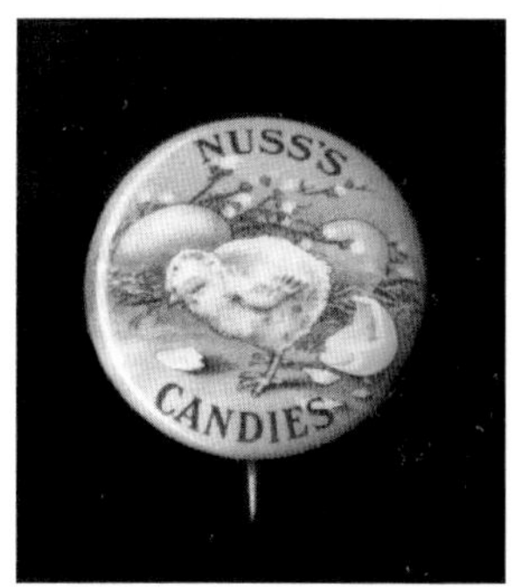

Above: An advertisement for Nuss Butter Cream Corn. *From the* International Confectioners Journal, *vol. 48 (1922).*

Left: A trade button for the Nuss Candy Company. *Schimpff Candy Museum.*

George Nuss was very involved in the local Cincinnati Confectioners Association and was part of the 1916 Candy Day committee, which was the forerunner to today's Sweetest Day. By his death in 1920, the company had grown at its 311–17 West Third Street location to seventy-five employees and a sizeable market capitalization of $100,000, which was fairly large for the time.

After his death, his daughter Isabel Nuss Dietz took over and ran the company for several more years. George's only son, Theodore, was a Catholic priest in Texas and was never involved in the candy business. The editor of the *Confectioners Journal* asserted in 1923 that the success Isabel attained for the Nuss company is evidence that "there are women as fully capable as men to perform the various duties called for in the affairs of the world." In

1922, under Isabel's leadership, the Nuss company patented a new product it called Indian Corn Candy, which was a larger-sized kernel of candy corn.

Isabel was involved in the Cincinnati Women's Chamber of Commerce and was very popular among a wide circle of friends in Cincinnati. She ran the Nuss Candy Company until its folding in about 1936. One particularly interesting worker at the Nuss factory was Noble "Kid" Chissell (1905–1987), who was a boxing champion, an actor with one thousand screen credits and a dance marathon champion.

THE ED MESSER COMPANY

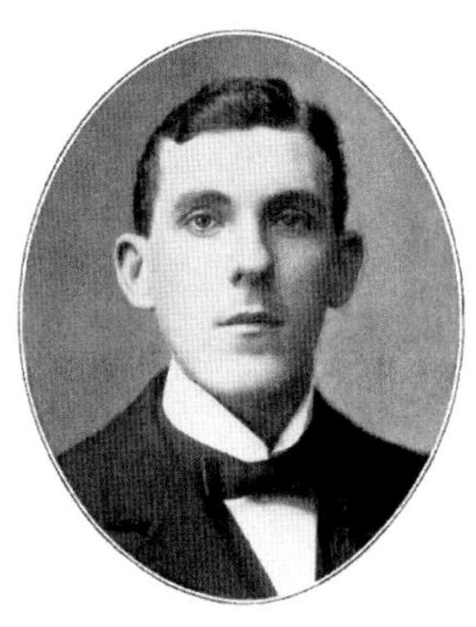

A dapper young Ed Messer posed for this photo in 1908 when he was president of the Jobber Confectioner's Association. *Carnegie Library of Pittsburgh, Pennsylvania.*

In 1922, a seasoned candy industry man named Edward Messer (1874–1952) came to Cincinnati to serve as vice-president of the Nuss Candy Company alongside Isabel Nuss. Messer had a family legacy in the candy industry but had his own entrepreneurial spirit and was looking for his own candy frontier to explore. His father, John Messer Sr., had owned the Messer & Son Candy Company in Pittsburgh, Pennsylvania, which was established in about 1884. John Sr. had two sons, Edward and John L. Jr. The singular son in the company name was Edward's older brother, John Jr., who took over the company when his father died. Edward did work in the family business, as a traveling salesman, in the 1890s. But he also had other candy accomplishments under his belt, separate from the family business.

Edward Messer was an avid inventor. By the time he moved to Cincinnati, he had several patents to his name, one for a retail candy container that kept out moisture and one for a method of marking candy. He had also served various leadership roles in several of the trade organizations, like the national Jobber Confectioner's Association, where he served as president in 1908. He also spent time around 1914 as vice-president of the Old Reliable Peanut Company Inc. in Suffolk, Virginia.

While involved in the Pittsburgh Jobber's Confectioners Association, Messer came up against an interesting candy issue. In 1901, an alcohol-infused candy called brandy drops was illegally being sold to kids in Pittsburgh-area candy stores. Although there weren't more than a few drops in these chocolate confections, it was thought that "their inebriate sweetness awakens a desire for strong drink among the children and will eventually give rise to a craving for intoxicating liquors." We already know that such conversation was heading toward prohibition. Messer said of this situation, "The association will do what it can to abate the practice [of selling brandy drops to children]. It isn't right that children should be taught intemperance in this way."

One of the more interesting and less appealing of the candies the Messer family made was a charcoal chewing gum that sold for five cents. Messer, however, had his eye on the buttercream candy market. Maybe Messer had heard about this new, profitable and popular candy within all the industry groups he was involved and wanted to learn its process and take advantage of the new market. At the time, with Goelitz and Nuss, Cincinnati was the place to learn how to make buttercream and the new candy corn that was sweeping the nation.

One of the primary pieces of equipment for its manufacture, the buttercream ball mixer, was made by a company in nearby Dayton, Ohio. This would also be the primary equipment that would be adopted locally by all candy makers who made opera creams.

In 1929, after learning the ins and outs of the buttercream market, Messer left the Nuss Company and started the Ed Messer Candy Company at 209–19 East Third Street, only a few blocks away from his former employer. He assembled a close-knit management team, including his only son, John E. Messer, as treasurer; Elmer Kalttenhasuer as secretary; and William Griffith as vice-president.

Here he embarked on making his version of candy corn, which he called Chicken Corn, along with other buttercream candies called Dandy Drops and Better Kremes. Messer adopted a cute baby chick taking flight as his company logo, oddly very similar to the logo of the Nuss Company, where he had started in Cincinnati.

In the mid-1930s, it seemed that Messer wanted to branch out into the burgeoning field of candy bars, obtaining a patent for making a new type of crunchy chocolate candy bar that "readily yields to the action of the teeth, said product being sufficiently firm enough to retain its shape when being handled and at the same time sufficiently fragile to be

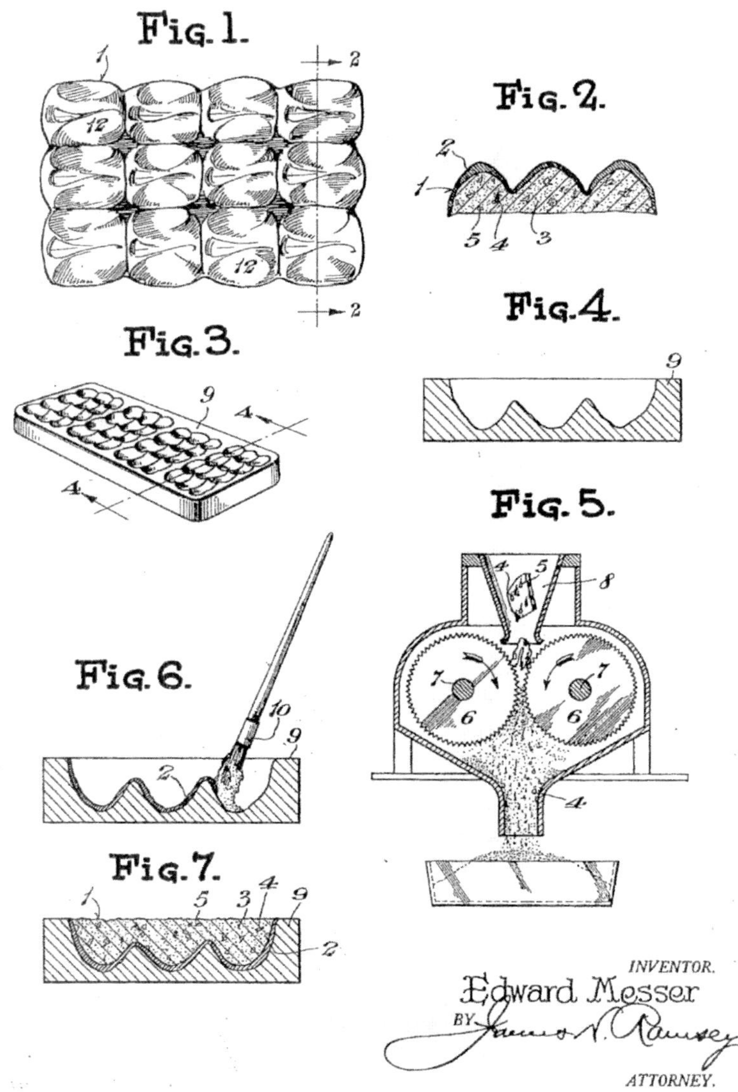

The 1931 patent for Messer's Edible Bar Brittles. *Public Library of Cincinnati and Hamilton County.*

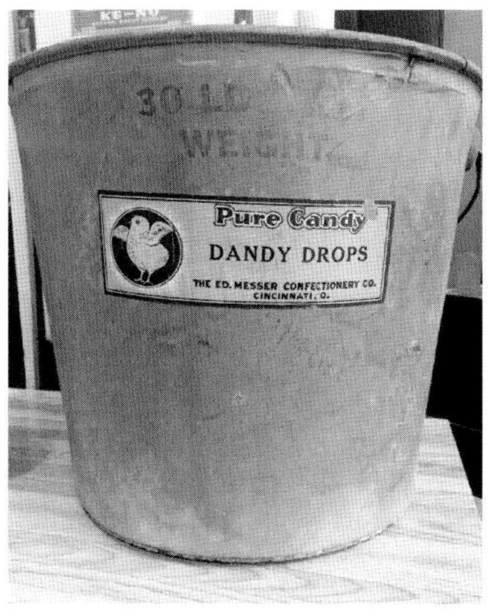

This 1930s-era Messer candy bucket transported its buttercream candies throughout the country. *Schimpff Candy Museum.*

easily broken into blocks or units of the desired size for eating."

The candy business allowed Messer a large house at 2496 Observatory Avenue in Hyde Park, near where the Goelitz family had lived in Cincinnati. It was in this house that Ed; his wife, Mary; his son, John E. Messer; and two daughters, Kathryn Messer Huenfeld and Mary Messer Heimann, lived. John Messer was part owner of the business and president before the company's closure. Afterward, John was an accountant for the William Powell Valve Company and secretary of the Foundations Savings and Loan.

On the night of April 9, 1936, after a staff of fifty girls making Easter candy had left for the night, a devastating fire engulfed the Messer factory building. The damages came to a $50,000 loss in Easter candy and the property. Unfortunately for Cincinnati, it would be the Easter without buttercream candies.

In 1941, at age sixty-seven, Edward Messer decided to retire and dissolved the business. Other companies like Kroger continued to make buttercream candies in Cincinnati.

Chapter 8

BETWEEN ACTS

THE CINCINNATI OPERA CREAM STORY

If you trace a recipe like the opera cream far enough back in time, you can get to the root of the original ingredients. But along the way, you also get great history—that of immigration, war and romance. Every region seems to have a proud native candy. Columbus, Ohio, has the creamy chocolate-covered peanut butter confection called the Buckeye. Lexington, Kentucky, has its boozy bourbon balls. Louisville, Kentucky, has the caramel-coated marshmallow treat called the modjeska, named after a Polish theater actress. And Cincinnati has its rich and silky opera cream.

It has become so popular that there are opera cream cupcakes made at local bakeries. The opera cream cake at the BonBonerie in O'Bryonville is legendary and a coveted birthday treat. One of our microbreweries, Braxton Brewery in Covington, Kentucky, even crafted a limited-batch opera cream stout in 2016.

There are two main forms of the opera cream in Cincinnati. There's the original, all-year-long version, which is a rectangular chocolate. Then there's the opera cream eggs that come out for Easter season. A third form is the virtual "unicorn" of Cincinnati candies because of its rarity: the opera cream cross. It's the most complex of the opera cream forms to manufacture and only available at Easter from a few companies. Putman's was one of the first to offer the opera cream cross in the 1980s, and Graeter's and Fawn are some of the few to still make it. The normal opera creams now come in dark, milk and even white chocolate.

The Cincinnati opera cream is an oblong chocolate, sometimes mistaken for the round buttercream. Each of the dozen or so local

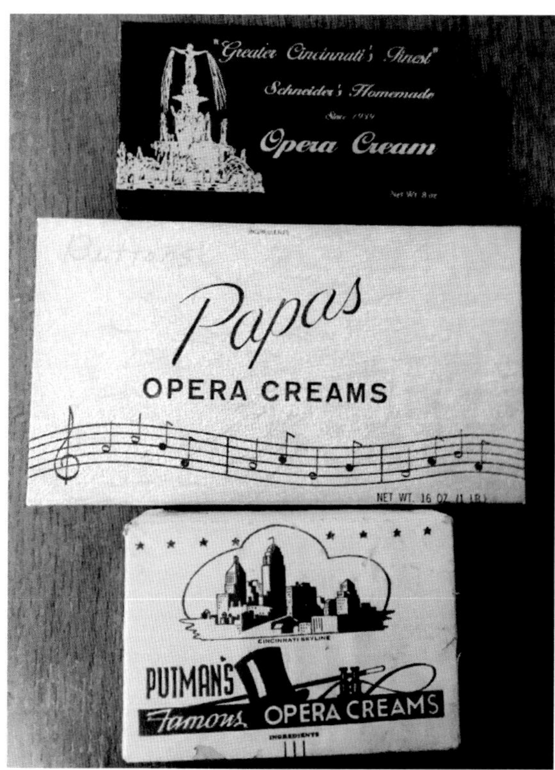

Candy boxes from three of the most prominent makers of opera creams in Greater Cincinnati: Schneider's, Papas and Putman's. *Author's collection.*

companies has its own recipe, each a bit different from the others. But the general makeup of an opera cream is dairy cream, sugar, vanilla and a homemade frappe, something like a thin marshmallow cream. It's cut into pieces and enrobed in either dark or milk chocolate. According to Bob Schneider of the Sweet Tooth in Newport, Kentucky, opera creams have a good shelf life for chocolates—about three to four months—but after that they can develop an off taste. The buttercream includes butter, which the opera cream does not, and also does not include the frappe. The filling can range from a creamy, gooey texture to a more chewy, caramel-like texture. And the difference between them is in the quality of the chocolate used to enrobe the filling.

The manufacturing process is a four-stage process. First, cream, sugar, vanilla and additives to prevent recrystallization are cooked to temperature in a double boiler. That "fondant" mixture is cooled down and then kneaded in a horizontal circular mixer called a ball cream beater that has been used since the early 1910s. That kneaded fondant is then cut into the sized pieces that will be used, and finally the cream center is enrobed in chocolate.

The first opera creams made by Putman were most likely hand beaten. But as the age of electricity came in, and volumes and demand of opera creams continually rose, a piece of equipment was needed to make opera creams. The answer to that production call was the ball cream beater, made by the Dayton Specialty Machine Company. Oddly enough, it's a similar piece of machinery to one used to emulsify meats to make Cincinnati bratwurst. The mixer uses a blade to horizontally mix cream and sugar together in a round motion. Zoutis and Droganes had one; Schneider's, Sweet Tooth, Fawn Candy and anyone else that makes opera creams use a ball cream beater.

In 1997, the *Cincinnati Enquirer* assembled a team of five foodies to taste and judge the best from ten Cincinnati opera cream makers. The panel judged them on a one to five scale for taste, texture and appearance. The entrants were Bissinger's, Sweet Tooth, Esther Price, Graeter's, Aglamesis, Lazarus Department Store, Fawn, Schneider's, Haute Chocolate and Divine's European Chocolates. Oddly enough, Papas, one of the oldest makers of the opera cream, was not included. Aglamesis won the best opera cream, which was described as "succulent and inviting, rich, dark chocolate, and cream thick centers."

Although there is contention in local sources as to who invented the opera cream—Bissinger's or Putman's—it's fairly clear that it was Putman's. Even the Papas family of Covington, Kentucky, claim that they invented the opera cream. So it seems to be a German-English-Greek contention as to who created the first opera cream. The earliest-known advertisement in the Cincinnati papers for the opera cream was in 1924 by Robert H. Putman Company. That was four years after the formation of the Cincinnati Opera Company. Legend has it that it supplied these opera cream candies to opera-goers at the Music Hall, where they received them free at intermission. A 1926 advertisement, which included all the chocolate companies in Cincinnati for October Sweetest Day, only showed Putman's supplying opera creams. Bissinger's only advertised fine French and American confections. A 1938 advertisement also extolled the World Famous Cincinnati Opera Cream, originated by the Robert H. Putman Company. Bissinger's first advertisement of the opera cream was in 1931. Another Putman advertisement said, "Putman Opera Creams—Often Imitated, Never Equalled."

ROBERT H. PUTMAN CANDY

Robert Hiner Putman (1858–1928) was a confectioner who came to Cincinnati from Tolesboro, Kentucky, in Lewis County, east of Maysville. He was born to Thomas Daniel (1825–1904) and Hannah Applegate (1836–1889). He started the company in 1893 with his wife, Margaret Ward Putman, after they borrowed $1,100 to gain the concession for the candy counter and soda fountain at a downtown department store called the Fair, then known as Cincinnati's progressive department store. Later, they opened a small store on Vine Street near Sixth Street. In 1900, they took over another confectionery and ice cream business downtown.

By 1907, the Putman Company was making fine candies at 1011 Main Street and 621 Vine Street, as well as running the candy department of the Fair. In 1922, it opened a new store in the Metrople Hotel (now the 21C Hotel). By 1922, Putman's had several branch stores in addition to the 226 East Fifth Street Main store: 628 Vine, 507 and 509 Walnut Street, 402 Walnut Street, 104 East Fourth Street and the new Metrople Hotel store. The next year, in 1923, after the death of Robert's wife, he transferred ownership of the company and retired.

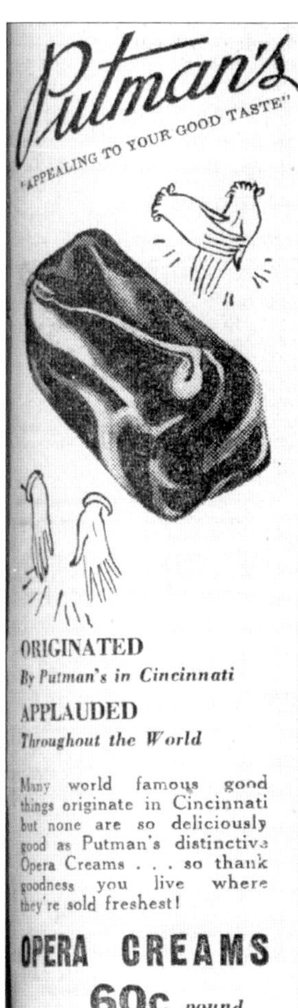

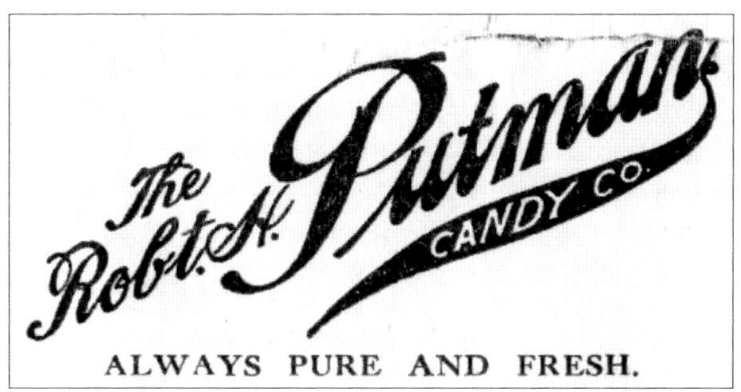

Above: A 1917 Putman ad from the *North Turner* newspaper. *Author's collection*.

Left: A 1938 ad for Putman's opera cream. "Originated by Putman's in Cincinnati." *Public Library of Cincinnati and Hamilton County.*

Robert involved three of his brothers in the business. Charles Monroe Putman (1865–1944) was the youngest of the brothers to run the business but also ran his own confectionery for several years in Lexington, Kentucky, around 1910. William H. Putman (1860–1942) started working for Robert in about 1910 and retired in 1932 from the business. William was responsible for many of the recipes and methods of candy making and certainly firmed up the famous recipe for the opera cream. The third brother involved in the business was John H. Putman (1863–1928). A nephew, Thomas Putman Lykins, son of their sister, Mary Alice, was also involved in the management of the business and would start his own offshoot after the company went out of business in 1931.

In 1907, Robert took on a seasoned candy industry partner, Roscoe E. Rodda, who was also a member of the Zion Christian Catholic Church. Robert and Roscoe recruited several of their candy workers to join the Zion Church in Cincinnati. An interesting account of Putman's workers attending services is preserved in an oral history of Christian Bang, a German confectioner in Cincinnati:

> *My brother, Henry Bang's wife worked at the Putman Candy Company as a chocolate dipper. One of her co-workers was Rosa Kieffer. Rosa was born in Cincinnati July 28, 1884, but her parents were born in Germany. She attended the Zion Church with my sister, Dora, and Henry's wife. We met at the Zions Church one Sunday when I went there with Dora. Rosa lived three or four blocks away from me, so I began to date her. I lived on Milton and she lived on Liberty Street. We went together for three years, then I proposed to her at her house. Her father gave his permission, and we were married at the home of the preacher on June 3, 1908. Rosa started helping me in the selling of candy, we both walked from store to store with big bundles of candy in each hand. We lived on Walnut Street at the time. Soon I started in a candy partnership with a friend of mine, but we split up, I took the retail end, and he the wholesale end of the business. I rented a store at 1431 Sycamore Street and called it Bangs Confectioner. I soon turned this store over to my mother to run so she'd have means of support. She ran the store for many years while I returned to the wholesale business for three years. I bought a wagon and one horse for a delivery truck about 1910. We'd go to the jobbing house, load up our wagon, and then deliver candy all over the city.*

The preacher who likely married Christian and Rosa Bang was probably Deacon Roscoe Rodda, partner in Putman's and the man who would later invent the Marshmallow Peep candy.

Robert's wife, Margaret Ward Putman, was very involved in the Zion Church and was one of the first ordained female bishops. She died on a business trip in Chicago, Illinois, in 1924. Robert Putman died at Zion City, the religious commune founded by their church, in 1928.

In 1931, the Robert Putman Company went into receivership and was sold. That same year, Thomas Putman Lykins, Robert Putman's nephew, started his own candy business at 31 East Court Street, a few doors down from what would become the Doscher candy factory.

Lykins operated the store for forty-five years, and when he retired, he sold it in 1976 to Thomas Schmidt, a former hairdresser and antique collector. Lykins had operated a small store and restaurant at Fourth and Walnut in what would become the Formica Building that he would be forced to close in 1967 due to urban renewal. At the time of the sale, a relative of the founder,

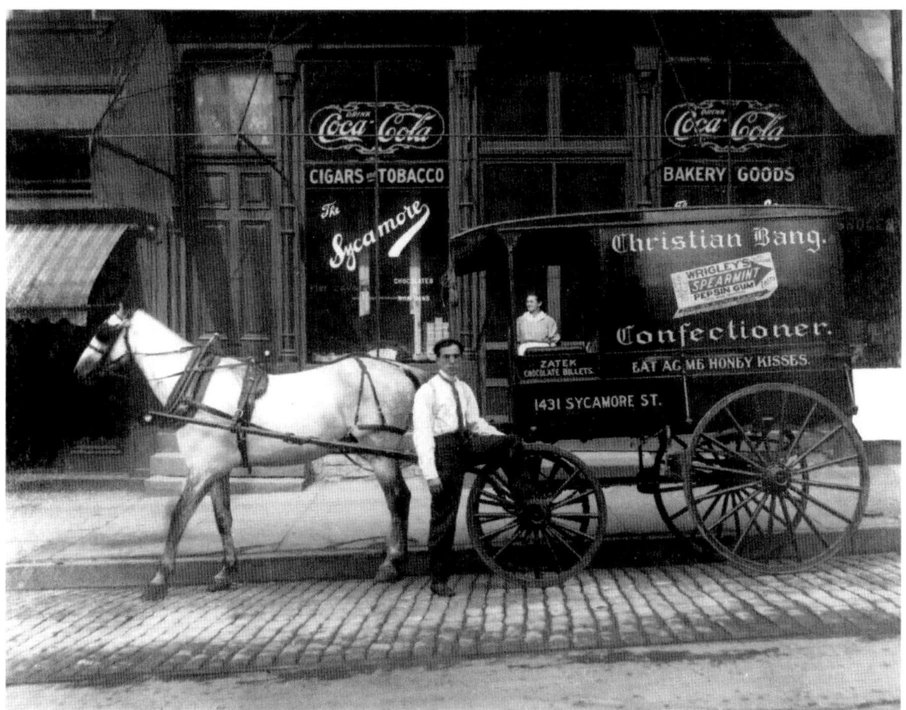

Christian Bang in about 1910 standing in front of his delivery wagon and candy store at 1431 Sycamore. *Marlene Fish.*

Thomas Putman, then seventy-six, was one of the two master confectioners still working for the company.

Schmidt lasted only one year in the business, selling it in 1977 to Steve Nordloh, a former officer in the Central Trust Bank. Steve would expand the company, investing several hundred thousand dollars in a candy plant in Madeira in 1979. He continued making the same Lykins brand recipes of thirty-five varieties of chocolate candies. Opera creams were still the highest seller.

In 1983, Nordloh sold the business to John and Ruth Puhlskamp, an accountant and teacher, respectively, with no experience in candy making. They would add a store in Northgate Mall on Colerain Avenue that would be bought by Fawn Candy.

Carl Papas bought Putman's in 1967 and continues to manufacture its legacy opera creams.

Bissinger's

The second entrant into the making of the Cincinnati opera cream, Bissinger's, has a history dating all the way back to the French empire of the 1600s and the extravagant Sun King, Louis XIV. The confections that Bissinger's provided in Cincinnati, aside from the opera cream, are from the same recipes that Louis XIV ate in his gilded palace as his imperial subjects starved in the streets.

In the year 1668, the German chocolate confection-making Bissinger family were living in Paris. That year, King Louis XIV proclaimed the family "Confiseur Imperial," or candy makers of the empire, because their candies were his favorite. Chocolate was extremely popular with Louis XIV and the members of his court at Versailles. When the Spanish princess Maria Theresa was betrothed to Louis XIV, she gave her fiancé an engagement gift of chocolate, probably Bissinger's, packaged in an elegantly ornate chest.

The Bissinger fame began to spread, and the family continued to make confections for the royals and nobles of Europe. The chocolate craze that took hold in Paris conquered the rest of France and kick-started its reputation as an aphrodisiac. Art and literature were thick with erotic imagery inspired by chocolate. Casanova was reputed for using chocolate and champagne to seduce his lovers. Madame de Pompadour was advised to use chocolate with ambergris (petrified whale vomit) to stimulate her desire for Louis XV (to no avail). Madame du Barry, reputed to be a nymphomaniac, encouraged her lovers to drink chocolate in order to keep up with her.

Chocolate had become so fashionable that in 1662, Pope Alexander VII took a look at this bewitching beverage during the Lenten fasting. His judgement was, "*Liquidum non frangit jejunum*," ecclesiastical Latin for "a chocolate drink did not break the fast, but eating chocolate candy did"—that was, until Easter. This is perhaps where the tradition of giving chocolate Easter candies originated.

The Bissingers continued making their chocolates for the French after the French Revolution, in the turmoil of empires and republics that followed. Legend has it that Napoleon Bonaparte I carried chocolate morsels into his military campaigns in the nineteenth century, eating them to conserve energy and, in a sense, inventing the first power bars. The Bissingers also dipped chocolates for the Rothschild banking family.

Karl Friedrich Bissinger (1828–1905) was the founder of the company in Cincinnati. His father, Karl Bissinger, was a noted maker of fine confectionery back in Germany. Karl Friedrich grew up in Mannheim, Germany, the largest city in the duchy of Baden, and after leaving college, he studied in Paris, France, learning the confectionery and catering trades. He became a specialist in preserving fruits, winning prizes for his confectionery in contests all over France, and he was caterer and confectioner to the noble house of Bonascea.

Karl Friedrich left Europe in 1845 to escape the rising turmoil and dissatisfaction with the French king, Louis Philippe, and settled in Cincinnati, continuing to make candies here. He brought with him the old family recipes. He opened his first confectionery in Cincinnati in 1863, but by then, the Bissingers were used to making chocolates during time of war. He married Theresa Meyer (1847–1925) in Cincinnati in 1874, and she quickly became involved in the business, becoming known as "Madame Bissinger."

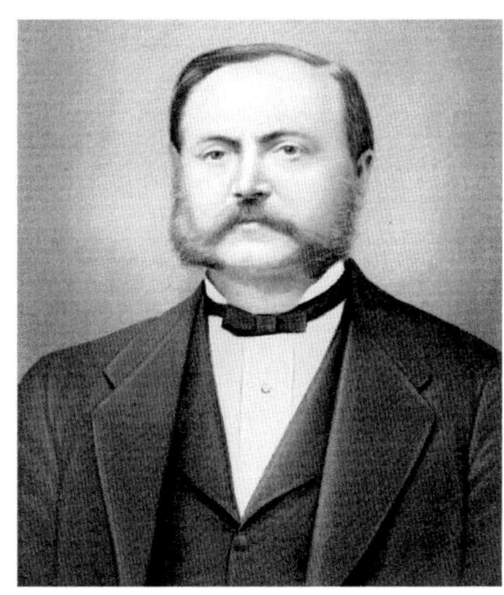

Karl Friedrich Bissinger, founder of the Cincinnati company of his name. *Public Library of Cincinnati and Hamilton County.*

The Bissingers left Cincinnati for Boston in the fall of 1881, selling their business to another confectioner, James

H. Empson, for $4,000, with the agreement that they'd not start another candy business in Cincinnati to compete for five years. Karl announced the sale in the September 18, 1880 *Cincinnati Enquirer*: "I have this day sold my business and good will together with all my private recipes and formulas to J.H. Empson. While thanking the public for their patronage in the past, I would respectfully solicit a continuation of the same for my successor." Empson was famous for his "peerless" caramels and Chinese orange confections, but he saw a good opportunity in providing the Bissinger fine chocolates.

Karl and Theresa stayed away for only one year, and Theresa was back operating a confectionery with help from Karl by 1881. Empson sued for breach of contract and won in court, and the Bissingers awaited the term of the agreement and started back up their confectionery by 1885, supplying to the large Peebles Grocery store in the Pike Opera building.

In 1898, at Theresa's earnest requests, William F.C. Cooper, an English immigrant, was brought into the business as plant superintendent. This brought about a bitter divorce case between Theresa and Karl Bissinger that aired in the *Cincinnati Enquirer*, with claims of infidelity, claims of a plot to get Karl committed to the insane asylum and death threats. During that time, son Karl Jr. was also accused by a cousin, Jake Meyer, of trying to poison his father, and Karl shot at him in public, thankfully missing him.

After Karl Sr. died in 1905, Theresa became one of the few female owners of a chocolate company in the United States. A year after her husband's death, she married William F.C. Cooper, and together they ran the business.

While son Frederick M. Bissinger (1890–1948) helped his mother with the business, Karl Jr. decided to spread his wings and moved to St. Louis, Missouri, after his mother's death in 1925. He opened the Bissinger's store there on McPherson in 1927, where it remained for the next eighty years until the move to Maryland Plaza in 2007.

After Theresa died in 1925, her son Fred became sole owner of the Bissinger Candy Company, then at 421 Main Street. He had been in charge of the factory since his youth. Fred fatally shot himself on the third floor of the candy company at 231 Main Street in October 1948, ending the Bissinger family ownership.

In 1931, Bissinger advertised that "if you aren't acquainted with the famous Bissinger Candy, then you are evidently a new visitor here. It's not only a tradition, it's a social necessity." In Cincinnati, the Bissinger Company operated at 127 West Fifth Street until 1965, when it moved to the Textile Building at 205 West Fourth Street.

Fine French Confections.

We have made arrangements with MONS. F. BISSINGER, for the sale of his Celebrated

CONFECTIONS AND BONBONS

Nothing can be made any PURER OR BETTER. They are made fresh daily.

Madame Bissinger has charge of our Candy Department.

Joseph R. Peebles' Sons,

Pike's Building, - - - - - Cincinnati, Ohio.

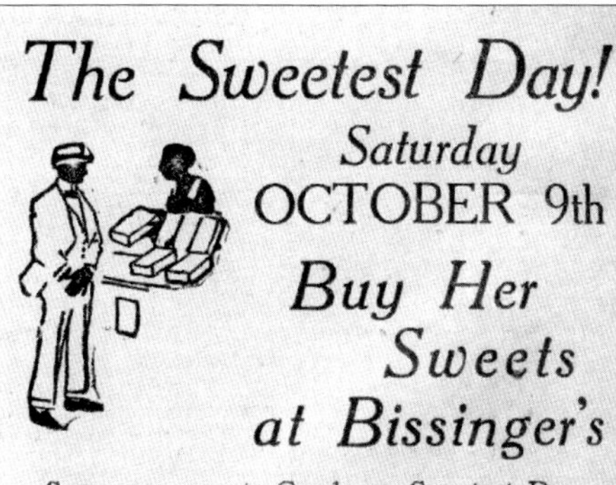

Some one expects Candy on Sweetest Day, so let it be Bissinger's.

Marvelous creations with thick, rich coverings of chocolate; surprisingly delicious centers of nuts and creams, and packed in beautiful boxes to further express your sentiments.

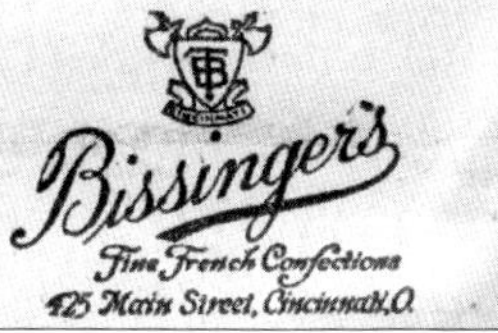

Above: An 1890s advertisements for Peebles Grocery touting Bissinger's candy. *Public Library of Cincinnati and Hamilton County.*

Left: A 1926 Sweetest Day ad showing the Bissinger family crest. *Public Library of Cincinnati and Hamilton County.*

The company celebrated its 100th birthday in October 1963, the second Cincinnati candy company to do so. Mullane's had celebrated its 100th in 1948. The president of the Cincinnati Chamber of Commerce presented a commemorative plaque to Ralph R. Zimmer, the firm's general manager, and Gene Kaercher, who had been Bissinger's long-term master confectioner. Kaercher was known for his walnut and pecan balls, cream caramels and specialty confections called neopolitans, as well as silistinas. He had worked at Bissinger's from 1921 to 1948, until the death of Fredrick Bissinger, after which he went to Sicardi's French Confectionery at 410 Main Street.

The Bissinger Company was bought by Bob Schneider of Sweet Tooth Candies in the late 1980s, but he had sold the name to the descendants of Karl Bissinger, in St. Louis, by 1997, calling the company Fine French Confections. The St. Louis company now uses the Bissinger name but does not make an opera cream. Coming full circle, the St. Louis Bissinger company's chocolates and gummy panda bears are in 2017 being sold at Greater Cincinnati Starbucks coffee shops.

PAPAS CANDY COMPANY

The third local legacy in the opera cream story is the Papas Candy Company. And the Papas family does claim that it was their patriarch, Chris Papas, who coined the name opera cream. With both the Putman and Bissinger Companies no longer in existence, Papas is the oldest continually operating manufacturer of opera creams. It is also quite possibly the largest manufacturer of opera cream eggs in the world.

The Papas Candy Company was established by Christus "Chris" Anthony Papas (1894–1984), an immigrant from Ermakia, Macedonia (now Frankovitza, Greece). Papas came to the United States in 1909 with his uncle Alex Thioharas on an Italian ship to avoid being drafted for a Turkish war in Greece. He was fifteen at the time and would have been drafted at age eighteen. He was the son of Anthony and Jahanna Papas and trained as a carpenter, like his father, with no experience in candy making. Coming through New York City, he traveled through Pittsburgh, landing in Cincinnati the same year.

By 1911, Chris was employed at the Monroe Hotel on Seventh and Race Streets, where he met his future brother-in-law, Chester Niederhelman. Chester introduced Chris to his sister Lilian, whom Chris married on

September 10, 1917. It was a German-Greek union from which came five children: Katherine, Alex, Gloria, Rita and Joyce.

After leaving employment at the Monroe Hotel, Chris started working with the Mehas brothers at their candy store in downtown Cincinnati on Fifth Street across from Fountain Square. It was a good position, as they had a reputation that landed the contract to supply the candy for the Mabley and Carew Department Store's candy kitchen. It was training with the Mehas brothers that launched Papas into his life's career. The Mehas brothers retired in 1920, but Papas continued the contract with Mabley and Carew, making candy in his house for the store until it closed its candy kitchen in late 1927.

Chris Papas became a U.S. citizen in 1918 and served his newly adopted country in Belgium and France during World War I with the 37th Division, Company G, 147th Infantry.

After returning from World War I, Papas had a variety of positions at local candy shops. He returned to the Mehas brothers until they closed their store in 1920. In 1921, Chris Papas opened his first store with his uncle Gustav Mahr at Eden and University Avenues in Clifton. But he soon bought his uncle's stake, and his uncle moved into another candy store at 2715 Vine Street. In 1923, Chris moved the store to Highland and Donuhue Streets across from the Children's Home in Clifton. Moving again, in 1924, Chris operated another candy store with his cousin Tom in Cumminsville, down the hill from Clifton, but that didn't last long, as Tom's wife seemed to be stealing from the candy jar. In 1926, he worked at the Agnes Sayre Confectionery at 1205 Harrison Avenue. The next year, he worked the soda fountain of Mabley and Carew on Fifth Street, near where the Mehas store had been. He still supplied candy to Mabley and Carew, made in his home. In 1929, he operated the former confectionery of his uncle Gustav Mahr at 2715 Vine Street, near Charlton in Clifton.

The Papas family claim that Chris made his first opera creams in 1928 and that due to the Clifton store's proximity to the zoo, where the Summer Opera was held, Chris coined the name opera cream. He supposedly sold opera creams on the street to people attending the opera. But this is unlikely, given the Cincinnati summer heat would have melted the chocolate and that most candy makers stopped candy production in the summer in favor of ice cream. This was also after Putman had invented the confection.

After 1929, Chris moved his family to Covington, Kentucky, where he and his young son, Alex, worked odd jobs through the Depression, like cleaning furnaces. Then, in 1934, Chris opened a storefront at Third and Crescent

Avenues in Covington, Kentucky. It was a good time, as the circus was set up near the store, and he had a steady stream of pedestrian traffic. On May 9, 1935, Papas set up a shop at 830 Madison Avenue and named it Lily's in honor of his wife. It was a family affair with both son Alex and daughter Katherine working the shop.

The store was remodeled in 1937 just in time for Easter, with a new soda fountain and candy display cases. At the time, the menu included fourteen-ounce sodas and sundaes for ten cents, banana splits for fifteen cents and twenty-six-ounce malts for fifteen cents. A final move of Lily's occurred in 1947, when Chris moved the store from 830 Madison Avenue to the corner location at 832 Madison.

Chris Papas retired in 1951. His daughter, Katherine Papas Hartmann, and her husband, Norb, operated the Lily's store, while Alex made the candy above the store. Alex moved the manufacturing to 921 Baker Street in Covington's Lewisburg neighborhood on the site of the former Lewisburg Brewery to address the growing wholesale business, for which their dark chocolate Easter eggs, opera creams and marshmallow eggs were in high demand. Chris would rename the wholesale side of the business Chris A. Papas and Sons.

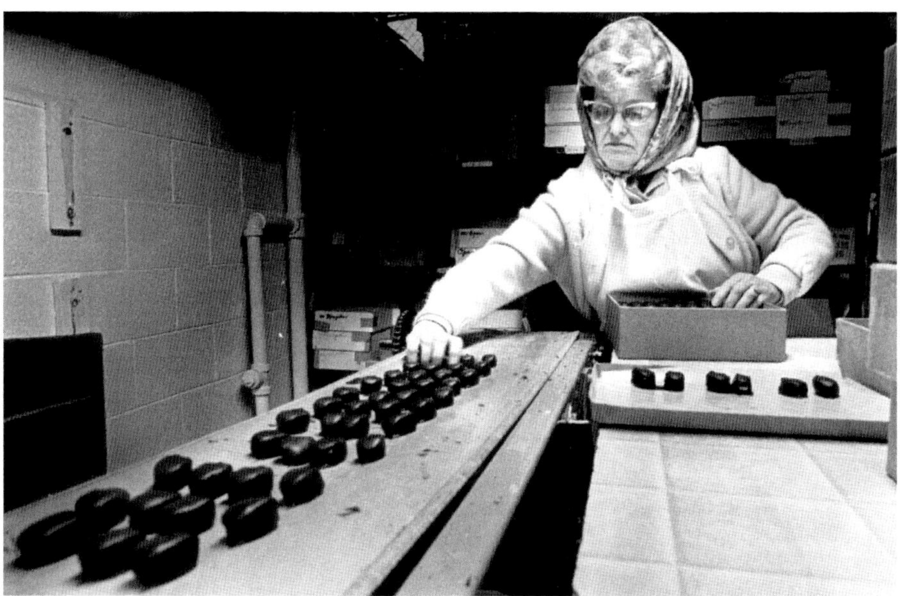

Evelyn Dwertman, worker at Lily's Candies, picking up chocolate-coated mints off the conveyor belt. *Kenton County Public Library.*

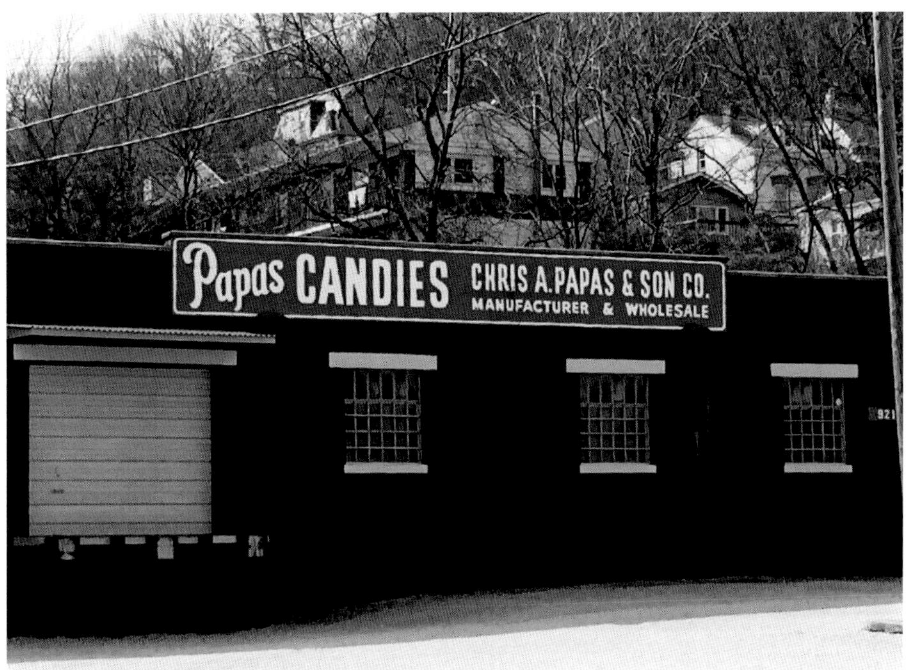

A panorama of the Papas candy factory at 921 Baker Street in Lewisburg, Covington, Kentucky. *Author's collection.*

Before he was inducted into the army in 1942, Alex met Ann Zappa and asked her to come work with him. She was making chocolates and he was stationed in West Virginia during the summer of 1943 when she traveled to marry him before he was shipped out. He would serve in Europe during World War II, fighting in the Battle of the Bulge.

After the war, he returned to Covington and the growing candy business. He designed machines to make candy in order to keep up with demand. During the 1950s and 1960s, Lily's was the place to stop while shopping in the downtown Covington business district or after seeing a movie at the nearby Madison or Liberty Theaters. The store windows were always decorated to the hilt for the holidays, and the candy counter was filled with delicious handmade candy. High school girls from Notre Dame High School were followed by the boys from other schools, where they might share a local favorite, the nectar soda.

Today, Papas opera creams are popular from Washington, D.C., to Arizona. The factory makes as many as 100,000 eggs in an eight-hour day during peak season—the three months before Easter. They're carried

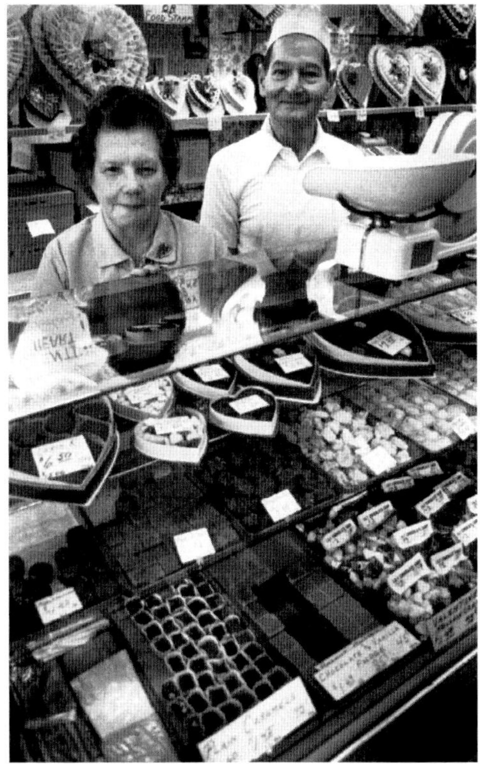

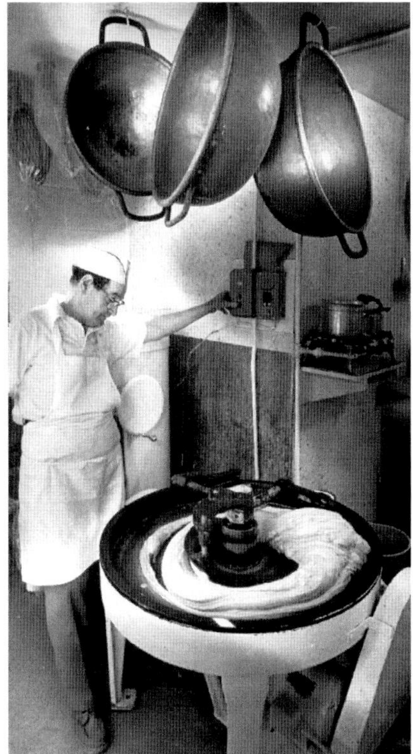

Left: Katherine Papas Hartmann and husband, Norbert, inside Lily's Candies in 1983. *Kenton County Public Library*.

Right: Norbert Hartmann in 1976 using the ball cream beater to make buttercreams at Lily's. *Kenton County Public Library*.

in retail stores across the Greater Cincinnati area like Jungle Jim's, Remke Markets and Kroger.

The company is perhaps best known for its Easter candy. Beginning in late December and early January each year, the staff begins working on the production of Easter eggs. During peak production, the company can produce eighty thousand eggs per day. While the opera cream egg is still the best-selling one, other popular flavors are vanilla cream, coconut, cherry cream, mint cream, maple nut, peanut butter, French cream and pineapple cream. There are a dozen flavors of Papas cream eggs in all.

Alex Papas bought the Putman business and trademark in 1967, making the original Cincinnati opera cream recipe. Alex's sister, Katherine Papas Hartmann, sold Lily's to her brother in 1986, but he only operated it a few months before closing it. Shopping had migrated to the new Florence Mall from the dwindling Covington small retailers, and retirement was calling to him, so in 1986 Alex Papas passed on the business to his two sons, Carl and Chris, as president and vice-president, respectively. Their sister, Pam Papas Stenger, helps make candy at the Lewisburg plant.

SCHNEIDER'S SWEET SHOP

Schneider's is a corner sweet shop on the main route through Bellevue, Kentucky, at the southwest corner of Fairfield and Foote Avenues. It remains in the same location that Robert Schneider Sr. started in 1939. The same time-tested recipes, equipment and methods are still being used to make the signature opera creams, chocolates, caramels and fudge.

Robert had learned the candy making business by working at Lily's Candies, owned by the Papas family. Robert would marry a Lillian (a common theme in the Cincinnati candy world) who would help run the candy shop and start a family of seven children.

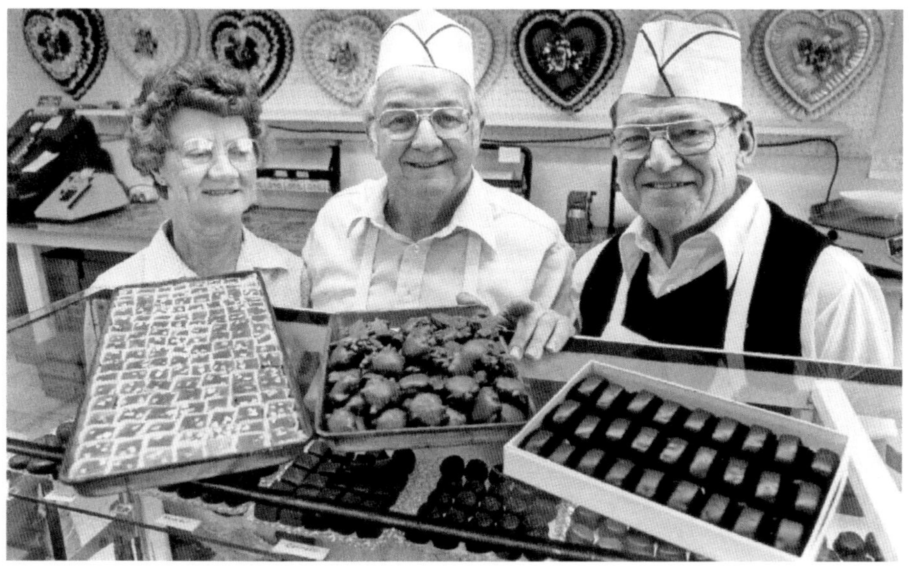

Lillian, Robert Sr. and Bill Schneider at the counter of Schneider's Sweet Shop in 1983. *Kenton County Public Library.*

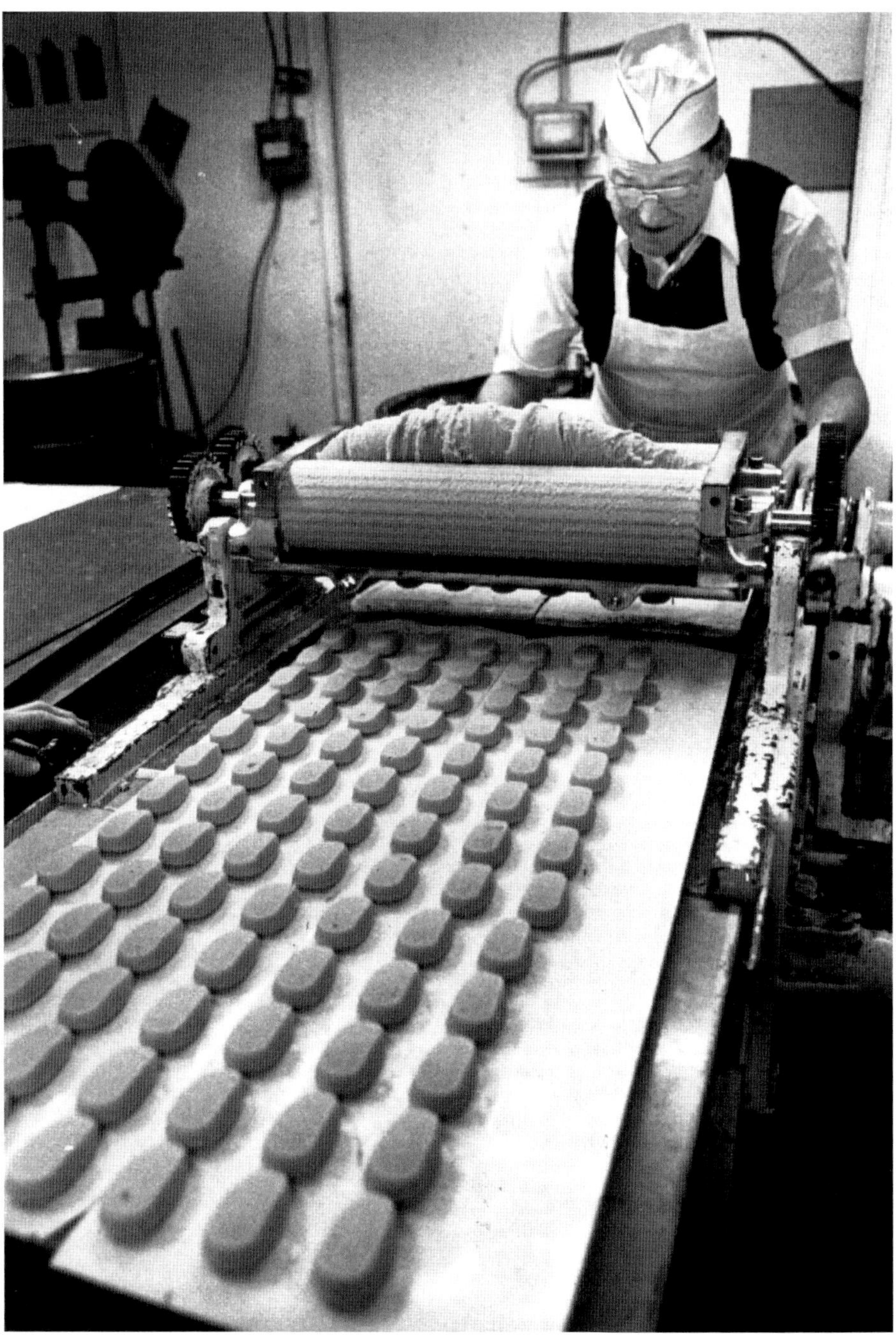

Bill Schneider running future Easter eggs through the cutting machine before coating them with chocolate at Schneider's Sweet Shop. *Kenton County Public Library*.

The original store in Bellevue had been purchased by Chris Papas for his son, Alex. After a year, Alex wanted out of the retail business, but his sister, Katherine, wasn't ready for that, so Bob Schneider, who had been working with Chris, offered to buy the store. Papas agreed and stayed on to help as an advisor, helping to launch another local candy legacy.

Before buying a chocolate coating machine, Robert would hand-dip the chocolates in the two-car garage behind the store, keeping an eye out for sneaky neighborhood children trying to snatch a free chocolate when he wasn't looking.

Robert Schneider Sr. retired from the business in 1986 with the intent to close it. His son, Jack, who had a career as an electrician at Cincinnati Milacron, wouldn't let the community icon die, so he quit his job. He and his wife, Kathy, took over the business, which they still run. Jack expanded the business with two new stores—one at Beechmont Mall on Cincinnati's East Side and one in Alexandria, Kentucky—but both are now closed. Even with one store, the business grows every year.

Opera creams make up one-third of Schneider's total business and are most popular at Easter. But Schneider's is also known for its ice cream, candy apples and several flavors of caramels. It celebrated its seventy-fifth anniversary in 2014 and plans to keep the business in the family—maybe passing it on to one of three daughters.

Sweet Tooth

Bob Schneider Jr. is the oldest of Robert's sons. He grew up in the apartment over Schneider's Sweet Shop with his brother, Jack, and started making candy with his father at age thirteen in 1955. Later, he branched out to expand his knowledge and landed a job at Bissinger's, where he learned its opera cream recipe. In 1970, Bob opened his Sweet Tooth at 125 Eleventh Street at the corner with Ann Street in Newport, Kentucky, where it continues to make this legacy recipe.

The candy shop has tables inside and benches outside where customers can enjoy their delicious handmade ice cream and confections. A sign on the front of the corner shop proclaims, "Shop Local—We try Harder." The candies include a wide variety of chocolate confections, like its very popular opera cream.

By 1988, Bob Schneider was advertising that he was making the original Bissinger opera cream recipe at the Sweet Tooth. But he would later sell the

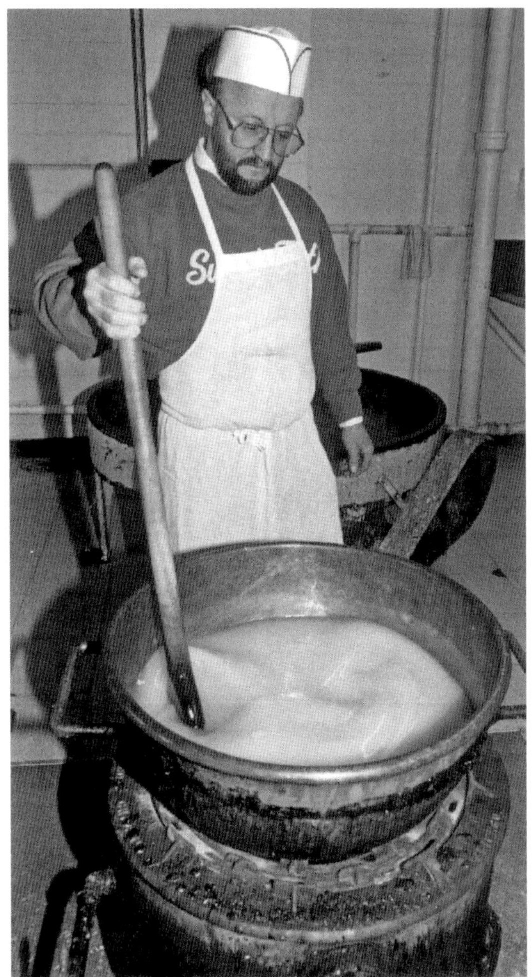

Left: Robert Schneider Jr. cooking what will become candy at the Sweet Tooth. *Kenton County Public Library.*

Below: A 1946 ad for G.A. Bellem Opera Creams, one of the many local makers. *Author's collection.*

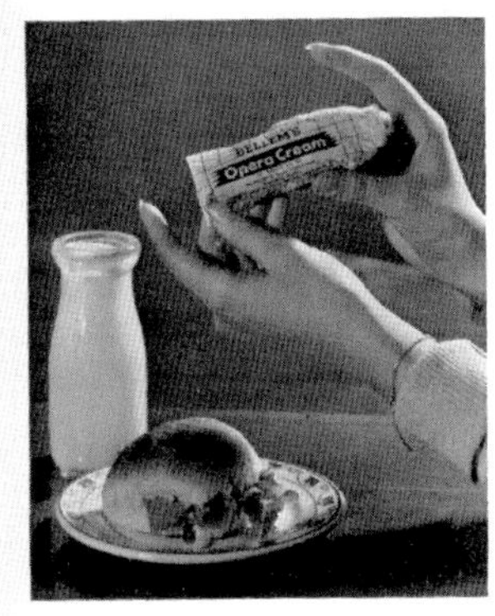

Bissinger name back to the Bissinger family in St. Louis, Missouri, where one of Karl Bissinger's sons moved in the 1920s, so it could legally operate under the Bissinger name.

Today, opera creams are made by Schneider's, Sweet Tooth, Papas, Fawn, Graeter's, Aglamesis and many others. Some, like Papas, make a milk chocolate–, dark chocolate– and even a white chocolate–enrobed opera cream egg. Whatever the origin, the opera cream continues to enrich Cincinnati's candy history after nearly one hundred years.

Chapter 9

SOLVING THE NATIONAL CRISIS

"CHRONIC HALITOSIS"

In 1914, Listerine became the first over-the-counter mouthwash marketed to kill germs that cause bad breath. The company used scare tactics in its advertising, showing couples eager for marriage but turned off by their partner's bad breath. Before then, bad breath wasn't considered a deal breaker, but an aggressive marketing campaign by Listerine put that fear of a new medical condition, "chronic halitosis," into the public mind.

So, mints and chewing gum companies started popping up all over the country, and Cincinnati caught on to the trend. The simplicity of mint making made it an attractive business in the early 1910s. All a manufacturer needed was sugar, flavoring oil and high pressure to make a mint. There had already been a legacy of products in America bridging medicine and candy. The medicinal lozenge was a precursor to these candy mints. The old saying, "A spoonful of sugar helps the medicine go down" was part of that legacy. Later, during Prohibition, mints would be marketed as a way to hide alcohol on the breath and were sold to the many speakeasies and lunch rooms that still offered alcohol.

The year Listerine mouthwash was released, two new mint companies were incorporated in Cincinnati. The Scott Mint Company was incorporated with $200,000 with E.R. Shaw, Anna Scott, C.H. Hungerford, A.C. Weber and C.E. Benedict. The Shamrock Mint Company was incorporated for $10,000 with E.A. Johnson, J.G. Blanerney, A.D. Blackwell and C.H. Trappe. But there were already several mint and gum companies pumping out products to cure bad breath in the Queen City.

Even the already established Dolly Varden Chocolate Company got into the mint craze. In 1914, it advertised Dolly Varden Mints as "A breath of Fragrance and Purity. Matchless in Flavor—unequalled in appearance, this fascinating confection is winning popular favor everywhere it goes."

Whiskey and Chewing Gum: The George Dorne Company

Across the river in Newport, Kentucky, George Dorne was one of the very first in Greater Cincinnati to start producing chewing gum. He sold his Toula Toula and Carnation chewing gums in Ohio, Indiana, Kentucky, Michigan, Illinois, Iowa, West Virginia, Wisconsin and Pennsylvania. George was son of Peter and Margaretha Dorne, who had immigrated in 1846 to Cincinnati, Ohio, from Hoesephweiler, Rheinpfalz, Germany, and moved across the river to Newport, Kentucky, in about 1859, when the St. John's German Evangelical Church was dedicated.

George Dorne (1856–1929) began as a grocer in the mid-1880s at Isabella and Harris in Newport. In 1887, he started a wholesale confectionery business in Newport and began the manufacture of chewing gum in the early 1890s. Originally, the business operated out of a one-room building on Orchard Street in Newport. Then it transitioned to larger quarters at 27 East Tenth Street. As business prospered, a new, three-story chewing gum factory, the Dorne Building, was built in 1912 to accommodate production.

One of Dorne's most popular and successful chewing gums was Carnation, patented in 1911 but released in about 1907. Dorne marketed this gum with slogans of "Taste the Smell" and "Spicy Lasting Flavor." As the name suggested, the flavor resembled the odor of carnations, hence the slogan. Dorne produced beautiful Carnation advertising items such as bookmarks and the highly sought-after Carnation Chewing Gum tip tray. Carnation gum posters also graced a lit poster stand overlooking Cincinnati's Fountain Square in 1914. Toula Toula gum was advertised as "Just right, none better." The company made both poplar wood and etched glass cases and cardboard counter displays to help retail grocers and other confectioners sell its products.

In addition to making delicious chewing gum, George Dorne was treasurer of the Monmouth Street Loan and Building Association, served on the Newport School Board and was a member of the Knights of Pythias. He married Amelia Reichert Dorne and had one son, Irvine Dorne, and two daughters, Murial Dorne Scharf and Elisabeth Dorne Hauck.

By the 1920s, George had brought Irvine into the business. In 1929, before closing the business, George and his son's reputation were tarnished by a charge of violating Prohibition. It was found that Frank Warner, a woodworker who rented the third floor of their factory, was operating a whiskey still in their building at Ninth and Orchard Streets. Testimony from reputable citizens of Newport got the six-month sentence of George and Irvine suspended and their good names cleared, but it didn't prevent them from closing the business.

SCOTMINTS

The Scott Mint Company was founded in December 1913 by lumberman Francis L. Scott, who realized that there was no well-advertised mint on the market. The company manufactured mints out of 301 Lincoln Court Inn Building. An aggressive marketing campaign produced sales in 114 cities in the country with more than 4 million people and supposedly took 30 to 50 percent of the mint market trade in those cities. Part of the advertising campaign were catchy streetcar ads in all those cities featuring a Scotsman in kilt and beany. Slogans like "Try Scotmints yourself—a wee nickel" and "Hae' ye seen the new bonnie-plaid package?" graced busy streetcars across

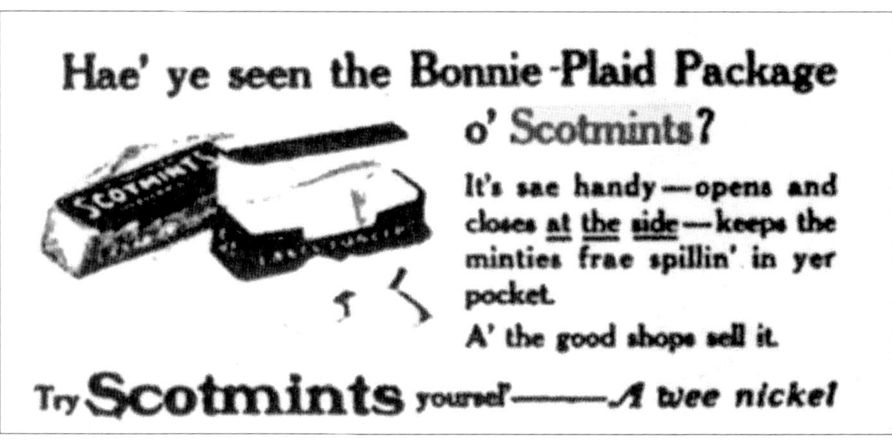

A 1913 Scotmints streetcar ad. *From* Printer's Ink, *col. 87, June 11, 1914.*

the country. By 1914, Scott had sold the company to a New York group but retained royalty rights and acted as advertising manager, and the operation moved out of Cincinnati.

Aromints

"Who hasn't heard of Aromints? The delicious confection which sprang into instant favor is made by the Aromint Company," said the 1914 *Queen City Newspaper Reference Book.* The company bragged that the Aromint was "Made in Cincinnati, eaten all over the world." The Aromint was invented by Canadian immigrant Robert D. Bogue. The company was incorporated in 1911 with brothers Robert D. and Henry L. Bogue, Charles F. Marlsbary, Charles Beaman, Victor Heinz and O.A. Ointe—Beaman was president, Robert Bogue vice-president and general manager and Henry Bogue secretary. F.E. Spiker served as treasurer.

The mints came in a lifesaver-like roll and five flavors—peppermint, cloves, cinnamon, wintergreen and black licorice. It also sold a product called Arco Matinee Mints, apparently targeting the moviegoing crowd. The mint lozenge, patented in 1916 and designed by J. Harris, was indented with a monogram of "AC" standing for the Aromint Company on one side and a raised Aromint with an arrow point into it.

Paul Varga, a Hungarian immigrant, was an engineer with the company who in 1918 designed the lozenge packaging machine it used.

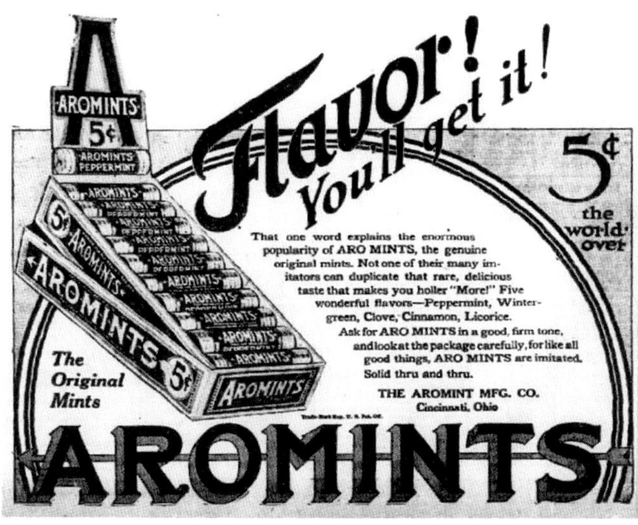

An Aromint ad showing the patented counter display case. *From the* Saturday Evening Post, *vol. 191, March 15, 1919.*

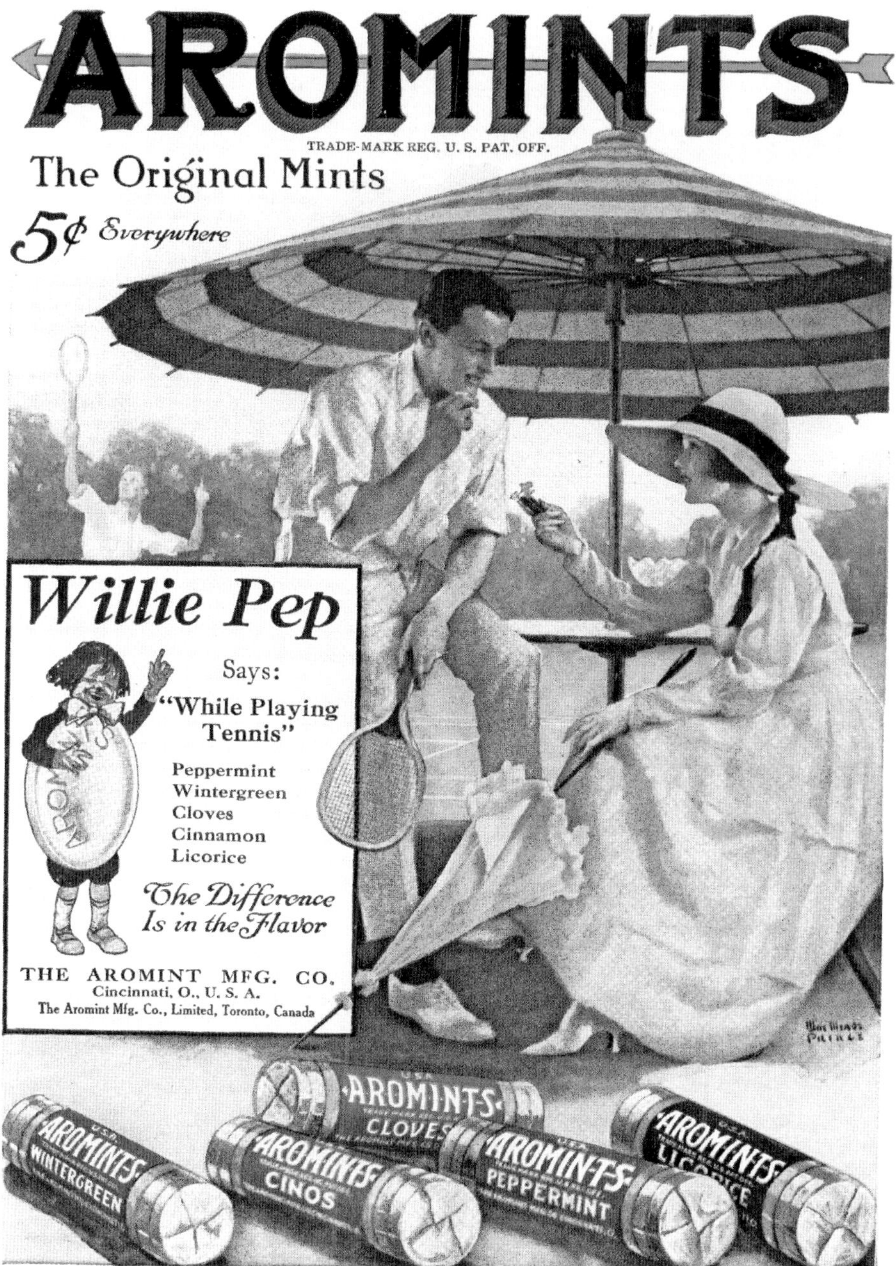

A 1910s *Saturday Evening Post* ad for Aromints, showing a couple sharing a romantic moment. *Schimpff Candy Museum.*

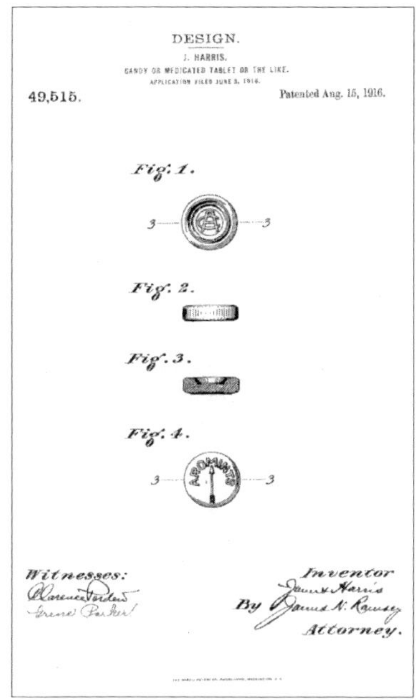

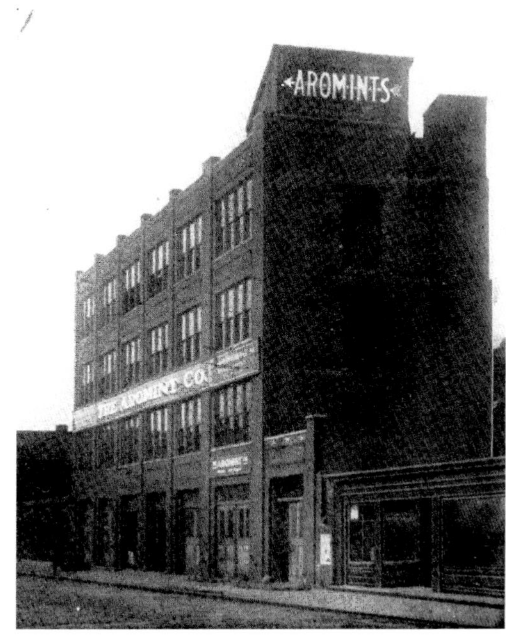

Left: The 1916 U.S. patent image, designed by James Harris, of the Aromint lozenge. *Public Library of Cincinnati and Hamilton County.*

Right: The large purpose-built Aromints plant on Central Avenue. *Public Library of Cincinnati and Hamilton County.*

A 1917 article claimed that Aromints were "[i]n line to become the best selling mints in the country. They plan to spend $200,000 in advertising next year." And sure enough, the output of a very expensive-looking campaign appeared in print in the next year's *Saturday Evening Post*. The ad was a cute graphic ad with a mint-boy mascot named Willie Peps speaking to a cheering crowd yelling, "The Story of Joy I've Come to Tell."

The plant at 1644 Central Avenue was designed specifically for the mint making and produced about four to five tons of mints per day on a machine that compressed the cane sugar and flavor oils with fourteen thousand pounds of pressure.

Aromint's ads read, "The Difference is in the Flavor. In all the world no delicious, satisfying sweetness like that of the Aromints!! The pure cane sugar blends perfectly with the rich flavors—Peppermint, Cloves, Cinnamon, Wintergreen or Licorice. They try to imitate them, but they can't get that snappy flavor. Made by a secret process—no cooking, no boiling. Insist that your nickel buys the best. Aromints the original mints. Still only 5 cents. Solid thru and thru."

HELMUT GUM COMPANY: THE ARTS AND CHEWING GUM

The Helmut Company was one that kept it all in the family—the Rosenthal printing and publishing family, that is. The company incorporated in 1909 for $10,000, with Joseph and Benjamin Rosenthal, Levi Block, George Smith and Joseph May, according to the *National Corporation Reporter*. Joseph B. Rosenthal (1886–1937) was president of the company. His brother Charles was vice-president, and his other brother, David, an artist, was secretary and treasurer. Joseph was also partner in the S. Rosenthal Printing Company, owned by his family. He got the family price on the printing of his gum packaging. He also got the family deal on his advertising.

The Helmut Company advertised in the *American Chauffeur*, owned by his relative Edward Rosenthal, which would become the F&W Publication powerhouse in the 1940s. The success of the F&W Publication Company helped fund many Cincinnati arts organizations, like the Contemporary Art Center.

David Rosenthal was a sought-after portrait painter in Cincinnati. He had studied at the Art Academy with Frank Duveneck and Lewis Meakin, whose brother also owned a candy company in Cincinnati. The Rosenthal family were pragmatic business people but weren't so confident that David would be able to make a living as a painter, so they set him up with an executive position with the Helmut Gum Company. Unlike the chewing gum Rosenthal and many of his customers rejected, his art found an appreciative audience when he was alive—and interest in his work has in recent years been renewed.

Helmut Gum were wholesale distributors, with a factory at 1021–25 Broadway. In 1914, the company moved from 28 Opera Place to a factory on Lockport Avenue three times its size. It offered an extensive line of official flavors, seemingly for everyone: Spearmint Algo, De Luxe, Dental, Caramel Tolu, Laxative Gum, Merry Widow, Baldees, Sweet Kiss, Panama, Lemonade, Dolly Dimples, Juicy Mint, Cream of Fruits and I.X.L. Spearmint. It also made ball gum and other flat and package gums to fit slot machines.

The Helmut Company was very sneaky in developing its wrappers to be similar to but different from Wrigley's gum. But Wrigley's realized the similarities and filed suit in a case called *Helmut Company v. William Wrigley Jr. Co.* on August 1, 1917. The suit was in reference to three Helmut brands: I.X.L. Spearmint (introduced in 1909), Helmut Spearmint Product (introduced in 1913) and Red White and Green Label Spearmint Product (introduced in 1910). Helmut was ordered to stop making products that simulated those of Wrigley's.

In 1915, Helmut Gum advertised "Make More Money—sell our new Grape Juice Chewing Gum" in *American Chauffeur*. It also advertised in another F&W Publications magazine, *Popular Mechanics*, from the 1920s to the '30s as a "dandy proposition selling chewing gum to dealers." It was "clean, profitable spare-time work." The company lasted until about the mid-1930s.

Chapter 10

CINCINNATI'S ROLE IN SWEETEST DAY

Sweetest Day, on October 17, is one of those guilt holidays on which you feel strangely obligated to buy something, usually sweet, for your romantic partner. It has a built-in inferiority complex to Valentine's Day, which is universally recognized as the day to buy your sweetie a gift. It feels like a manufactured holiday, and indeed it was—by the U.S. candy industry. But its origins were not romantic. The origins were in philanthropy, namely in doing small, sweet acts of kindness directed at the less fortunate. However, outside Ohio, Michigan, Illinois, Wisconsin, Indiana and the western edges of New York and Pennsylvania, most people have likely never heard of the holiday. And those of us in those states are even less likely to be able to tell the story of how it all got started.

The forerunner to Sweetest Day was the 1916 Candy Day, organized to be a countrywide event by the National Confectioners Association. It all started on May 10, 1916, at the thirty-third NCA convention in Detroit, Michigan, held at the now demolished Statler Hotel. Members approved a motion at the convention that a given Saturday in October each year would be designated as "Candy Day," declaring, "A little effort and hard work by all hands in our industry will make Candy Day the happiest day of the year." All the large candy manufacturers went back to their respective cities to plan their versions of the celebration. Cincinnati's candy barons were supremely inspired and formed a committee to plan an over-the-top Candy Day.

The planning paid off. Cincinnati took the crown for the most successful Candy Day in the country on October 14, 1916. "Speaking collectively

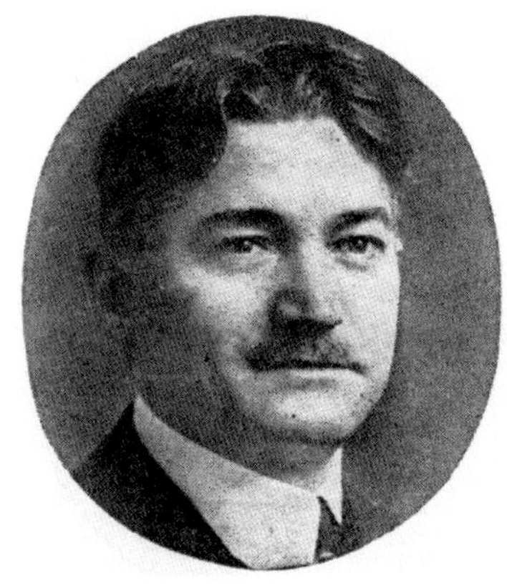

Charles Eisen was president of Dolly Varden and Cincinnati Candy Day Committee chairman. *Public Library of Cincinnati and Hamilton County.*

the reports indicate as we go to press that Cincinnati carries the honor. The originality and completeness of detail that were made for the celebration of Candy Day far exceeded anything reported from any other city. And it was some celebration!"

The man behind the event in Cincinnati was Charles Eisen, the president of the Dolly Varden Chocolate Company and chairman of the Cincinnati Candy Day Committee. The Cincinnati committee made sure that packages of candy were distributed to the orphans of the city with help from many volunteers. The generosity was said to create a pay-it-forward motion of those who received to make someone else happy on Candy Days to come.

In addition to Eisen, the campaign committee in Cincinnati consisted of Oscar Graeser of Peter Echert Company (then part of the National Candy Company); George Nuss of Nuss Candy Company; Herman Roehr and George Ast, retailers; Charles Mullane of Mullane's; and Charles Meakin of Meakin's.

William B. Melish, president of the Cincinnati Chamber of Commerce, released this letter to the public:

> *To the Good Citizens of Cincinnati:*
> *Believing that the most valuable asset to any community is Happiness, and knowing from experience that nothing will tickle the palate of both children and grown-ups more than to partake of good wholesome sweetmeats, prompts me to bring to the attention of our good citizens that little happiness bringer—Candy—which although in Ye Olden Days was considered a luxury, is now classed as a food product. The foreign nations at war have included candy among the rations they are supplying to their soldiers.*
>
> *The manufacture of candy is now one of the leading industries of the country, Cincinnati having the reputation of manufacturing the highest quality—ranking seventh in point of production.*
>
> *In view of the above and knowing that there are many who may have little quarrels to patch up; many who want to make HER lot brighter; many who would send candy to orphans; many who would buy candy for*

countless other reasons; prompts me to heartily commend Candy Day, and to call upon members of the Chamber of Commerce and all other good citizens, especially the "man with the sweet tooth" to observe Saturday, October 14 as Candy Day.

Yours for "Kandy for Kids"
William B. Melish.

Large amounts of money were spent on advertising in the press and on billboards leading up to the event. It was even promoted in the material for the Automobile Show that year in Cincinnati, which conveniently happened the same week as Candy Day. Notices were displayed in movie theaters and store windows, canvas streamers were made for cars and wagons, streamers were displayed on the streets and posters were made for community bulletin boards. Hearts with sashes printed with "Have a Heart" and "Remember Candy Day" were distributed by pretty girls at the Business Men's Club and the chamber of commerce and at all the main streetcar transfer points in the city. There was even a man with a megaphone shouting Candy Day messages on Fountain Square. The distribution of free candy to orphans, hospitals and similar organizations required more pretty girls. In the evening, a Candy Day parade was held with balloon sendoff and fireworks.

On Candy Day, Eisen presented the "All-Day Sucker," the size of a football, in jest to Executive Secretary Culkins of the Cincinnati Chamber of Commerce for a photo opportunity and some double entrendre. The events commenced with a large banquet, where all the candy barons patted one another on the backs for their success increasing sales.

It seems like every retailer either sold out or underestimated volumes of candy needed. It was the largest sale day outside of the holidays. Mabley & Carew noted, "This was our biggest day since we have been in the candy business"

Mehas Brothers candy store said, "Candy Day was our biggest day since Christmas, and sincerely hope that this day will be made a yearly event."

Peebles Grocery in Walnut Hills said, "From 11 PM until night we were so rushed in our candy department we did not have near enough help. We sold out every pound of candy we had in house."

Fred W. Becksmith, a candy jobber, said, "My business Candy Week showed an increase from $150 to $200. My trade were all very well satisfied with the results." Fred had started as a grocer with Eagle Grocery and expanded into a wholesale candy distribution business that lasted into the

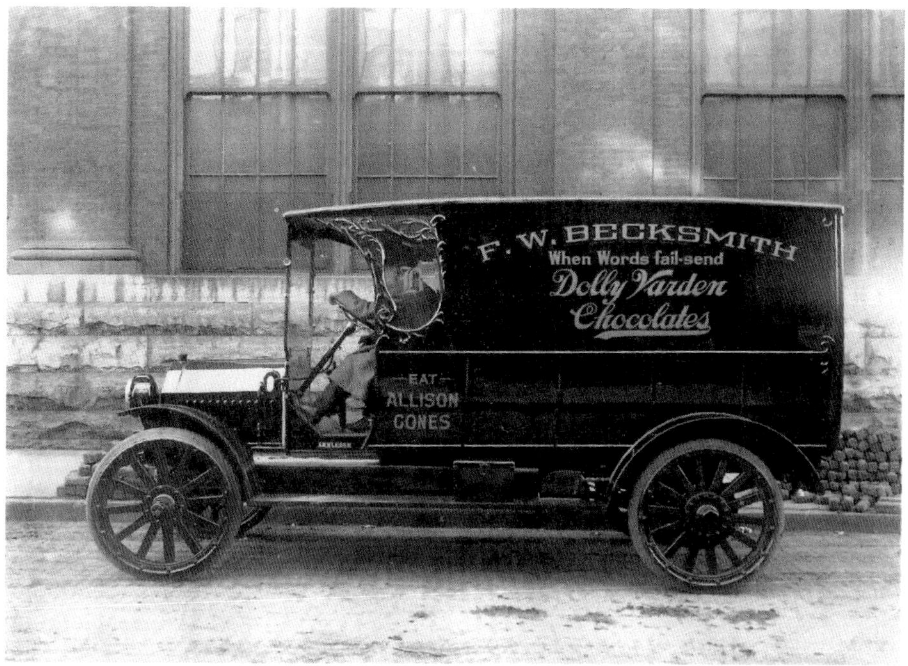

Candy jobber Fred W. Becksmith parked his fleet of candy trucks behind his 2707 Ida Avenue home in Norwood. *Martha Becksmith Uhl.*

fifth generation—the longest family-run candy jobbing business in Greater Cincinnati. From a warehouse behind his home at 2707 Ida Avenue in Norwood, Becksmith distributed chocolates, candy and fountain drink supplies to drug and sweet shops throughout Cincinnati. The business was then moved to Barrow Avenue in Oakley in the 1950s, where it remained until Fred's grandson, Raymond Becksmith, closed it in 2002.

Unfortunately, the success of Candy Day was short-lived. One year later, on October 6, 1917, the Candy Day event was canceled due to a minor roadblock: World War I. It was quickly halted when Herbert Hoover, then head of the U.S. Food Administration, firmly reminded the NCA that Candy Day ran contrary to the war effort to conserve sugar. Concerned at being called unpatriotic, the NCA sent urgent telegrams instructing its members to immediately stop all further planning and publicity related to Candy Day.

As World War I came to an end, Candy Day was shelved until Herbert Birch Kingtson, the president of a Cleveland advertising company, reimagined the holiday as a way to help the less fortunate. He gathered eight of Cleveland's largest candy companies and organized the first "Sweetest Day in the Year" on October 8, 1921. As part of the promotions, Cincinnati-born silent movie star Theda Bara, the original queen of Goth, came to Cleveland to help, passing out candy at local theaters. The *Cleveland Plain Dealer* reported that ten thousand boxes of candy were distributed to Cleveland's orphanages, old folks' homes and other charitable institutions. The day became a sort-of national holiday after that, morphing into a second Valentine's Day, but it got its biggest push from the most successful Cincinnati Candy Day in 1916.

Chapter 11

ROSCOE E. RODDA

THE INVENTOR OF THE PEEP AND HIS TIME IN CINCINNATI

A Progressive-Era Cult and the Inventor of Marshmallow Peeps

One of the most iconic American Easter candies is the Marshmallow Peep. The cute, sugary, marshmallow treat has graced Easter baskets as the Peep since the 1950s and even earlier as a Mallow Chic or another name. There are two very different schools of thought on how to eat them. Some like them fresh and chewy, while the other side likes them a bit stale so the outside sugary layer becomes crunchy. They've been integrated into s'mores, as cake decorations and even microwaved down into other culinary creations. There's even a cult that uses them to create dioramas of historical scenes and famous paintings.

One of the most interesting candy stories in Cincinnati is that of the man credited for inventing this candy. His name is Roscoe E. Rodda, and he spent sixteen years, more or less, in Cincinnati at the helm of several companies influencing the candy industry. Whether he came up with the idea of the Peep while working through the candy industry in Cincinnati, we'll probably never know. But his time here was very interesting. While in Cincinnati, Rodda was involved in a very controversial Progressive-era religious cult called the Church of Divine Healing, or the Christian Catholic Church of Zion. It was sort of like the Church of Scientology of its day, and it was considered the forerunner of the modern Pentecostal Church. This Cincinnati part of Rodda's story is one not well known.

Roscoe E. Rodda (1862–1941) was born in Michigan, near Lake Superior, son of Simon and Elizabeth Rodda, from Cornwall County, England. He first dipped his bonbon in the candy trade as a teenager, working from 1879 to 1887 for the Detroit candy firm of Gray, Toynton and Fox. This firm would later become part of the National Candy Company in 1902. Rodda married Luella Chetham in Illinois in 1885, started a family and moved in about 1891 to Cincinnati, where he is listed as a confectioner from 1891 through 1900. This was at a time when Cincinnati was already on the candy map, with several large national wholesale candy manufacturers.

Rodda probably came to Cincinnati as part of the pioneering group of the Church of Divine Healing to expand outside Chicago. By 1900, Rodda had become a deacon of the Church of Divine Healing in Cincinnati, headed by Dr. John Alexander Dowie of Chicago. Rodda and his family were living at 607 Crown Street in East Walnut Hills at that time, near what is now the Essex Studios.

Dowie, the leader of the Zion Church, was an over-the-top character. The center of the church was Dr. Dowie praying for the healing of church members who paid him dues. He considered himself the reincarnated Prophet Elijah and dressed in ancient priestly robes as Elijah the Restorer. He was totally against modern medicine and relied solely on his divine healing. He claimed to be the object of many Old and New Testament prophecies and the fifth angel spoken of in the Book of Revelations.

Dowie gained fame by renting property adjacent to the Chicago World's Fair in 1893. There he staged elaborate "Divine Healings" in front of large audiences. Many of these "healings" were staged using audience "plants" and other dubious methods. At other times, carefully screened individuals were brought on stage to be healed. Dowie's following grew, and in 1894, he established the Zion Tabernacle downtown and was holding regular services for large crowds at Chicago's Central Music Hall, in sort of a mega-church fashion.

Rodda first shows up in connection with the Church of Divine Healing in an 1897 church publication at a meeting. In the transcript, he confirms to the audience that he went to the Zion House in Chicago with his family and blind daughter. His daughter's sight was restored and his own tuberculosis cured by the prayers of Dr. Dowie. He was most probably one of the "plants" in that healing demonstration.

In another 1900 church publication, *Leaves of Healing*, Rodda credited Dowie's prayers to the healing of his nine-year-old son, Emmons, involved in an accident in Cincinnati. Rodda said, "I thank God for the wonderful

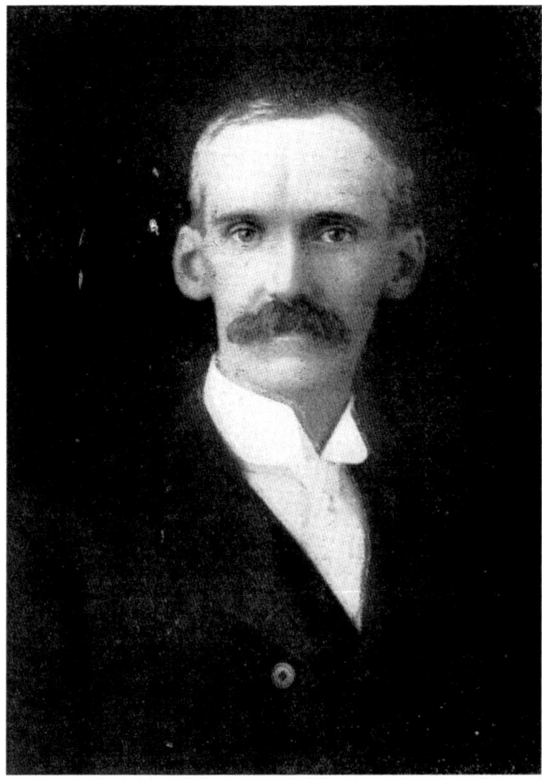

Roscoe E. Rodda, inventor of the Marshmallow Peep, shortly after he left Cincinnati to start the Zion Candy Plant. *Zion Illinois Library*.

healing of my little boy, who was knocked down by a streetcar in Cincinnati. God did not permit a bone to be broken or a scratch upon his body, although he was knocked unconscious."

With about six thousand followers, Dr. Dowie sought land north of Chicago and bought up a large amount of real estate secretly. In 1900, he announced the founding of the city of Zion, forty miles from Chicago, where he owned all the property. He established a theocratic political and economic structure and prohibited smoking, drinking, eating pork and any form of modern medicine. The indulgence of eating candy, however, was not prohibited, and Rodda would be intimately involved in that enterprise with the church. Dowie also established a range of businesses, healing homes and a large tabernacle. Followers from across the world descended on Zion.

By 1901, Dowie was already being accused in the press of hypocrisy for the lavish lifestyle and empire he had established for himself. One report by Elder Stokes, a former officer of the church, noted, "He is a fraud. He has given himself over to commercialism: he is only after the money he can get. He claims to do all for God: yet all the property is in his own name and he receives thousands of dollars a day from deceived ones all over the country as tithes and offerings. Zion is a mess of tattles and spies."

By 1902, Rodda was the general manager of the Peter Echert Company in Cincinnati. Due to his affiliation with the church and his role as a "plant" in healing demonstrations, Rodda was brought to Zion in May 1902 when Dowie decided (probably at the persuasion of Rodda) to open a candy factory there. In September, the Echert Company became part of the National Candy Company, so Dowie probably knew that was coming and made Rodda decide to move to Zion. The move was announced in the *Cincinnati Enquirer* on May 12 that year:

> *Dr. John Alexander Dowie is to start a large candy factory at Zion City, Illinois. The concern will be known as the Zion Sugar and Confectionery Association. The factory will be three stories high and about 100 by 150 feet. The plant is now in the course of construction. The new factory will be near Dowie's lace mills and other industries at Zion City. The General Manager of the plant will be R.E. Rodda, now general manager of P. Echert's candy factory at Court Street, Cincinnati. Rodda will leave Echert's employ June 1, 1902.*

A description of the Zion factory and its operations in Dowie's 1902 *Leaves of Healing* publication noted:

> *The Zion Sugar and Confection Company began its existence fifteen months ago in a little tent with a corps of two employees* [Roscoe Rodda and Horace Cook]. *Today the factory covers 19,000 feet of floor space, employs about 100 hands, and is unable to turn out goods nearly rapidly enough to supply the constantly increasing demand. Plans have been made for a great factory, four hundred feet in depth, with all the finest and most modern equipment. Within the coming year agencies will be established in all parts of the United States, and in many foreign centers. The Manager and Assistant Manager, of this Association, both of whom have enviable reputations as expert confectioners give their personal attention to the manufacture, and the result is that Zion Candy is known throughout the country as absolutely pure beautiful in workmanship, and unexcelled in quality. The plant is run by electric throughout, ensuring perfect cleanliness. A specialty is made of pan work,*

the finest and most complete line of these goods made by any factory in the world being produced in large quantities.

At first, the Zion Candy Company turned out a general line of hard candy, but by the 1920s, it was producing candy bars. One of the most popular of those bars by the 1920s was the Fig Pie candy bar, inspired by the Bible. Other candy bars were the Cheer Leader, the Cocoaroon and the Cherry Sunday.

Rodda led an exhibition of all the candy they made at Madison Square Garden in New York City in October and November 1903, along with the other industries at Zion.

In 1904, after only two years in operation, the Zion confectionery company in Illinois was shut down because of lack of funds to buy raw materials. It was a shame because of all the businesses in Zion, candy was the most profitable. Zion candies were known for what they advertised to be—genuine—and won wide acclaim with candy dealers and the public.

From this point on in his career, Rodda fought through estrangements with partners in other candy firms that he joined or in which he bought significant shares. Whether his rise to the top of the candy industry was wily or legitimate, the next nearly thirty years of his professional life were riddled with candy wars that mirrored the financial allegations Dr. Dowie faced in Zion.

With as much aggression as the oil and railroad robber barons, the titans of candy protected their sweet empires with all types of corporate shenanigans, including hostile takeovers, shady bond deals and frivolous copyright infringement lawsuits meant to drain the resources of upstart competitors. It was a time of large consolidations within the candy industry. In 1902, the Peter Echert Company of Cincinnati merged into the National Candy Company, headquartered in St. Louis. By 1902, when Rodda was general manager there, National Candy was a consolidation of fourteen other candy companies in the United States.

In 1905, the Reinhart & Newton Manufacturing Company was incorporated in Columbus as a partnership and took over the candy manufacturing business of the former Reinhart & Newton company, which manufactured taffy and chocolate-covered marshmallow products. This was after founder George Newton retired, selling his interest to Captain John D. Reinhart. The new stockholders were John D. Reinhart, principal holder, and D.J. and Charles Reinhart, Henry Wehking, Basil Duke, George W. Nippert, R.H. Ranson and Roscoe Rodda, listed as former general manager of Dowie's Zion candy factory. The new company continued doing business in the Bottoms, the downtown manufacturing district near the Ohio River.

Only two years later, in 1907, Rodda was living in Norwood and partnered with Robert Hiner Putman, a confectioner from Tolesboro, Kentucky, credited with creating the opera cream candy. Together, their company made fine candies at 1011 Main Street and 621 Vine Street, as well as running the candy department of the Fair, "Cincinnati's Progressive Department Store." Putman had been making candy in Cincinnati since 1895 and was also a member of the Christian Catholic Church of Zion. However, he was on the opposite end from Rodda involving a split in the church. In Cincinnati, the church met at the tabernacle at Fourth and John Streets in the West End.

Putman also testified to a healing, of sorts, in the Zion church publication *Levels of Healing* with the headline "God Rebukes the Devourer in Answer to Prayer": "Dear Friend and Brother: Early in the summer about a dozen of my fine peach trees were assailed by an insect, which was fast destroying them. I wrote you, telling the situation, and asking you to pray for those trees. I heard nothing from you, but within one week the plague disappeared and the trees were soon in beautiful foliage, and have since been healthy and thrifty."

As Dr. Dowie got crazier with his claims and more feeble in age, he was forced out and the church was taken over by Wilbur Glenn Voliva. Voliva had been a minister in Washington Courthouse, Ohio, but became aware of Dr. Dowie's ministry and was ordained in his Christian Catholic Church. Voliva would direct the church's work in Chicago and Cincinnati before immigrating to Australia in 1901 to direct its work there. After Dowie suffered a stroke in 1905, he summoned Voliva from Australia to oversee Zion, Illinois. Arriving in Zion in early 1906, Voliva, with the support of church elders, promptly took over the town and the church.

However, there were some who weren't supportive of Voliva and broke off, wanting to remain independent. Rodda was the leader of supporters of Voliva in Cincinnati, and his candy partner Putman was on the other side of the quarrel.

Voliva even visited the congregation in Cincinnati to try to mend fences in March 1907, staying with Rodda, making big news in Cincinnati: "Bolters from Zion Have Split: One Faction, Headed by Confectioner Rodda, Supports Voliva and Holds Regular Meetings." Then, in April 1907: "Voliva in a Belligerent Mood. Successor of Dowie Comes to [Cincinnati] to Check Spread of Insurrection Among the Local Zionists."

The fences weren't mended. Voliva was ousted in May, and as a result, on May 27, 1907, Rodda left the partnership with Putman and incorporated himself in Cincinnati as the Roscoe E. Rodda Candy Company. Robert Putman went into partnership with his brother, William, and in 1908, Roscoe moved his candy business to Lancaster, Pennsylvania, near another famous candy baron, Milton Hershey. But Rodda did not leave Cincinnati and its candy businesses behind like he did the Zion church.

Like his predecessor, Voliva increasingly developed an overtly lavish lifestyle, amassing a $5 million personal fortune by 1927, which began to alienate his followers, especially after the hardships brought on by the Great Depression. This forced Zion Industries into bankruptcy. In 1942, after being diagnosed with terminal cancer, Voliva made a tearful public confession to his followers that he had misappropriated church funds for his personal use and committed other misdeeds.

So, Rodda had already learned the art of chicanery from the whole Zion church episode. It looks like Rodda then first learned a trick with mergers and stock inflation from the managers of Headley Chocolate, the next candy company on his radar. In 1915, the controlling shareholders, Frank O. Headley and his VP, Henry W. Matthews, forced the company to pay themselves excessive salaries and then sold their control block of $150,000 to a new buyer—none other than Rodda—as well as some others. Matthews ended up suing Rodda for damages of $50,000 in September 1916 after the sale.

Rodda at the time co-owned the American Caramel Company in nearby York, Pennsylvania, with partner Daniel Lafean, who was its president. The purchase of the Headley stock made Rodda more of a majority owner than its founder, William C. Bidlack, and Rodda began operating it jointly with the American Caramel Company.

In 1916, Rodda battled his estranged partner, Daniel Lafean, on charges and countercharges of fraud, collusion, breach of contract and secret and unlawful profits. Lafean had tried to seize controlling interest of the American Caramel Company by buying up a majority of the Rodda Candy Company stock. Rodda was forced to pay Lafean his original salary up to the merger.

On January 1, 1920, Rodda plunged back into the Cincinnati candy industry when he was made vice-president of a conglomerate that consolidated his Headley Chocolate Company of Baltimore; the Lancaster Chocolate and Caramel Company of Lancaster, Pennsylvania; and Reinhart & Newton of Cincinnati, which would buy the Dolly Varden Chocolate

Company in 1924. William C. Bidlack was president, Rodda vice-president, Clayton Crone secretary and treasurer and Russell Ranson of Cincinnati (then manager of Reinhart & Newton) general manager.

The Lancaster caramel company was founded by a young Milton Hershey in 1886. He sold it in 1900 to the American Caramel Company, in which Lafean and Rodda were executives, before going into the chocolate industry that made him an American candy icon.

The new conglomerate would shut down operations of Reinhart & Newton and Dolly Varden by 1926, when another candy war was started by Cincinnatian Bertha Ruehl Selbert. Selbert was the wealthy Walnut Hills widow of Albert Selbert, owner of a Cincinnati paper company. She was a large stockowner in Reinhart & Newton. She named Rodda as a co-defendant, accusing him of colluding with Bidlack in manipulation of stocks and moneys of the merged corporation resulting in illegal profits, payment of excessive salaries (which had been done during the Headley takeover) and dissipation of assets of Reinhart & Newton and thus devaluation of that stock for shareholders. This litigation followed Rodda up until the last case was settled in 1926. Rodda died in 1941 and is buried in Pennsylvania. His company was sold to Samuel Born, a Russian immigrant confectioner, in 1953. Sam Born is credited with inventing "jimmies," chocolate sprinkles, and the chocolate coating on ice cream novelty bars.

Wholesale candy catalogues from the early 1920s from the Rodda Company show his concentration on a variety of Easter candy, including chocolate-covered mallows, but no candy that looked like Peeps. This was probably because at the time, non-coated marshmallow products didn't have a good shelf life and wouldn't travel well and therefore wouldn't have been sold on the wholesale trade, but they would have been sold in the local retail trade.

When Rodda first invented Marshmallow Peeps, they were hand-piped in pastry bags by up to eighty women. They would spoon small batches of freshly made marshmallow batter, which included whipped raw egg whites, into regular pastry tubes and then squirt out the baby chicken through the tiny fluted steel tip. This was before the worry of potential salmonella poisoning from uncooked eggs. The chicks were not baked, but rather air-dried into a mushy yet firm type of meringue. This long manual process took some twenty-seven hours and included little piped wings on the little chicks that were later snipped off by Samuel Born when he bought the company in 1953. This was probably because the wings were too laborious to add, and this made them easier to automate and less expensive to produce.

It was Born who renamed the marshmallow meringue chicks Peeps and popularized them, putting them in nearly every American Easter basket. With the automation of the process, Born was able to make the Peep a shippable product that could be mass-produced and had a better shelf life than the unstable original meringue product that Rodda had invented as an Easter novelty.

So the complex story behind the inventor of the Marshmallow Peep started in Cincinnati and involved another popular local Easter candy, the opera cream, and its inventor, Robert Hiner Putman. The corporate shenanigans of Roscoe Rodda, in and outside Cincinnati, led to the demise of two of Cincinnati's largest surviving candy companies, Reinhart & Newton and Dolly Varden. He also connected us to the most recognizable name in chocolate, Milton S. Hershey.

Chapter 12

A PEPPERMINT PATTY AND A THREEWAY

CINCINNATI GREEKS IN THE CANDY INDUSTRY

The Cincinnati chili industry was founded by Macedonians and, later, Greeks. But the Cincinnati candy industry also had a large Greek influence. Greeks are not necessarily known for their candy confections. They do have a wonderful baking tradition with baklava and cookies, but they don't have a rich candy tradition in their own country. Their neighbors the Turks were much more known for their sweets, like Turkish delights or "rahat," a candy based on a gel of starch and sugar, with nuts and dried fruits embedded.

So, how did the Greeks get so involved in the candy industry in the United States? They went into a business in which their earlier compatriots had been successful. Through a series of chain migrations, those here first discovered the candy industry and its low cost of entry. Those pioneers set themselves up and hosted family members and fellow countrymen. They worked at their fellow immigrants' candy shops and then opened their own. They mirrored the process of the Cincinnati chili pioneers, most of whom worked at the original Empress Chili Parlor before opening their own parlors. In the same way, Greek immigrants, most from Sparta, worked and learned the candy and ice cream trade at other establishments before starting their own.

In Cincinnati, there's a connection between candy and Cincinnati chili. A long-standing tradition exists of eating a fifteen-cent York Peppermint Patty after a bowl of Cincinnati chili to quiet the spices and freshen your breath. But how did this tradition start?

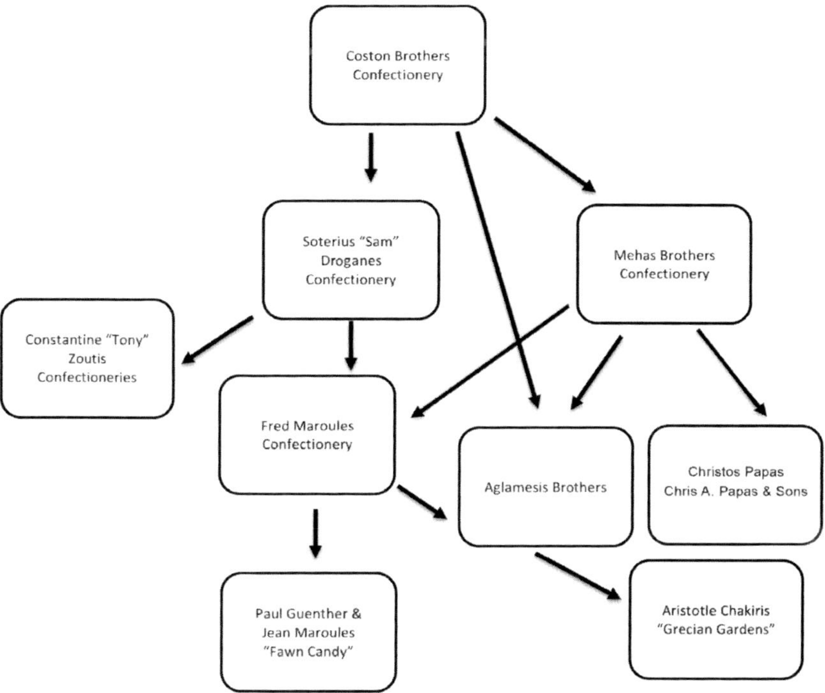

The Cincinnati Greek confectioners' family tree. *Created by the author.*

For the Greek immigrants, ice cream and candy went hand in hand. The American ice cream sundae—integrating fruits like cherries, pineapples and other "fancy fruits"—is a Greek invention, according to community folklore. Like the creation of Cincinnati chili, Greek confectioners played to an American audience, selling and making traditional American confections like caramel, taffy, chocolates and hard candies. The Greek Confectioner's Association even urged its members to blend in with American clients in a proclamation in the early twentieth century. This ensured their success in a very xenophobic society in America before and around the First World War.

The two main waves of Greek immigration came in 1900–1920 and 1950–70. The first wave was primarily from Sparta and the latter from northern Greece. It was the first wave of immigration that fed into the candy and chili businesses. The main reason for immigration from Greece to America was opportunity for a better life, as well as to escape mandatory military service during the Balkan Wars. Sometime before World War I, there were enough Greeks in Cincinnati to form something of a community, and a Greek Orthodox church was formed on Lower Vine Street. In Greece, the church was the center of community life, and so it was in Cincinnati. To the immigrant, the church provided, and still provides, a place to meet countrymen, speak Greek and preserve cultural traditions.

Both candy and ice cream were seasonal and perfect complements. Combining the two into a business meant you were set for the year. Some even added other seasonal businesses or fireworks to their arsenal. Ice cream sold well during the hot summer months, but candy didn't. Without air conditioning, it was hard to store and sell chocolate candy that melted quickly or even hard candy that would stick together with humidity during the summer. Then, during the cold winter months, candy sold better, while ice cream didn't sell as well.

By 1906, Chicago was the candy wholesaling capital of the United States. The Greek community was operating nine hundred candy shops. According to a 1915 editorial published in the *Salonika Greek Press*, "On every great business corner in Chicago you will find the brightly lighted, clean, neat and attractive Greek confectionary store…almost two thirds of the confectionary business of Chicago is in the hands of the Greeks." Chicago's McCormick Place still hosts the largest candy show in the country every year, the Sweet and Snacks Expo, sponsored by the National Confectioners Association.

In Cincinnati, our long-running candy and ice cream companies were founded by Greeks, the majority of whom were from the area of Sparta. How there was no Spartan brand of candy in Cincinnati is amazing. The Macedonians in Cincinnati flocked more to the chili and restaurant businesses, while those families from Sparta went into the ice cream and candy businesses. The families hosted one another, intermarried and shared ice cream and candy recipes among their businesses. We already discussed the Macedonian/Greek-founded Carl A. Papas Candy Company and its role in the popularity of the opera cream in Cincinnati.

Nicholas Sarakatsanis, the founder of Dixie Chili, worked first at a candy store on Fifth and Elm Streets in Cincinnati in 1917 and then at the Chris Malavazos Candy Kitchen in Portsmouth, Ohio, before returning to Cincy and landing in the chili business. He started working for the Kiradjieff brothers at Empress Chili before moving across the river to open his own chili parlor. With both industries in his wheelhouse, he was a double threat.

So perhaps this large connection to the Greek-dominated U.S. candy industry is why the York Peppermint Patty is paired today at Skyline and other Cincinnati chili parlors. In addition to the York Peppermint Patty, another common mint sold at chili parlors is the Andes chocolate mint. The Clifton Skyline Chili parlor reported that it goes through 1,600 peppermint patties per week. Another anonymous Skyline location confessed to selling three to four boxes of 175 patties per day. Averaging two boxes per day, multiplied by eighty-four Skyline locations in Greater Cincinnati, a rough estimate of 29,400 YPD (Yorks Per Day) for Skyline Chili alone is quite a lot of mint consumption! That's 882,000 patties per thirty-day month and 10,731,000 per year.

Who started the tradition is hard to pinpoint, but certainly it was someone who had a cousin, brother, in-law or other family member who owned a Greek candy store and was helping them out by offering an after-dinner mint. Back in the early days, maybe instead of a York or Andes mint, it was a Mehas chocolate mint or a Coston mint that sat on the counter of the neighborhood chili parlor. There were certainly more than a handful of the Greek-owned ice cream and confectionery shops in Cincinnati and Northern Kentucky that could have supplied their homemade chocolate mints to the various neighborhood chili parlors.

The Coston Brothers Confectionery

One of the first Greek families who came to Cincinnati and began their own candy business were the Coston brothers, James (1870–1930) and George (1879–1957). James Coston had been a colonel in the Greek army and was a prominent spokesperson for the immigrant Greek community in Cincinnati. When Greek king Constantinos XII was assassinated in March 1913, James organized a memorial service at the Greek church for him and those Greeks who fell in battle. At the end of the Balkan Wars in 1914, Coston led a banquet for the community and a local campaign to correct the false reports of cruelty to women and children in Macedonia by Greek soldiers during the wars.

James had immigrated to Cincinnati in 1884 and started with a confectionery on Warsaw Avenue in Price Hill. His brother, George, followed him to Cincinnati in 1902. By 1909, James was running a confectionery at nos. 5–7 in the Emery Arcade downtown, with the backing of his brother-in-law, Herman J. Berlage. This would be the location he would apprentice the Aglamesis brothers, Nicholas and Thomas, for three years before they opened their own confectionery in Norwood and then Oakley.

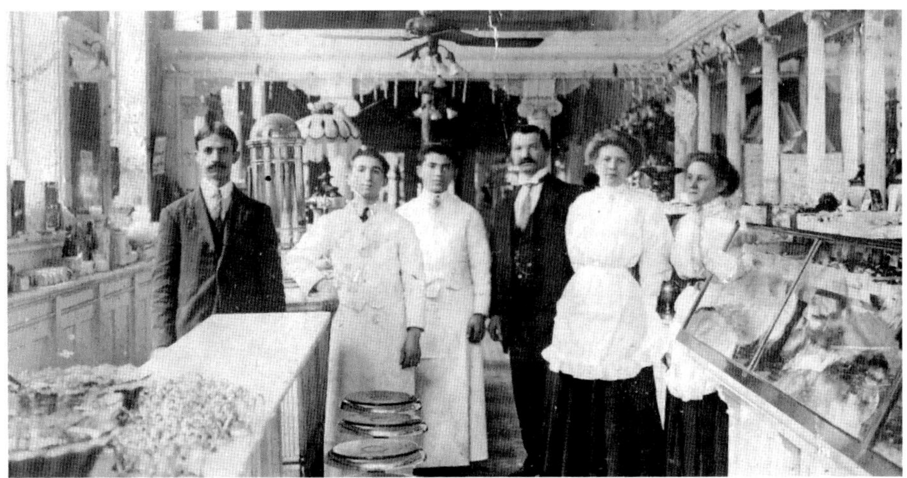

The Coston Brothers confectionery in Covington, Kentucky. *Sam Droganes.*

The Emery Arcade was built in 1877 connecting Race Street with the Emery Hotel. The glass roof of the arcade was forty feet high, with two stories on each side, housing stores (among them at least two Greek-owned candy stores), offices, a restaurant and a hotel. The arcade was torn down in 1929 to make way for the Netherland Hotel and Carew Tower, but it might be considered the birthplace of all Greek confectioneries in Cincinnati.

In 1909, the Costons branched out from their original store, opening one in Hamilton, Ohio, and one in Covington, Kentucky, at Sixth and Madison. The store on Madison Avenue in Covington would be where Soterious "Sam" Droganes would learn the business before buying the Costons out and then opening his own store. Another Coston, Nicholas, would open a confectionery in Oxford, Ohio, on High Street around 1910 to satisfy the sweet tooth of the college crowd at Miami University. James had the ice cream and candy concession for several seasons at the Ludlow Lagoon amusement park on the Ohio River in Ludlow, Kentucky. Many other Greek immigrants were hosted and taught the confectionery industry by the Coston brothers.

Another family operated a confectionery at the Arcade, according to the July 6, 1962 *Cincinnati Enquirer*. George P. Zervos (1883–1962) came to Cincinnati from Geraki near Sparta, Greece, in 1905. For twenty-four years, he operated the Maroudas Confectionery at the Emery Arcade at nos. 46–48, previously operated by his four uncles who returned to Greece. George was one of the first trustees of the Greek Orthodox Church in Cincinnati.

Mehas Brothers Confectionery

The Mehas brothers—Peter, George and Nicholas—built the largest Greek-owned wholesale and retail confectionery business in Cincinnati. They started from an ice cream pushcart, later moving into a chain of six large downtown store operations, plus two to the north in neighboring Hamilton, Ohio. The brothers were born in the village of Geraki in Sparta, Greece, to Andrew and Lilly Chorgas Mehas.

By 1917, the brothers owned about $200,000 in downtown real estate. They owned the flagship Fountain Square store building and another at the corner of Fifth and Plum Streets.

In 1886, brothers Peter (1865–1940) and Nicholas (1870–1936) came to Cincinnati, starting with one small store. In 1900, their youngest brother, George, joined them and was brought into the business. Together they built a name for their ice cream and extensive line of handmade candies and chocolates. George became a victim of the 1918 flu epidemic, and Nicholas and Pete decided to retire in 1922.

The Mehas retail store locations were at 28 East Fifth Street; 819 Vine Street; nos. 5–7 in the Old Emery Arcade, taken over from the Coston brothers; 1223 Vine Street in the Rialto Block; and two stores in Hamilton,

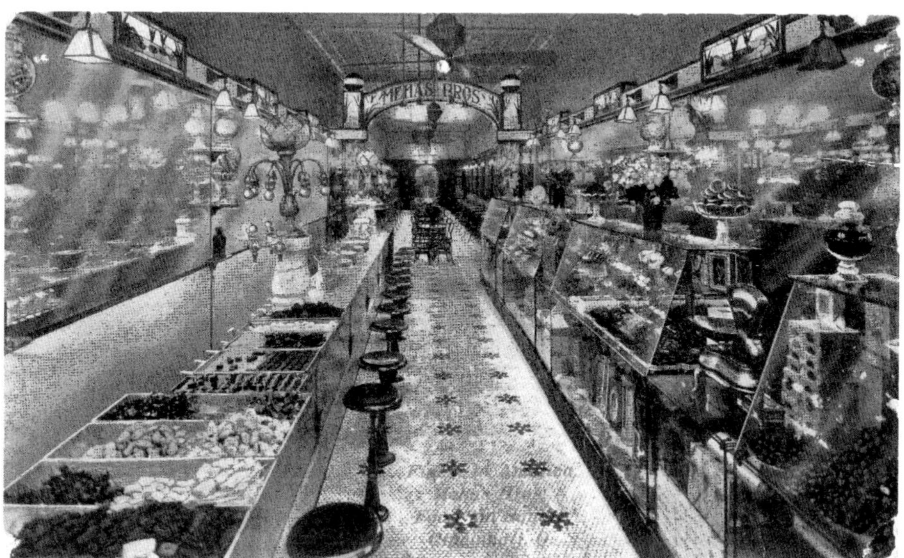

This postcard of the Mehas Fountain Square location shows its extensive line of candies. *Public Library of Cincinnati and Hamilton County.*

Ohio, at 28 and 221 High Street. The candy was made at a factory on Fifth and Plum Streets in downtown Cincinnati.

The most prominent of the stores was the Fifth Street location opposite the Tyler Davidson Fountain and next to the beautiful Bijou Theatre. It was remodeled in 1918 at a cost of $2,500 by famed architectural firm Tietig & Lee. One side of the store was the marble-topped soda fountain. The other side was a candy case, displaying the variety of handmade chocolate confections that could be boxed in the signature foil box with the image of the Tyler Davidson Fountain.

The Mehas brothers also owned a confectionery in Norwood at 3961 Montgomery for a short time, only a block away from the Aglamesis brothers' Metropolitan Confectionery. Peter Mehas's daughter, Viola Mehas, would marry Thomas Aglamesis, and their son, Jim, would carry on the ownership of the Aglamesis Brothers Ice Cream Parlor in Oakley when it moved from Norwood.

The brothers hosted others from their village, including nephew Peter Michel Mehas, son of their other brother, Michel, who was able to open barbershops in Hamilton, Ohio. The cities of Hamilton and Middletown also had a sizeable Greek immigrant population, spawning confectioneries and lunchrooms as in Cincinnati.

Jonson Brothers Confectionery

The Jonsons were another set of brothers who immigrated from Sparta, Greece, to Cincinnati. John came in 1902, Nicholas in 1908, Charles in 1912 and George in 1914. The brothers received their educational training in the schools of Sparta, where their family owned considerable property and farming lands. After arriving in Cincinnati, John learned the confectionery business from a friend already established. His brothers followed the same training as they arrived over the next several years. In 1910, John and Nicholas Jonson opened a confectionery store at 937 Central Avenue, Cincinnati, the firm being known as Jonson Brothers.

On November 23, 1915, Nicholas Jonson came to Hamilton, where he purchased the interest of Peter Vlachos in the confectionery business of Mehas & Vlachos at 221 High Street, now the site of the Firststar Bank. The firm became Mehas & Jonson, and the brick-and-mortar site was named Jonson's Sweet Shop. The Mehas brothers had bought out the interest of the Politz brothers to partner with the Mehases at that location. It was a revolving door of Greek ownership. The Jonsons added restaurant service in 1919 and in 1929 moved across Journal Square to 235 High Street, where Nicholas operated until 1968. In 1964, Jonson bought the building that housed his restaurant. In earlier years, Nick joined his brothers, John, Charles and George, in operating other downtown establishments, including the Ideal Confectionery, the Boston Bakery and the Mayflower.

On April 26, 1918, Nicholas Jonson left Hamilton for Camp Sherman and one month later went with the 331st Infantry to France. With only the equivalent of a fifth-grade education, Nick mastered five languages—Greek, English, Spanish, French and Italian. Owing to his knowledge of the French language, he was promoted to the rank of corporal and served as an interpreter, seeing eight months of active service overseas. He was sent back to the United States and honorably discharged at Camp Sherman on February 8, 1919, following which he returned to his business in Hamilton. On March 1, 1919, Mr. Jonson purchased the interest of his uncle Mehas in the business and admitted his brothers to partnership under the firm style of Jonson Brothers.

Nick Jonson wasn't the first Greek in Hamilton, but he was the first Greek immigrant in this community to become an American citizen. He then served on the Americanization Committee of the American Legion, urging and helping not only Greeks but also other nationalities to become citizens.

Nick Jonson died on December 27, 1968, and his restaurant closed a little more than two years later on December 31, 1970. It was sold to John Kurlas and George Mitchell of Cincinnati and was operated as a Skyline Chili franchise from June 1971 until August 1997, after which it became High Street Chili.

Peter Courlis Confectionery

Peter Courlis was born in Philicon, Sparta, Greece, and came to Cincinnati in the 1890s, establishing himself in the Greek candy community with his own confectionery. His son Jerome joined him in Cincinnati in 1903; his other son, Harry, arrived in 1904, and then in 1905, his wife, Catherine, and mother joined, reuniting the family. A typical story of immigration, Courlis worked and saved, bringing family members over as they could afford to. Peter and Catherine retired and returned to Greece in 1910, but Jerome would move to Springfield, Ohio, and start his own confectionery there in 1907.

Aglamesis: Made the Sincere Way

Immigrant brothers Thomas and Nicholas Aglamesis saw their ideas and hard work built into one of the most widely known confectioneries in Cincinnati. Starting as many immigrants from Sparta did, on a farm, Nicholas Aglamesis came to Cincinnati in 1905, two years after the arrival of his brother, Thomas. The two had spent their childhood on the family farm in a small town outside Sparta, Greece. The brothers, reunited in Cincinnati, settled on West Fifth Street downtown, which was the enclave of the Greek community—refugees of the Balkan Wars.

The brothers found employment in the Coston brothers' confectionery in the old Emery Arcade, serving three years of apprenticeship to learn the candy and ice cream business. Destined not to fail, the two saved their money and, equipped with new ideas, opened the first Metropolitan Confectionery at 4631 Montgomery Road in 1908, three doors from the present Norwood City Hall and near the Plaza Theatre. The brothers developed a reputation for the fastest horse wagon delivery in Norwood, above the several other competitors they had in the Norwood Theatre District.

At the time, there were several other Greek-owned confectioneries in Norwood. The Mehas Brothers Confectionery was at 3961 Montgomery; the Lambros and Athanasakos Confectionery at 4634 Montgomery Road; Grecian Gardens, owned by Constantine Chakiris, at the corner of Sherman and Allison; and the Malas Brothers Confectionery at 4607 Montgomery Road. The Malas brothers, George (1895–1941) and Peter (1887–1956), both from Geraki, Sparta, Greece, had bought out the Butler Candy & Ice Cream at the same location in 1916. Butler had been there since 1911.

The reason why there were so many confectioneries in Norwood was that it had a thriving theater district. The earliest theaters were the Plaza at 4630 Montgomery Road (1910), a short-lived Pike Theatre at 4643 Montgomery (1909–10) and the Minette Theater at 4608 Montgomery (1909–12). The Norwood Theatre at 4720 Montgomery Road at Maple opened in 1913. The Norwood Hippodrome at Smith Road opened in 1918. The Ohio Theatre at 4646 Montgomery was south of the Norwood Theatre, north of the Plaza Theatre. The outdoor Airdrome Theatre at 4431 Montgomery and Mills Avenue lasted from about 1912 to 1920.

Despite the competition, the Aglamesis business flourished, and in 1913, a second store was opened at the Madison Road address in Oakley. It was one of the first buildings to be constructed on Oakley Square when little else was there and freight was still transported by horse wagon.

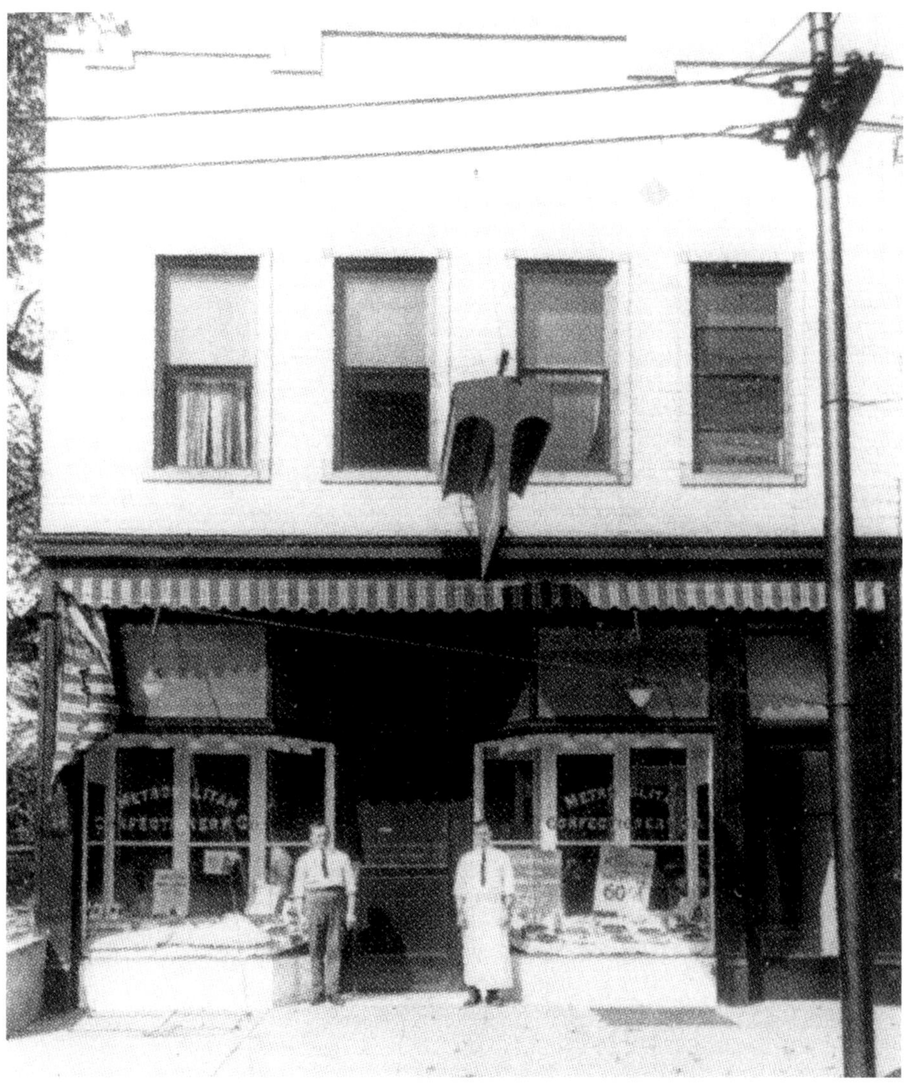

The Aglamesis brothers in front of their Norwood Metropolitan confectionery. *Aglamesis family.*

The Oakley store was built with marble imported from Portugal, and the counter was dotted with soda fountains with tulip-shaped Tiffany lamps. Patterned terrazzo tiled floors, pressed tin ceilings and an authentic player piano created an ambiance that made it a popular meeting place. Nine years later, the brothers added an ice cream plant with modern refrigerated cooling machinery to the Oakley location.

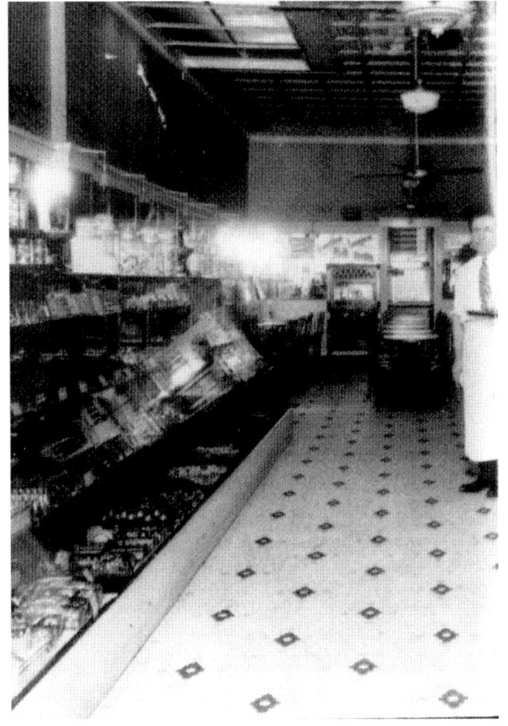

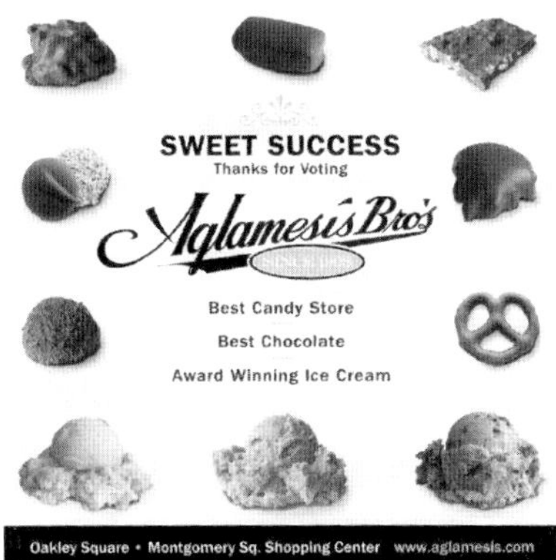

Above: A 2017 ad showing the Aglamesis candy and confection lineup. *Aglamesis family.*

Left: The candy counter of the Aglamesis brothers' shop in Oakley Square. *Aglamesis family*.

Thomas may have softened the competition in Norwood when he married Viola Mehas, the daughter of Peter Mehas, owner of the other confectionery. Thomas and Viola had three children: Mary, Jim and Peter. They all went to Withrow High School and the University of Cincinnati.

The brothers found that operating two stores was more than enough, so they sold the Norwood establishment to fellow Spartans Peter and Demos Geovanes during the Depression around 1922. The Geovanes family opened another Metropolitan store one block away at 4711 Montgomery Avenue, and Peter's son, George, operated it.

The sale of the Metropolitan allowed the Aglamesis brothers to experiment more with their homemade ice cream and candy for which they soon became widely known. The Aglamesis brothers had learned how to make confections while working at Coston Brothers and later with Fred Maroules at the Mabley and Carew Candy Store in downtown Cincinnati.

Nicholas Aglamesis passed away in 1950, and his brother took on the business. Nicholas was active in the St. Nicholas Greek Orthodox Church and was a member of the Oakley Chamber of Commerce and the Oakley Civic Association.

When Thomas suffered a debilitating stroke, his son, Jim Aglamesis, took over the business. Jim had served in Korea and returned in 1952, turning down two corporate marketing jobs to carry on the business. He had grown up with his siblings in the apartment above the store in Oakley. One of his jobs to help the family business was cutting up the fresh strawberries they used in their ice cream.

The Oakley store is nearly the same today as it was back in 1913 when it opened, minus the player piano. The original Portuguese marble countertops and Tiffany tulip-topped glass fountain take you back to the turn of the last century. Oddly enough, the same floral-topped, fluted, marble-based soda fountain was in the original soda stands at Sam Droganes's original store in Covington, Kentucky; the Mehas Brothers store on Fountain Square; and two Meakins locations at Opera Place and Vine Street. There must have been a very successful supplier of these soda fountains in Cincinnati in the early 1900s.

The original family apartments upstairs now house the production facility for chocolate and candy that is fully staffed by an army of women.

Aglamesis today makes all sorts of chocolates, dark and milk, with and without nuts, turtles and chocolate-dipped pretzels and fruit and opera creams. It still makes the opera creams using the old "creaming process of mixing the fondant just right." The Aglamesis slogan is "made the sincere way," and that means it has a commitment to using quality ingredients.

In 2016, Vice-President of Operations Randy Young showed that commitment to quality ingredients in a press release to customers about the increasing price of the bourbon vanilla they use:

> *The world vanilla bean market has seen an unprecedented increase in pricing due to a reduced crop in Madagascar, where roughly 70% of the world's finest vanilla bean crop is produced. At Aglamesis Brothers we use pure Bourbon vanilla extract (having nothing to do with the liquor bourbon).*
>
> *In order to preserve the quality and integrity of our products, despite this cost increase, we will not make any substitutions in our ingredients or changes in how we make our products.*
>
> *We have made this decision using the same basic principle many times over the years when sugar, milk, cocoa, and other commodities have jumped in price. We remain dedicated to the quality of our products that you have come to know us for in our 108 years of business.*
>
> *We are proud to continue producing Cincinnati's finest ice creams and confections and ensure an exceptional product for years to come.*

Aglamesis candy bestsellers are the assorted chocolates, followed by turtles and the opera creams. At Easter, the back of the store is like a scene out of the Willy Wonka candy room. Baskets filled with chocolate bunnies, eggs and assorted chocolates are stacked rows high on any available flat surface.

Jim Aglamesis just celebrated his ninetieth birthday in April 2017 and still regularly works at the store. Third-generation Randal Young, Jim's stepson, handles manufacturing and wholesale accounts, while his sister, Dianne Aglamesis Lytle, handles the retail, marketing and accounting.

Sakelos Confections

The Aglamesis brothers weren't the only Greeks in the ice cream and confection business in Oakley. From 1936 to 1952, Peter Sakelos and his wife, Jean, operated the Sakelos Ice Cream Shoppe at 3056 Madison Road, opposite St. Cecilia Catholic Church, only blocks away from the Aglamesis stores. Apparently, there was friendly competition, but in the end, Aglamesis won.

Sakelos had emigrated from Geraki, Sparta, Greece, around 1908 with his other brothers, John and James, and had operated a confectionery shop in downtown Cincinnati on Vine Street in the early 1920s, moving it to 3527 Reading Road by 1922.

All the brothers pitched in for about fifty years in the ownership of a popular restaurant hangout for University of Cincinnati students in the Ludlow Avenue Business District. The Sakelos family owned the Busy Bee Restaurant from the 1930s into the 1980s.

Grecian Garden in Norwood

In the 1920s, Aristotle Chakiris opened the Grecian Garden in Norwood, Ohio, which was a soda fountain, beer garden, confectionery and lunch stand. It served malted milk sundaes, candy, ice cream sodas, sandwiches and beer. It became popular with Norwood residents and created a good living for the Chakiris family. Aristotle, along with his wife, Ekatarina, and son, Stylianos "Steve," immigrated to America from Turkey in 1916.

One of the first jobs Steve landed was at a Greek confectionery in Norwood called the Metropolitan, owned by Thomas and Nicholas Aglamesis. With this knowledge, Steve helped his father with the confectionery. But Steve had dreams of acting on the silver screen and moved his family to Hollywood, California, in the late 1930s. Although Steve's dream for himself never materialized, his son, George Chakiris, became a successful actor, winning an Academy Award for best supporting actor as Bernardo, leader of the Sharks, in the 1961 film *West Side Story*.

Droganes Confectionery

As a young teenager in the village of Neochorion in Sparta, Greece, Soterios Droganes read letters from his cousins George and James Coston about how free and wonderful America was. His cousins had established themselves in the confectionery business first on Warsaw Avenue in the late 1890s at the Emery Arcade in Cincinnati. Droganes knew that his future was mandatory military service at seventeen, which would insert him into the ethnic border wars around Sparta. Although he wasn't against serving for his native land, when his mother died, he decided that it was best to take up his cousins' offer and immigrate to America for a better life. So he left his father and brother and a life of shepherding for a new country.

With no knowledge of the English language and literally no money in his pockets, he made his way in 1908 to Ellis Island, where Soterios became Samuel. Along the way, he met a countryman, Mike Sholio, who would become his brother-in-law in Covington and operate the Queen Garden Restaurant on Madison. They would marry sisters Mary and Isabel Exterkamp.

Sam first worked with his Coston cousins at their candy store at nos. 5–7 Emery Arcade in Cincinnati, which they sold in 1910 to Fasmoulos and Tsorgas and moved from Cincinnati's downtown Arcade to Sixth and Madison. After working a few years at the Sixth and Madison business, Droganes had saved enough money to buy them out of the business. That building was condemned by the city, and in 1911, he moved to an existing business at 205 Pike Street. This fountain would have the same Tiffany glass tulip lamp soda fountain that the Aglamesis, Meakins, Mullane's and many other Greek confectioners in Cincinnati had on top their soda counters. Then, in 1918, Droganes built the three-story building at 207 Pike Street, in the vacant lot next door, where the business existed for nearly one hundred years.

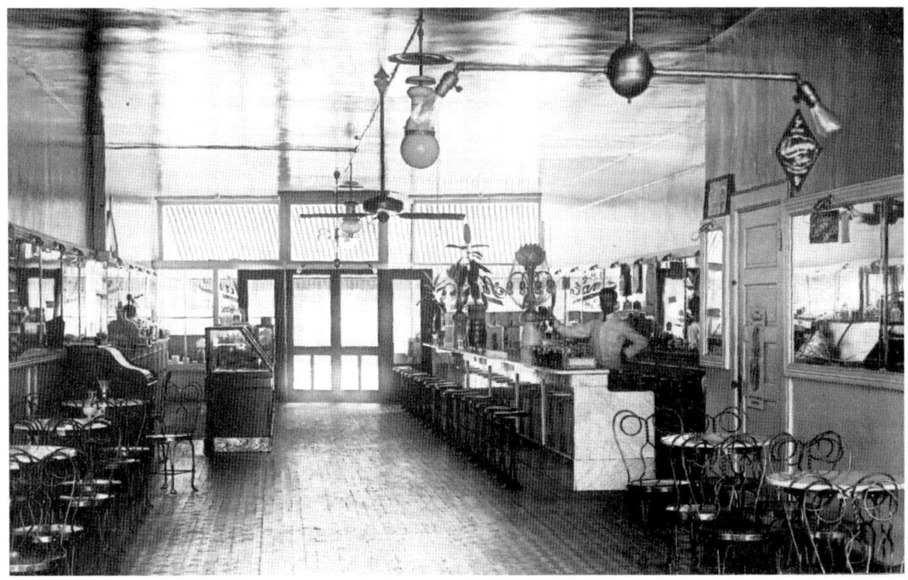

The original Pike Street confectionery of Sam Droganes, with the same tulip lamp fountain as at Aglamesis. *Sam Droganes.*

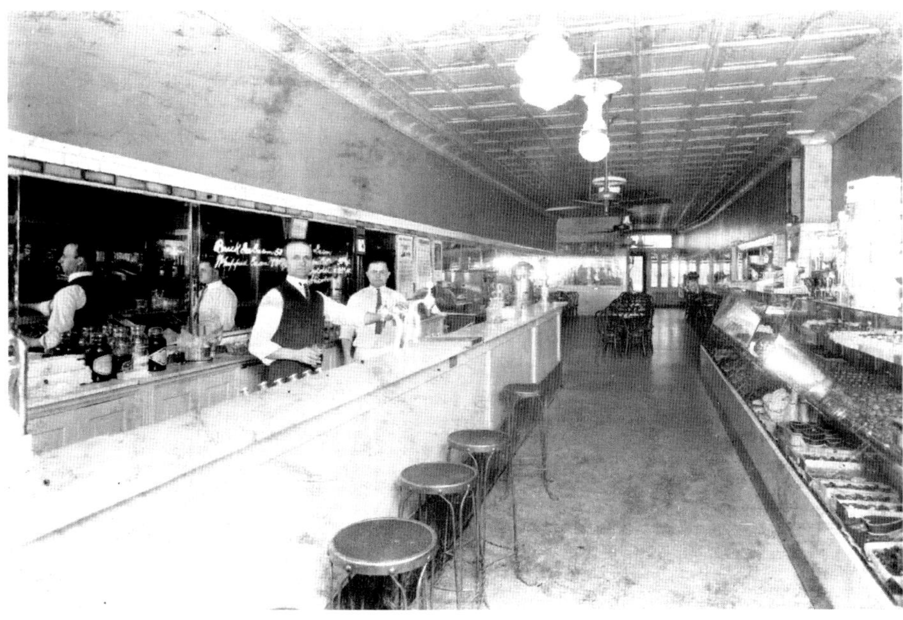

The final location of Droganes Confectionery on Pike Street. *Sam Droganes.*

The Costons had also hosted and trained Aglamesis brothers Nicholas and Thomas around the same time at their Arcade confectionery.

They made a variety of candies in the basement, including handmade chocolates, taffy and peanut brittle, as well as homemade ice cream. Sam's wife, Mary, was a master decorator and made over-the-top chocolate Easter eggs seasonally that became well known throughout the neighborhood. Sam never had more than a taste of his own ice cream—oddly enough, he was lactose intolerant.

In 1923, Sam would open a second store at 506 Madison Avenue, as a former saloon closed during Prohibition. That store would handle the high school customers from Notre Dame, while the Covington store handled high school crowds of Covington Latin, Villa Madonna and LaSalett.

Sam and Mary were blessed with two sons, Sam Jr. and Ollie, both of whom would work for their father.

Paying it forward, Sam and his wife hosted Tony Zoutis in their store and gave him a home with them. He would later move to Cincinnati and open his own confectioneries. The Droganeses also hosted one of the Maroules brothers, teaching them the confectionery trade.

Sam Sr. stopped the candy and ice cream making in 1967, turning the business totally over to the sale of novelties and fireworks, which was in operation until 2016.

Zoutis Confectionery

Constantine "Tony" Zoutis (1885–1985) exemplified the song lyric "The Candy Man can." He weathered several moves downtown due to urban renewal that caused many of his compatriots to quit and retire.

A sign in Zoutis's shop proclaimed, "Laughter is God's hand on the shoulder of the troubled world." He was small in stature—barely tall enough to peek over the candy counter—but tall in spirit. His stocked candy stores also served sandwiches, coffee and doughnuts, as well as at least five flavors of ice cream.

Zoutis got his start in the candy business at the Sam Droganes confectionery in Covington, Kentucky. He was also part of the wave of immigrants from Sparta who settled in Cincinnati. Born in a small village fifty miles south of Greece in 1885, he grew up tending his father's flock of five hundred sheep and goats. He drove them in the mountainsides during the day, playing his panflute to pass the time, and made cheese from their milk at night with his thirteen other siblings. He immigrated to America in his teens and went from city to city until he landed in Cincinnati at age fifty-one. By the time he opened his first candy store in Cincinnati in 1939, he already had twenty-four years of candy making experience from the other cities he had gone through.

His first store at Eighth and Walnut Streets was followed by three others, at 34 East Sixth Street, 105 West Fifth Street and 625 Walnut Street. All four stores were within a block of one another, but his work ethic drove him to work hard in his new country. He claimed to an *Enquirer* reporter that he missed the 1940s because he was working twenty hours a day supporting all four stores. Tony made hand-dipped chocolates, including opera creams, fudge and other confections.

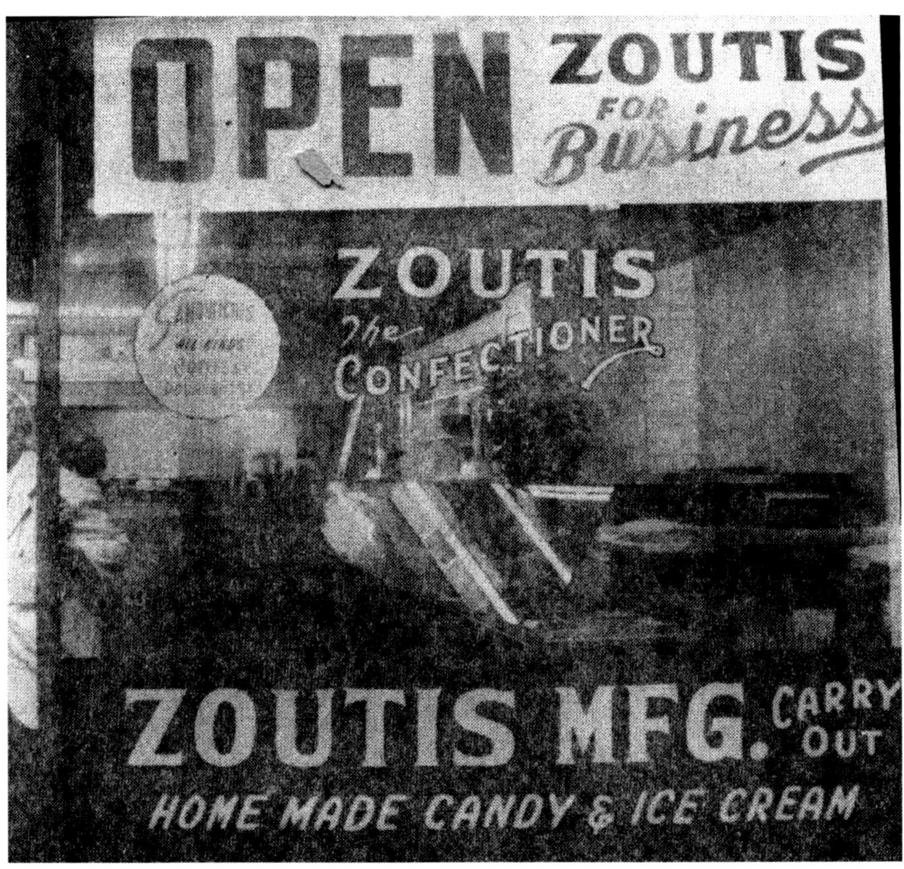

A view into the last Zoutis store at 703 Main Street in 1977. *Public Library of Cincinnati and Hamilton County.*

He was evicted in the late 1970s from his shop at the Temple Bar Building at the Court and Main Streets location due to an urban renewal project, but he quickly reopened at another location at Main and Seventh Streets. He also had stores in Price Hill and at Government Square for a time.

Tony was one of the first candy makers to go non-smoking in his establishments. He thought that the smoke would affect the quality of his ice cream and turn off those customers who didn't smoke, a fairly progressive stance in the age of smoking.

Tony finally married at age fifty-nine, to the much younger Calliope Fotos (1924–1987), and had three sons and a daughter, none of whom followed him into the candy business. They lived at the corner of Clifton and Woolper Avenues, right across from the old Clifton School. Tony Zoutis worked twelve-hour days with hired help into his nineties and lived to be one hundred years and three days old.

In 1949, the Zoutis Candy Shop on Government Square became Cincinnati's own version of the Greensboro, North Carolina Woolworth lunch counter. The shop became the focus of the effort to integrate Cincinnati's segregated community when a group of white and black folks from the Cincinnati Committee on Human Relations (CCHR) entered and were refused service. They sat in place at the counter for several hours. The group returned on another date; they were offered special menus with greatly inflated prices, were roughed up and sprayed with soda water and again refused service. After two more nonviolent visits and sit-ins, and registered letter writings to Zoutis, the group received a letter from Marshall Bragdon of the Mayor's Friendly Relations Committee, who told the CCHR that Zoutis would now serve everyone. A fifth visit proved this, and the group found the service extremely cordial. Interestingly enough, Sam Droganes Confectionery in Covington, Kentucky, where Zoutis learned the business, had a "Colored Entrance" in the back of the shop but served African Americans alongside whites at the counter.

Christos & Drivakis Confectionery

Winton Place in the 1920s had a wonderful confectionery and ice cream shop that is still in the memories of many. At 701 East Epworth, on the corner with Edgewood, there was a magical place called Christos & Drivakis Confectionery, owned by John Drivakis (1864–1929) and George (1891–1978) and William Christos (1888–1975). With true Greek pride, they

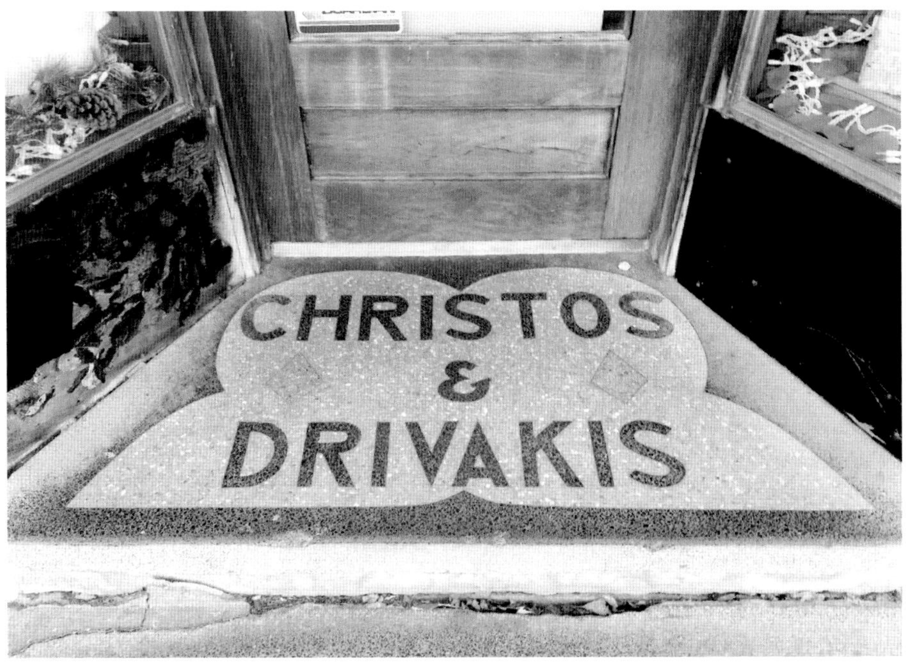

The original 1918 terrazzo entryway for Christos & Drivakis Confectionery. *Author's collection.*

emblazoned their name for posterity in tile in the terrazo entryway of the building. Thus, every restaurant or sandwich shop that came after at that location bore the names of the original founders. The Christos brothers and John Drivakos were born in Sparta, Greece, just like many of the other wonderful confectionery proprietors in Cincinnati.

Brothers George and William built and opened the Christos & Drivakis Confectionery in Winton Place in 1918. William Christos retired in 1974, and George Christos continued to operate the store for several more years into his eighties. William Christos was married to business partner John Drivakis's daughter, Katherine, so it was one big Greek family enterprise.

The family ran a soda fountain, which served lemon phosphates for a nickel and other ice cream drinks, along with offering a variety of candies. Many remember the amazing smell wafting up from the room in the basement where they made their chocolate candies. Christos & Drivakis was also famous for its fountain cherry coke, its hot fudge sauce and its coconut haystack candies.

George and another brother, James Christos (1914–1980), bought Arnold's restaurant in 1959 from the original Arnolds family and created a dish known as Greek spaghetti. James "Jim" Christos (he used the last name Christakos, which was probably shortened to Christos) was a wrestler who, as the pride of the Central Parkway YMCA, was crowned Cincinnati's amateur light-heavyweight champ in 1934 and went on to compete in professional wrestling. Christakos was good enough to pair up with Jack Londos, the Hulk Hogan of his day. George Christos was also a local wrestler, so they both offered an imposing presence to their customers.

After George died in 1978, their confectionery became a vegan restaurant, and from 1996 to 2001, it was the Henke Winery.

Kalomeres Candy Shops and Cincinnati's Sweet Barbecue Sauce

As sons of George and Stamata Kalomeres, Nicholas (1892–1964), John (1885–1964) and Charles Kalomeres (1888–1961) came to the United States in 1910 from Sparta, Greece, with other family and cousins. They would open the Kalomeres sweet shop, a confectionery, grocery store and sandwich shop, at 701 Central at Seventh Street and operate it from 1924 to 1949. From that store they made fresh candies daily. In 1926, the Kalomeres brothers opened a branch of their downtown confectionery near a funeral home in the Kennedy Heights suburb. Charles Kalomeres would run that store for twenty-three years until his retirement in 1949.

The brothers sponsored another cousin from Sparta, William Cheroneres, who became their candy salesman.

Things weren't easy for the new Greek immigrants. A 1927 *Cincinnati Enquirer* article reported that John Kalomeres applied for citizenship but was denied on a technicality:

> *Because he had spent approximately two of the last five years visiting in Greece, his native land, and, incidentally, wooing a young woman* [Angelica Mourtzekos], *whom he married and brought back to this country with him, John Kalomeres, Greek, Seventh street and Central avenue, confectioner, was denied citizenship by United States District Judge Smith Hickkenlooper yesterday. The Court's action was taken because, under the naturalization laws, an applicant for citizenship must have resided continuously in this country for five years before he is eligible to admission as a citizen and must produce witnesses who have known him*

> *for that period, and who have been continuously in touch with him so they are in a position to testify concerning his character and reputation during the five-year period.*

An advertisement in the December 2, 1921 edition of the *Cincinnati Enquirer* proclaimed Kalomeres candies as "[t]he better candy for every occasion. No candy is quite as tempting, quite as pure and delicious, quite as satisfying."

Charles Kalomeres's daughter, Matula, would marry Ted Gregory and in the 1950s create the sweet barbecue sauce behind the Cincinnati icon the Montgomery Inn. Charles helped out in the production in the early days of Montgomery Inn. Every year, an estimated 1.4 million bottles of Matula's sauce are sold in retail grocers like Kroger. And perhaps her father's candy background is why the Montgomery Inn signature barbecue sauce is so sweet.

CUPID ICE CREAM

Charles Ponticos (1892–1974) emigrated from Kapsi, Lamia, Greece, in 1912 and operated ice cream and candy shops in Elmwood Place and Northside. In 1919, he incorporated the C&S Ponticos Confectionery Company with Steve Ponticos, Nicholas Sarros and Joseph B. Derles. Then, in 1921, he formed the Cupid Ice Cream Company with his cousin Gregory Porticos. They specialized in ice cream novelties for sale by truck and pushcart vendors. His son, Jim Ponticos (1926–), worked with his father in the company until they sold to French-Bauer Ice Cream Company in 1966. French-Bauer Ice Cream dominated the soda fountains of Greater Cincinnati before Graeter's and United Dairy Farms became dominant.

Jim grew up in Clifton, graduating from Hughes High School and serving in Europe as an army sergeant during World War II. Like many of the Greek immigrants, Jim Ponticos was an active member of Holy Trinity–St. Nicholas Greek Orthodox Church, serving as finance chairman when the church in the Finneytown suburb was built in 1972.

Evangeline Candy Shop

In the 1930s, James Pulos, a Greek immigrant, operated the Evangeline Candy Shop in Price Hill at 4405 Glenway Avenue, named after his wife, and it is still fondly remembered by many on Cincinnati's West Side. It is not to be confused with another candy company by the same name that opened in 1920 at the Havlin Hotel at Race and Opera Place in a shop decorated by Rookwood Pottery artists. This candy company was incorporated by E.E. and A.J. Thomas, K. Holly, A.B. Kautz and K.A. Bauer. The company was named after the character Evangeline, from the Acadian story and poem written in 1847 by Henry Wadsworth Longfellow. In the epic poem, Evangeline and her fiancé, Gabriel, are separated by British soldiers, and she spends two decades searching the Americas for him. When she finally finds him, he is dying; she holds him in her arms as he takes his last breath. The reference was meant to inspire men to bring their sweetheart a box of Evangeline chocolates when they were in the city.

There were certainly many more Greek-owned confectioneries in Cincinnati than discussed in this chapter. Like the Cincinnati chili industry, the candy industry gave recent immigrants a way to integrate into their new country and make a living. And the connection between these two industries is still evident in our local custom of having a peppermint patty after a threeway.

Chapter 13

NINETY YEARS OF BLACK LICORICE IN CINCINNATI

Long before Twizzlers reigned supreme, black licorice was the favored flavor. Now black licorice is polarizing—you either love it or you hate it. The red raspberry–flavored variety is what kids today know as licorice. The Queen City can boast of a company that manufactured black licorice candy for nearly ninety years and was known nationally. Today, the majority of licorice confections use anise oil for flavor, but back in the day, the John Mueller Licorice Company used real Spanish licorice. That's probably why those who tasted Mueller's black licorice miss it so much. Unfortunately, none of the three buildings where they manufactured the candy is standing today, so all that's left are memories.

The company was founded in 1885 by John Mueller. John was the son of 1848er Andrew Mueller, an immigrant from Anweiler, near Alsace Lorraine, who came to Cincinnati in 1848 to escape the failed revolution in the German states. John's birth in 1865 on Christmas Day, one of the largest days for the candy industry, foreshadowed his career.

John grew up on his father's farm in an area then known as Turkey Bottoms, which is now the area of Lunken Airport on Cincinnati's East End. After finishing his schooling at age fifteen in Cincinnati, he worked at the Goode Candy Company for five years, learning the candy trade from candy baron George Wilhelm Goode, who had partnered with a Louis McNamara a few years before. Being an entrepreneurial young man, John decided to leave Goode in 1885 and began manufacturing candy for himself.

In 1901, he, with several other investors, incorporated the John Mueller Licorice Company, focusing on the manufacture of black licorice confections. It's not known where he learned how to make black licorice candy or why he decided to focus on it, but Mueller created a profitable national niche for his company in the candy industry. For those of us who love black licorice, what a treat it must have been to live near the Mueller factory and smell the black licorice being boiled into candy.

One of the first brands Mueller trademarked was Neldynes, which was registered with the U.S. Patent and Trademark Office in 1905. Neldynes, crowned "king of all licorice candy," was guaranteed not to stick together in the summer.

Another ad described Neldynes as "[l]icorice-candy! Oh boy! Combined in one dainty tit-bit-all gooness and deliciousness of pure licorice as only Mueller can make it, AND candy of such a quality as to make the mouth water…Result, an unusual treat—something that will thrill the kiddie and delight the grown-ups, to whom licorice candy will bring back all the licorice joys of their own childhood. Pure licorice base, with a flavor you'll never forget. In short, a chewy confection that's 'NELDYNES' and nothing else in the world like it!"

An interesting story about licorice is why we call the long ribbons of the candy "licorice whips." A trade advertisement from Twizzlers (seen on the following page) before the turn of the nineteenth century shows us the reason. The licorice twist was originally fashioned as shown in the trade image, as a buggy whip. The end had a smaller ribbon attached to the end that curled so the candy looked like a whip. It was a real pain for manufacturers to make the licorice whip, and obviously they were happy when automobiles came on the scene because the whip came to an end—now the standard twist portion remained. Imagine how many injuries happened back then with kids whipping one another with their licorice!

The Mueller company's first location was at 2117 Reading Road in Mount Auburn. When it outgrew that location, it moved to a location at Wade and Freeman Streets in Cincinnati's West End. By the 1930s, the U.S. industry was importing some thirty-five thousand tons of licorice root per year, for flavoring tobacco, pharmaceuticals and candy. Mueller was one of the largest U.S. importers of the root.

Mueller's sold through the jobber network to retailers all over the country. To get the word out, Mueller was a dedicated marketer, running wonderfully descriptive ads in the *Confectioners Journal* in the 1920s. By 1922, it was leading the candy industry with candy cigars, candy pipes and Famous brand

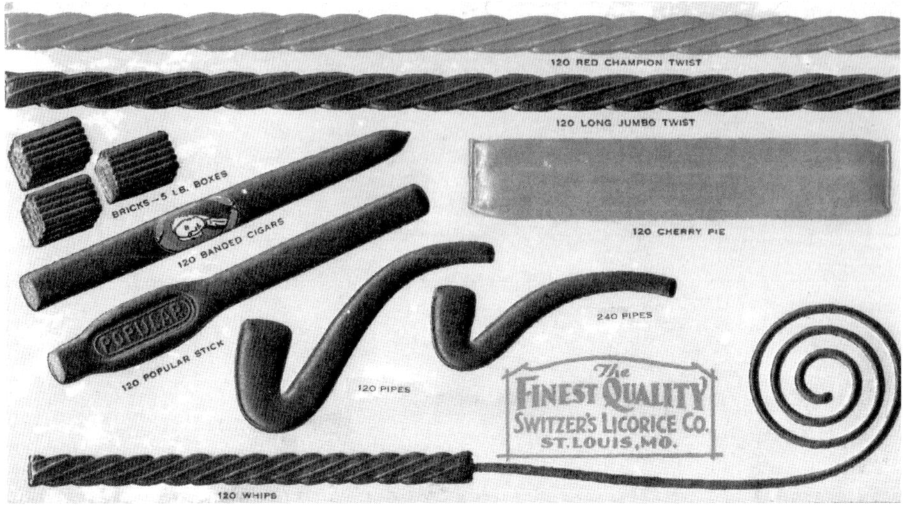

This nineteenth-century Twizzlers advertisement shows the original licorice whip that resembled a buggy whip. *Schimpff Candy Museum.*

black licorice candy cigarettes, a line it would carry into the 1980s. Other candy manufactures followed and introduced lines of candy cigarettes by the 1930s. Back then, smoking wasn't the health concern it became, so the American public didn't bat an eye at allowing children to pretend to smoke these candy imitations. Slogans encouraging kids to smoke "Just Like Dad" would cause trouble in the 1950s, when the first reports of smoking's health hazards surfaced. Early brands were modeled after the real cigarettes—Marlboro became Marboro, Winston became Winstun and Camel became Acmel. Although national legislation was proposed in 1970 and 1991 to ban the sale of candy cigarettes, the only state to outlaw them was North Dakota, from 1953 to 1967. The word *cigarette* disappeared from all national candy cigarette brands and was replaced by "candy sticks."

A package of Mueller Famous Candy Cigarettes came with a premium: animal trading cards. One package showed Elmer the Elephant and advertised "24 different animals to collect for your scrapbook." So, you got a premium and an enticement to buy more candy cigarettes to collect all of the series, something a number of candy manufacturers did. Mueller continued the trading cards with its candy cigarettes into the 1950s, with its Space Age brand, patented in 1959, and its Slims brand, patented in 1965. Kids could collect twelve different cards of various airplanes and flight machines while enjoying their candy cigarettes.

By 1922, Mueller had been around for nearly thirty years and employed thirty people in the factory. It played to its legacy with slogans like "made famous and kept famous by two generations." Not only did it produce the loops and whips of black licorice, but it also had a full line of innovative licorice candies, like a candy train set with licorice tracks, a licorice wristwatch and even a huge oblong-shaped hunk of black licorice they called the XLCR.

In 1922, it had the following candy lineup: Neldynes, XLCR, Famous brand candy cigarettes, banded candy cigars, whoppers, twisters, wristwatch, train assortment, whips, 120 tubes, 120 Famous stick busters, chocomels (a unique type of chocolate–black licorice/caramel that sounds amazing!), Big 4, bricks, lozenges, plugs, trio tubes, travelers companion and 240 tubes.

In its ads, Mueller played to the health and safety of its workers: "All our goods are manufactured in an updated, sanitary plant where sunlight and fresh air contribute to the health and happiness of all workers." Its West

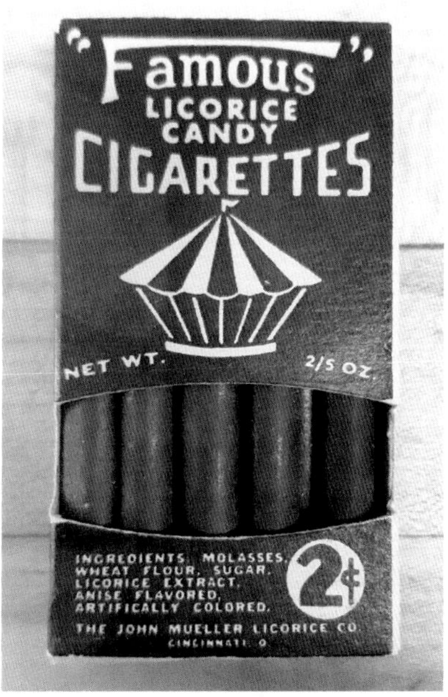

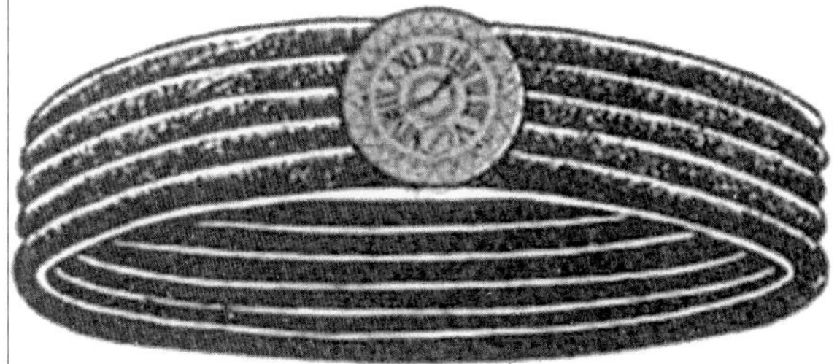

Top: One of the Mueller Famous Candy Cigarette packages sold to kids. *Schimpff Candy Museum.*

Bottom: The black licorice candy wristwatch made by John Mueller Company. *From the* International Confectioners Journal, *vol. 28 (1922).*

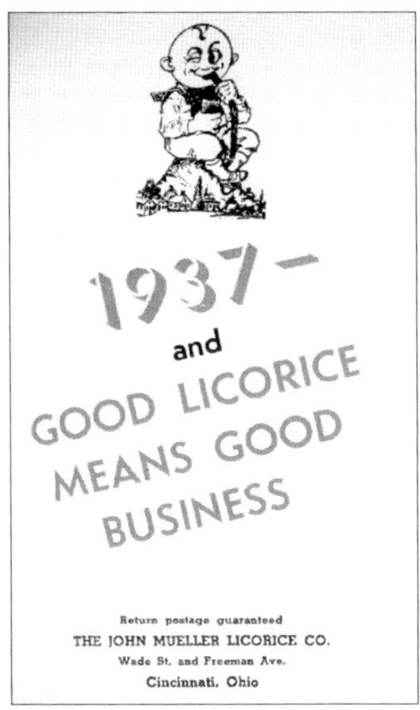

Left: A 1937 advertisement shows the Mueller licorice mascot, a pudgy, smiling kid stuffing his face with a licorice whip. *Schimpff Candy Museum.*

Below: A 1930s John Mueller Licorice package showing the variety of products. *Schimpff Candy Museum.*

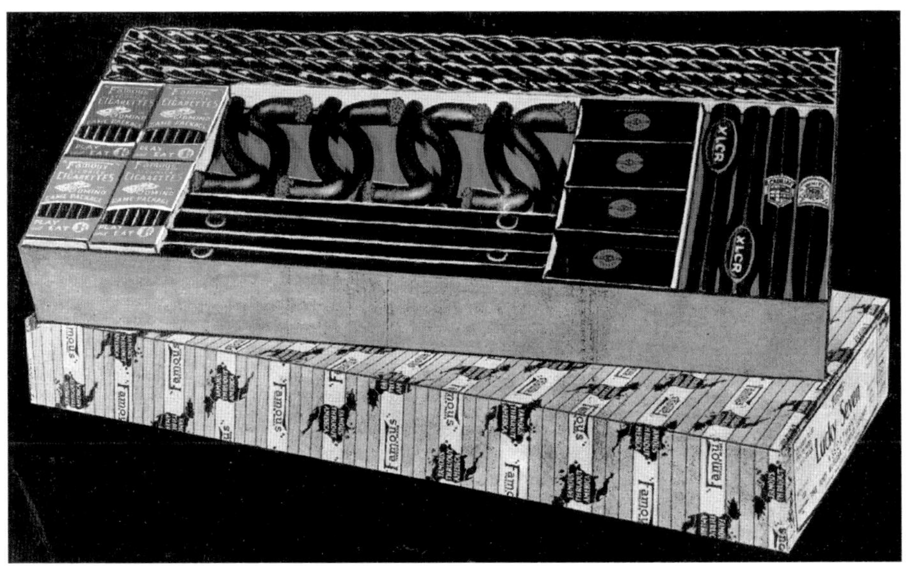

End plant was flooded in the 1937 flood, but it cleaned up and continued manufacturing after the waters subsided.

The house that black licorice built—the Mueller red brick family homestead at 1722 Queen City Avenue, on the West Side of Cincinnati in Fairmount—is still standing. As a Fairview community member, John Mueller exhibited the traits of a true candy baron. He volunteered as treasurer for his church, the German Emmanuel Church on the corner of

Tremont and Lawnway in Fairmount, for twenty-three years and supported the local Republican Party. In his industry, he was active in the Candy Jobbing Confectioners' Association, the Candy Salesman's Association and the Travelers' Protective Association.

Having only one daughter, Nelda Mae, after whom his Neldyne brand was named, he and his wife, Elizabeth Dennert, had no sons to pass on his business. So, in 1920, only a few years before his death, Mueller sold his business to Walter H. Pritz, who had been president of the company, for $66,000. Pritz ran the company until his death in 1950. At that time, Mueller was said to be one of only four manufacturers of black licorice candy in the world, all of which were in the United States, including American Licorice, founded in 1914 in Chicago; National Licorice, founded in 1848 in Brooklyn, New York; and the Switzer Company, founded in 1887 in St. Louis, Missouri.

Pritz introduced black licorice mixes in the 1940s, like Miami Mix, Lucky 7 and the Fair-N-Warmer mix. He also extended the line of black licorice cigarettes with a brand called Domino. One of his candy makers, Edward Schoettle, patented a black licorice cigar candy in 1940 for the company. Schoettle would take over the company after Pritz's death in 1950 and move the company to Norwood in the early 1950s.

The new plant was a Teamsters union–run factory at 2011 Ross Avenue in Norwood, just north of downtown Cincinnati. The area is now inhabited by the newly built Paycor and the Urology Center facilities on the Norwood Lateral. Here the company continued introducing new lines of black licorice candy until it went out of business in 1973. In 1970, John Mueller licorice trademarked its last candy, called Kettle Treats. For all its years in Cincinnati, the John Mueller Licorice Company was a leader in the U.S. black licorice confection market and an under-known sweet asset to our city.

Chapter 14

GREATER CINCINNATI CANDY TODAY

Although there are no longer the huge candy wholesale manufacturers in Cincinnati, there are more than a few candy makers left, as well as several wonderful candy shops and retailers left to carry on the legacy of Cincinnati candy.

Kroger Candy Manufacturing

It's no surprise that even our local retail grocer got into the candy making business. Kroger was founded in 1889 by Bernard "Barney" Heinrich Kroger, son of German immigrants, in Over-the-Rhine. It grew from a one-location general store to become one of the largest grocery retailers in the United States. By the 1920s, the Kroger candy plant had become one of the largest in the country, located at Florence Avenue near Eden Park. It had been making its own candy at least since the early 1900s.

In 1909, Kroger's lineup of candies included gum drops, chocolate peanut squares, Boston baked beans, French creams, hard candy, caramels, cream kisses and coconut bonbons. At Easter, Kroger made a line of buttercream chicks, bunnies and ducks, in competition with the local Nuss Candy Company and the Ed Messer Candy Company. Kroger even made its own candy corn. In 1912, it got into the mint craze, making mint and wintergreen chips.

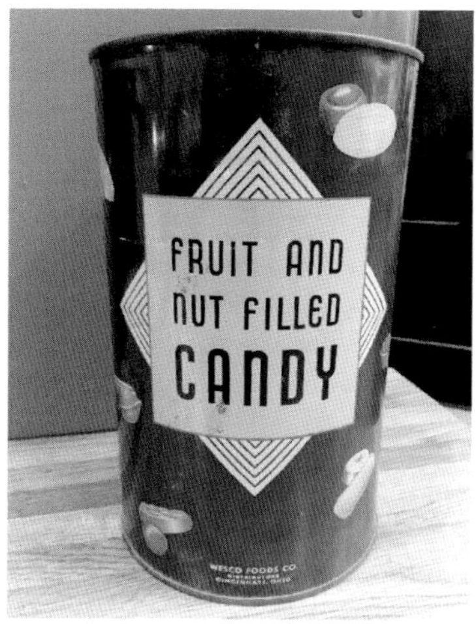

This candy container shows the filled chocolate candies that the Kroger company distributed under the WESCO Food Company subsidiary. *Schimpff Candy Museum.*

In the 1930s, Kroger added peanut brittle and circus peanuts to its growing list of candies. By 1949, the Kroger candy plant employed five hundred employees, managed by plant superintendent Norman Beatty. It had also added orange slices, chocolate-covered cherries, chocolate drops and caramels, among other candy varieties.

In the summer of 1964, Kroger announced that it was going to build a large candy plant in Springdale, double the size of its downtown plant. The 617,500-square-foot facility on 113 acres was built in three stages, completed in 1968. Kroger distributed the candy under the WESCO foods brand, a subsidiary of Kroger that was formed in 1930 to inspect produce it bought at local farms. The Kroger candy plant was second in size only to the Brach's candy plant.

In 1970, the plant produced, among two hundred varieties of candy, specialty fruit- and nut-filled chocolates, turtle candies, orange slices and some 1 billion marshmallows annually.

Kroger closed the candy plant in December 1982, idling more than 325 employees and exiting the candy manufacturing business altogether. At the time, Kroger was the second-largest retail grocery chain in the country, but its candy making business was only marginally profitable and had steadily declined since 1968, which was a peak consumption year in the candy business. The site was redeveloped into a Roberd's Grand Furniture Store, Golf Galaxy and a gaming site.

Peter Minges & Son

Peter Minges is the last evidence of Cincinnati's great candy manufacturing days. When Peter first entered the wholesale candy business in 1905, our city still had many large manufacturers of candy, similar to Chicago, Illinois. With all of the manufacturers like Mueller Licorice, Dolly

Varden Chocolates, Reinhart & Newton and the Echert Company, Peter decided that they needed a sales representative to run around and sell their candies.

So, Peter Minges became what was known as a candy jobber. He started his business delivering candy with a donkey and an old milk wagon to local retailers. Some of his early customers were Hathaway's Restaurant in Carew Tower, the Golden Lamb Gift Shop and candy stores in Lebanon, Indiana. Antiquated candy cases were stocked with sweet memories.

In 1924, he opened Peter Minges & Son, Wholesale Candy & Confections, at 138 West Court Street downtown, getting into the retail business as well. That same year, Peter's son, William B. Minges (1912–1999), started working in the store after school at Westwood Elementary and on weekends. He would devote a total of seventy-five years of his life to the family business, helping it become a leading candy wholesaler in Ohio, Indiana and Kentucky. After the Depression hit, he started working full time for the business.

In the decades after World War II, when the distribution of candy merged with that of tobacco, Bill Minges decided not to distribute tobacco. He chose instead to add specialty bulk candies to his line of gum and candy bars.

Peter W. Minges, grandson of the founder, took over the business in 1999 and then passed it along to daughter Leslie Betts, who holds down the fort, managing the candy store. She still has her great-grandfather's rare 1940s-era candy sample case, filled with items like Amish fruit, hoarhound lozenges and small prizes. The family sold the business to SNACC Distributing but still work at the store.

Galerie

Galerie founder Richard Ross is a creative entrepreneur with a passion for confections. His company at 3380 Langley Drive in Hebron, Kentucky, has a mission "to provide outstanding customer service while delivering fresh, innovative confectionery gifts of the highest quality and value."

Galerie's products and solutions have a unique combination of quality ingredients and materials, creative packaging and design and an overall value for the consumer. Continuing on with the legacy of nineteenth-century "prize packages" supplied by early Cincinnati candy companies like H.D. Smith, Galerie delivers a broad range of products that includes ceramics, plush, sequin, tin and interactive toy items. Galerie continues to be a design-driven enterprise, bringing more than 1,200 items to retailers across the world every year. In addition to the Galerie brand, its licenses include Disney, Star Wars, Hershey, Minions, Trolls, Peppa Pig, Marvel, Warner Bros. and NASCAR.

Inducted into the National Confectioners Association's Candy Hall of Fame in 2015, Rick has been involved in the candy industry since he was fifteen, first as a buyer for his mother's gift and candy store in Dayton, Ohio, then as a distributor and retail entrepreneur and finally as CEO and president of Galerie. Oddly enough, his father was a dentist.

Born in Columbus, Ohio, on May 26, 1961, to Helen and Allen, he graduated from Fairview High School in Dayton in 1979 and enrolled in the University of Cincinnati, majoring in business. At nineteen, he took a leave of absence from school to become a distributor for Jelly Belly Candy Company in Alhambra, California.

Rick opened his first Jelly Bean Factory store in a Salem, Ohio mall in 1978. Two years later, his first permanent store launched in the Cincinnati Union Terminal, followed by a larger-format outlet in the Cincinnati Westin Hotel, Galerie Au Chocolat, featuring premium chocolates and an automated bean-dispensing wall fixture offering shoppers a choice of seventy-two flavors.

Eleven more stores in major cities followed in short succession. By 1981, Rick was featured on the front page of the *Wall Street Journal*. Orders from other retailers for the company's novelty wares eventually drew Rick from retail to wholesale and the founding of Galerie, which designs and fabricates more than 1,500 gift and novelty items annually, including premium private-label confectionery items.

Galerie has been ranked among the Deloitte Cincinnati USA "100 Best Places to Work" five times and earned the Northern Kentucky Chamber of Commerce International Trade Award of Excellence in 2008 and its Economic Vitality Award in 2001.

Rick was the National Confectioners Association State of the Industry Conference Committee chairman for four years and a member of the association's executive board. He has also served three terms on its board of trustees and is very involved in several charities in the Greater Cincinnati region.

Perfetti Van Melle

Most people in Greater Cincinnati don't know that a Dutch-Italian candy maker has been in Erlanger, Kentucky, since 1979 and manufacturing candy-based products since 1982. Perfetti Van Melle makes candy brands Airheads and Mentos in its twenty-thousand-square-foot plant, employing three hundred workers.

The company is part of the Perfetti Van Melle Group, a privately owned global manufacturer and marketer of sugar confections and chewing gum. It was established in 2001 by the merger of Perfetti S.p.A., an Italian company founded in 1946 by brothers Ambrogio and Egidio Perfetti, and Van Melle NV, a Dutch company founded in 1900 by Izaak Van Melle. They represent the third-largest candy and gum manufacturer in the world.

Airheads come in bar, bite and belt form, and the factory in Erlanger is equipped with the machinery for all of it. Airheads travel about one mile through the plant before being shipped. The factory produces Airheads five days a week, twenty-four hours a day, but the new Airheads Extreme candy line runs seven days a week. From the mixing of sugars and sweeteners to the thinning and forming process and the packaging, machines churn out a total of three thousand pounds of taffy, which equates to about 4 million bars a day.

Airheads are a tangy, taffy-like, chewy candy that come in twenty-four different flavors such as cherry, watermelon, strawberry, orange, pink lemonade, grape and even birthday cake.

The Mentos candy was born in 1932 when brothers Michael and Pierre Van Melle set off for Poland to learn a procedure to produce soft fruit chew candies. They brought back the recipe and procedure for the original "Tell Dough" to the Netherlands, leading to the creation of Fruittella. Based on this recipe, the brothers created a peppermint-flavored candy that became known as Mentos. The Mentos brand became known in the United States for its zany Dutch commercials.

The candy packaging and artwork promote a fun and bright brand. The logo for Perfetti Van Melle's European Chupa Chups lollipop brand was sketched by Spanish surrealist artist Salvador Dalí in 1969.

Continually innovating, the company in 2013 launched Mentos NOWMints, a sugar-free formulation that comes in eight flavors—eucamenthol, spearmint, sweetmint, peppermint, licorice, strawberry, orange and berry. In March 2017, the company announced an $11 million expansion to its Erlanger, Kentucky plant, adding new lines and expanding production and local candy jobs.

Marshmallow Cones and Marpro Products

Another delicious candy confection was created in Cincinnati in 1936 and is still on the market today. The first non-meltable ice cream cone, the Yum Yum Marshmallow Candy Cone, is still made by Marshmallow Products, or Marpro.

Marpro was founded in 1936 by John V. Arbino, who was a tailor. During the Depression, he noticed that people couldn't always afford clothes, but they did always seem to have pennies for candy. So, Arbino experimented with a mixer and made marshmallow candies at night, while tailoring during the day. He made an extensive line of marshmallow candies and would job them out on consignment on Saturdays to local groceries.

John passed the business on to his son, Jack, in 1964, headquartered at 2354–2400 Symmes Street in Walnut Hills. Jack grew the business his father had left him, but by the 1970s, it was evident that the top product was the marshmallow-filled ice cream cone. So, he reduced all the other products and focused on that one unique item. Jack would sell the business in 1999 to a Cincinnati couple, Fred and Sandy Runk, who had owned the Murray Brothers Old Time Stores, a small chain of retail candy stores. Dan Runk operates the manufacturing arm of the business, Runk Candy, at Fischer Place in St. Bernard.

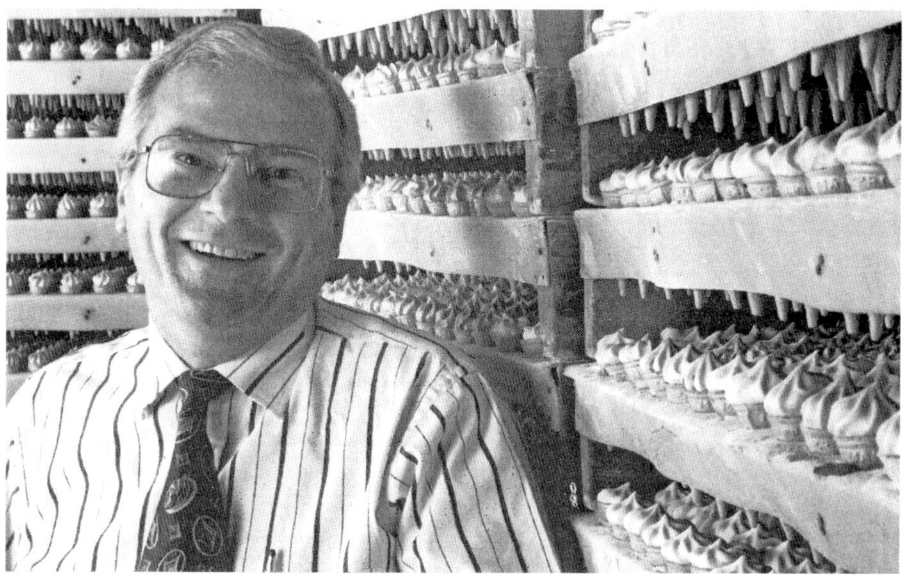

Jack Arbino, second-generation owner of Marpro Products. *Public Library of Cincinnati and Hamilton County.*

The Runk family has been in the trade since 1858 and acquired Murray Brothers Old Time Store, one of Ohio's oldest candy stores, in the late 1990s. So the Runks were no strangers to the charm of the old-time candy brands they represent. Runk Candy Company purchased the rights to BB Bats and Kits in 2011, candies that were first released in 1924.

Today, with the same recipe for the Yum Yum cone as in 1936, Runk is distributed throughout the country. The wafer cone is baked in house in rotary gas-fired baking ovens, and the marshmallows are made in stainless steel kettles.

Fawn Candy Rookwood

The Fawn Candy Company family has a German name, with Greek beginnings. In 1946, the founder, Paul Guenther (1923–2002), returned from service with the Navy Seabees in Okinawa, Japan, during World War II. Like many returning servicemen, he wanted to go into business for himself. Nicknamed "Pep" because of his energy, the only thing he knew about candy was how to eat it.

But his wife Jean Maroules's parents, Fred (1874–1939) and Helen Maroules (1898–1963), were part of the Greek candy making community and had operated candy stores in Northern Kentucky. Fred and Alex Maroules operated the Peerless Confectionery at 720 Madison Avenue in Covington, Kentucky, with help from their brother, Louis. Fred Maroules taught the Aglamesis brothers how to make ice cream, which he had learned from Sam Droganes in Covington, Kentucky. Fred met the Aglamesis brothers while working with them at the candy department at Mabley and Carew Department Stores in downtown Cincinnati, whose candy had been supplied by Mehas Brothers from the early 1910s to 1922.

Fred Maroules had emigrated from the Ionian island of Ithaca in Greece and served in the United States Army during World War I. One of the sweetest of Cincinnati candy stories starts when Fred left on September 19, 1917, for the war. That day, he gave Helen Smith, his then girlfriend, a box of handmade hard sugar candies, each decorated with a different flower or a patriotic symbol like the American flag. Helen saved that box of candy and passed it on to her son. The Guenther daughters framed the box and proudly display it in their flagship Bridgetown store. Fred and Helen married in April 1921 at St. Stephens Catholic Church in Newport, Kentucky.

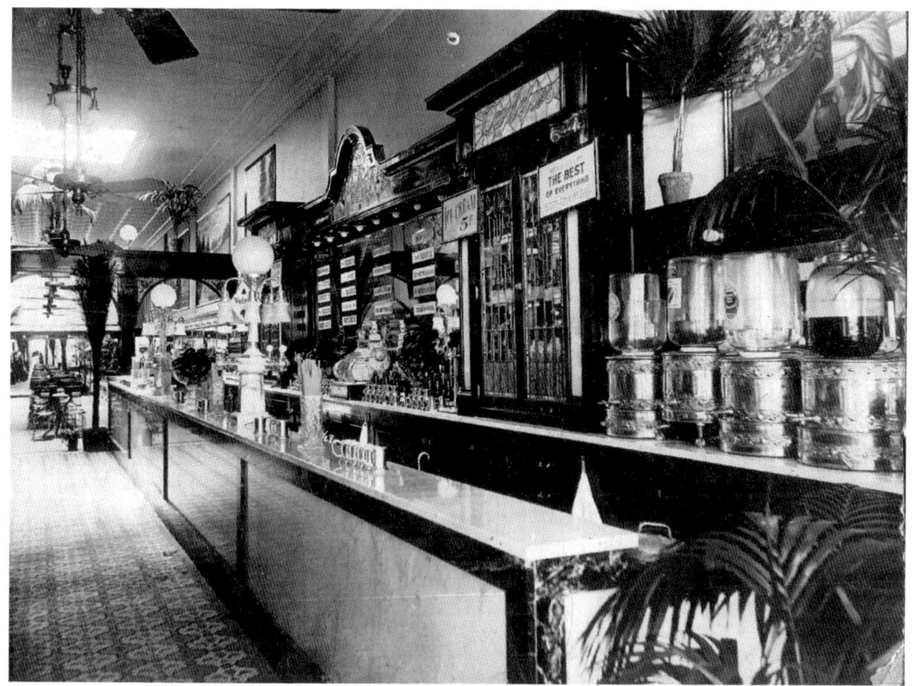

Above: An interior shot of the Maroules Peerless Confectionery in Covington, Kentucky, in the 1930s. *Guenther family*.

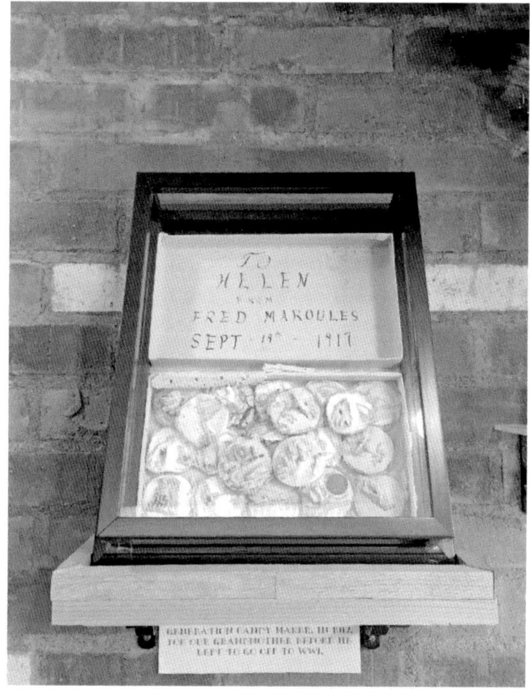

Right: The box of handmade candies that Fred Maroules gave his future wife, Helen, in 1917 before leaving to serve in the army. *Guenther family*.

When Fred Maroules passed away in 1939, his wife, Helen, took on the dairy and confectionery business at 39 West Corry Street in Cincinnati and continued to sell ice cream to local soda fountains. One of those she sold their ice cream to was the Fawn Fountain, at the corner of Lovell and Harrison Avenues in Westwood. She knew that the two couples who owned it were feuding and wanting to sell. So, knowing that her son-in-law was looking for a business, she brokered the deal in 1946. Paul and Jean took a leap and bought the Fawn Fountain, getting into a sweet new business. They already had a dedicated ice cream supply chain and the family candy making knowledge. After first getting their feet wet with ice cream and the soda fountain, they experimented with candy.

By 1970, Paul had moved their candy kitchen to 4271 Harrison Avenue and began focusing on candy rather than ice cream. Paul and Jean made their home in the apartment above the candy kitchen until they retired. The candy kitchen in the basement of the Harrison Avenue store is filled with vintage candy making equipment. A chocolate enrobing line extends the length of one wall, with a chocolate mold filling station in one corner. A large ball cream beater used to make opera creams sits next to an old gas-fired double boiler, where most of the candy process starts. A dent in the basement foundation reminds of the day the ball cream beater was brought in and installed in place. Various mixers, a pan coater (used for their chocolate-covered cherries), a taffy puller and wooden candy racks made by Paul Guenther's stepfather, a carpenter, line the other walls.

A first expansion of the business in the 1970s was a small candy kiosk at what was then a shopping mall at the Union Terminal, now the Museum Center. They operated a store in downtown called Executive Sweets in the Skywalk, until the city closed the Skywalk. Hathaway's Diner in the nearby Carew Tower sold its Savannah Cream candies in large quantities during the Christmas season. Then, in 1984, Guenther "retired" and passed the business on to four of his daughters—Jean, Jane, Jackie and Kathy. He was originally skeptical of his daughters being able to handle the work, but they proved him wrong. In 1988, the sisters bought the former Lykins Candy Shop at Northgate Mall, which had been the successor of the Putman candy business. They operated that store for nearly twenty years.

In 1994, at the objection of their father, the Guenther sisters opened their first East Side outlet in the old LeBlond machine tool factory's clock tower at Rookwood Pavilion near Hyde Park. They chose the location because they felt the shopping center had great anchors. It turned out to be a good location decision. The Rookwood Complex would continue to grow,

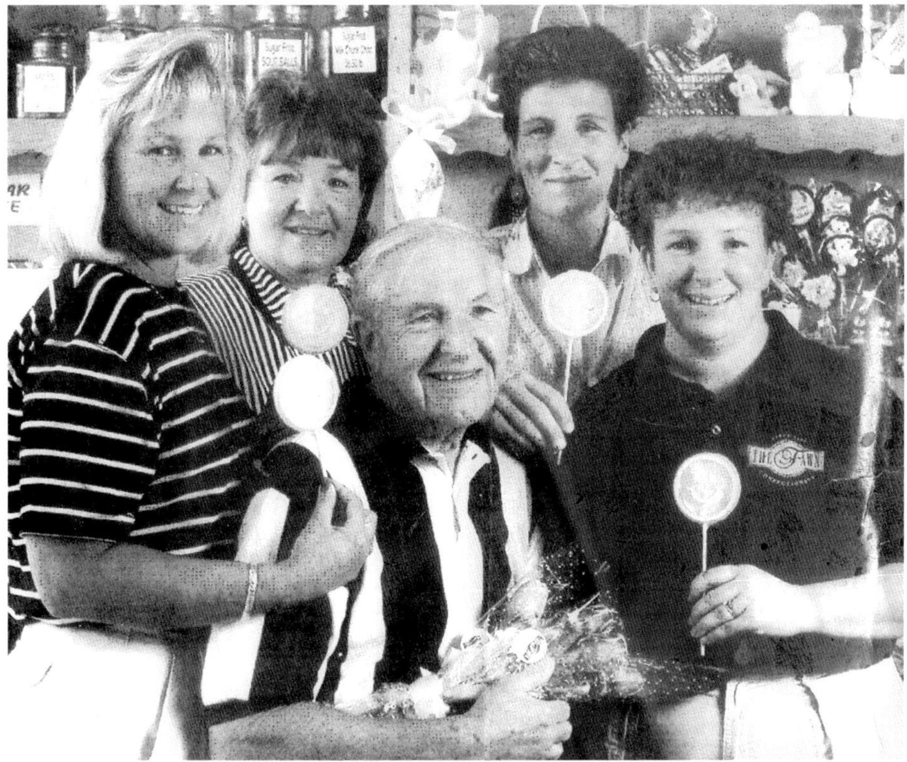

The Guenther candy making family. *From left to right*: Jackie Copenhaver; Kathy Guenther; Paul Guenther, the founder; Jean Guenther Ranz; and Janie Guenther Oka. *Guenther family*.

doubling in size with the addition of Rookwood Commons in 2000 and then in 2013, expanding across the street to Rookwood Exchange, a complex of boutique offices, hotels and restaurants.

A brother, Paul Jr., and his wife operated a Fawn Confectionery for a few years at Harper's Point in northern Cincinnati. Paul Guenther's only form of advertising had been in local church bulletins. Nowadays, the Guenther sisters use social media and have an incredible Facebook page. They even took advantage of their Rookwood store as a Pokestop in the mobile game *Pokemon Go*, giving customers who showed their download a special treat.

Fawn makes a variety of hand-dipped chocolates, including handmade opera creams, truffles, fudge, caramel apples and specialty confections like bourbon balls, bourbon cherries and even chocolate-covered bacon and potato chips. During Valentine's Day, it sells nearly a ton of chocolate-covered cherries. But Easter is its largest-volume holiday. At Easter, in

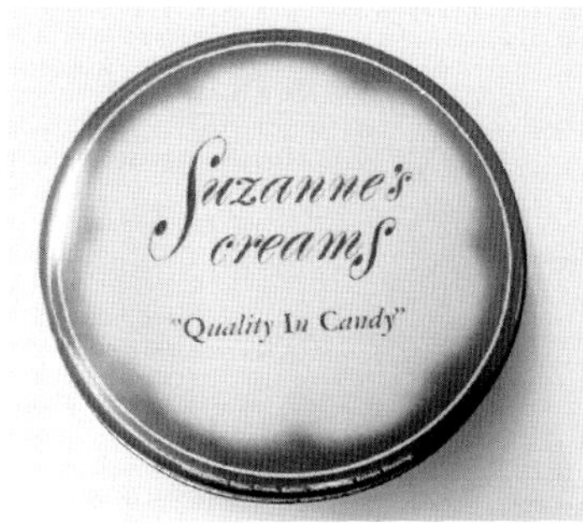

An original Suzanne's Creams tin, which would become Fawn Savannah Creams. *Guenther family.*

addition to making the delicious opera creams, it makes coconut "Goodie Eggs," a West Side favorite, and chocolate rabbits and other seasonal favorites. Fawn doesn't limit itself to the largest holidays. It makes an "Irish Potato" candy for St. Patrick's Day, which is a nearly century-old candy tradition in Pennsylvania, made of buttercream rolled in cinnamon to make it look like a potato. They even dip wine bottles in chocolate as a special service. Always trying new limited-time candies, Fawn recently made Troll Chocolate Pops in time for the November 2016 *Trolls* animated movie.

Fawn's opera cream recipe, once voted best by *Cincinnati Magazine*, is the recipe Paul Guenther first made and hasn't changed in more than seventy years. He learned it from another local candy maker, just as has happened with all the opera cream recipes. In addition to the standard opera cream, Fawn makes an opera cream egg, an opera cream cross and an opera cream fudge. Fawn's most popular candies are its chewy sea salt caramels and opera creams. The traditional turtles are a popular candy for Valentine's Day.

Another unique product Fawn makes is the Savannah Cream, a buttercream candy, which used to be called the Suzanne's Creams. This "old Kentucky pull candy" is a super-rich buttercream that melts in your mouth. The delicate texture and buttery-vanilla flavor make the Savannah Cream a favorite. Paul Guenther bought the recipe from Nick Sullivan, who owned Suzanne's Candy Kitchen in Fort Mitchell, Kentucky. Sullivan had named the treat after his daughter, Suzanne. After the Guenthers integrated it into their line, they decided to name it after Savannah, one of Paul's granddaughters.

Fawn works with local companies to produce specialty chocolates for customer gifts. It produces chocolate logos and business cards that local plumbing businesses and others use to give to clients at the holidays. One of its largest customers of this specialty service is HillRom in Indiana, for whom it makes a chocolate casket the size of a small candy bar, probably one of the most unique of all Cincinnati chocolate confections.

Fawn Confectionery continues to make perhaps Cincinnati's most extensive line of handmade candies into the third generation. And Cincinnatians depend on its scrumptious legacy candies for their Easter baskets, Christmas stockings and Valentine's Day gift boxes.

Chocolates Latour

For Shalini Latour, owner of Chocolates Latour, chocolate making is in her blood. She had been a pastry chef for twenty years, making wedding cakes and working in New York and Cincinnati. Her mother is Belgian, from the region of the world's most renowned chocolates. So, growing up, she had years of experience tasting the Belgian chocolates her mother's family would send them at Christmas. About four years ago, she started playing with making her own chocolates.

Latour prides her products in being fair trade, made with locally sourced ingredients and in sustainable packaging. All the herbs she uses either come from her own garden or from local Carriage House Farm or Wind Dance Farm. The cream she uses is sourced from Snowville Creamery. She is open minded to suggestions from all the local sources she uses for other ingredients like fruits and nuts for new and interesting flavors.

Her hand-painted truffles and caramels are true pieces of art. In addition to these delicacies, Latour also makes nut brittle, turtles and a variety of uniquely flavored chocolate bars, like the Bollywood, a bar with coconut, curry, turmeric, golden raisins and mango.

In November 2016, Chocolates Latour moved out of a home kitchen in the Northside neighborhood to the Chocolate Bee, also in Northside, sharing the space with Sam of Bee Haven Honey. Now out of her home kitchen, Latour can expand out of the state of Ohio and has already to West Virginia and several other states. Locally, her products can be found at Findlay Market, many local coffee shops, bookshops and specialty stores.

Maverick Chocolate Company

Ohio's first bean-to-bar chocolate company is Maverick Chocolates, started in 2014 by Paul and Marlene Picton, who were aided by their sons, Benjamin and Scott. There are only about eighty bean-to-bar chocolate companies currently in the United States. Paul is an engineer, and Marlene is a seasoned chocolate connoisseur. When Paul would travel for work in his life as an engineer, he'd bring back chocolate from the various countries where he traveled. When the job ended in 2013, and their supply of good chocolate was gone, they started experimenting on their own.

After a visit to Askinosie Chocolate in Springfield, Missouri, they enrolled in Ecole Chocolat's Bean-to-Bar chocolate making course. They purchased

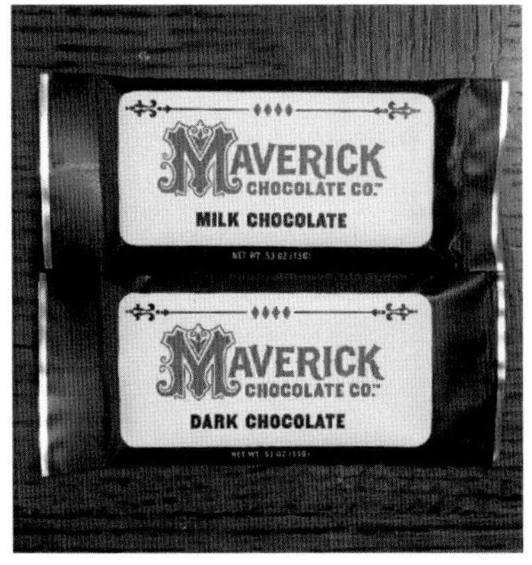

A pair of Maverick bean-to-bar chocolate bars. *Author's collection.*

used equipment from Potomac Chocolate in Washington, D.C., ordered beans online and went to work, signing a lease on a store in Findlay Market in December 2013.

The image on each packaged Maverick chocolate bar features some type of early flying machine, a nod to Paul's aviation engineering background. It also explains the company's business mentality. All those early experimenters of flight were mavericks—pushing the limit, and the envelope, trying new things and being bold. That's how the Pictons approach making chocolate.

Bean-to-bar is a recent chocolate trend and means the retailer actually makes his or her own chocolate directly from the cocoa bean. Most confectioners will buy chocolate already processed in chip or block form and just melt and mold it into their products. In Maverick's factory, beans are roasted and hulled and the cocoa nibs removed from the hull. Rather than being discarded, the hulls are sent to local brewers like Rivertown and Braxton Brewery, which use them to make a beer. Rivertown makes one called Captain Maverick's Flyer. The nibs are stone-ground for days until they are liquefied, and sugar and other ingredients are added. It's then sent through a tempering machine to make sure it's stable at room temperature. Once tempered, it can then be poured into molds and aged at least a month so that acidic volatiles are released. Then the chocolate is packaged for consumption.

In addition to breweries, Maverick has also partnered with local Macaroon Bar in Over-the-Rhine, which uses its spicy Fahrenheit 513 chocolate for a Valentine's Day special macaroon.

Maverick produces about eight tons of chocolate per year from its Findlay Market location. Each ton yields about fifteen thousand bars of chocolate.

Its factory retail store is on Elder Street at Findlay Market and carries a full line of chocolate bars, drinks and truffles. Cheery associates will let you taste small chips of each of their chocolates in the store. And you will learn the true taste nuances between a chocolate made from a bean from Belize versus a bean from the Dominican Republic. The product is currently retailed in ten states, including California.

Graeter's Confections

Graeter's is most known for its ice cream, but it has been making handcrafted confections for more than one hundred years. In 1868, a young Louis Charles Graeter, oldest son of Louis Carl, came to Cincinnati from Germany and founded the company two years later in 1870. Their French Pot ice creams are famous for large chips of Graeter's signature bittersweet chocolate. According to family legend, it was a young Wilmer Graeter, son of the founder, who stole chocolate from his mother and poured it into a pot of ice cream, inventing the now famous chocolate chunks. It's this process of pouring liquid bittersweet chocolate into the ice cream that makes them a bit like snowflakes—no two are exactly alike or the same size. These dispersed chips make eating a bowl of Graeter's ice cream like mining for a chocolate treasure.

Graeter's Black Raspberry Chip is one of its signature and most popular ice creams. It's so popular a flavor that it partnered with a local Northern Kentucky's Braxton Brewery to create the Black Raspberry Chip Milk Stout, which received rave reviews in the beer world.

In the mid-1800s, the Graeter family emigrated from Baden, Germany, to Madison, Indiana, where the patriarch, Louis, was a barber. Louis Carl Graeter left home in about 1870 as an early teenager and came to Cincinnati, where he began making ice cream by hand at the base of Sycamore Hill. After meeting with success there, he moved up to Walnut Hills, where he began making candy in addition to ice cream at his new shop on the corner of Gilbert and Curtis. In 1879, Louis, along with his brother, Fred, and Fred's wife, Anna Hubert, moved their growing ice cream and confection shop to 473 McMillan Street. They operated the business together until 1888, when Louis left Cincinnati for California.

Fred and Anna moved the shop in 1889 to Vine Street and continued the ice cream and confection business without brother Louis for the rest of the 1800s. In 1896, due to an illness, Fred had to close his business. He gave preference to his brother for the purchase of the business, which Louis did and returned to Cincinnati, leaving a wife and son in California.

In 1899, Louis returned to Cincinnati and the next year married Regina Berger, more than twenty years his junior and daughter of Anton Berger, who was president of the Julius J. Bantlin Company and the Calhoun Loan and Building Company. Together they opened a store at 967 East McMillan Street in Walnut Hills that eventually grew into the modern-day Graeter's. The two made ice cream and confections in the back room,

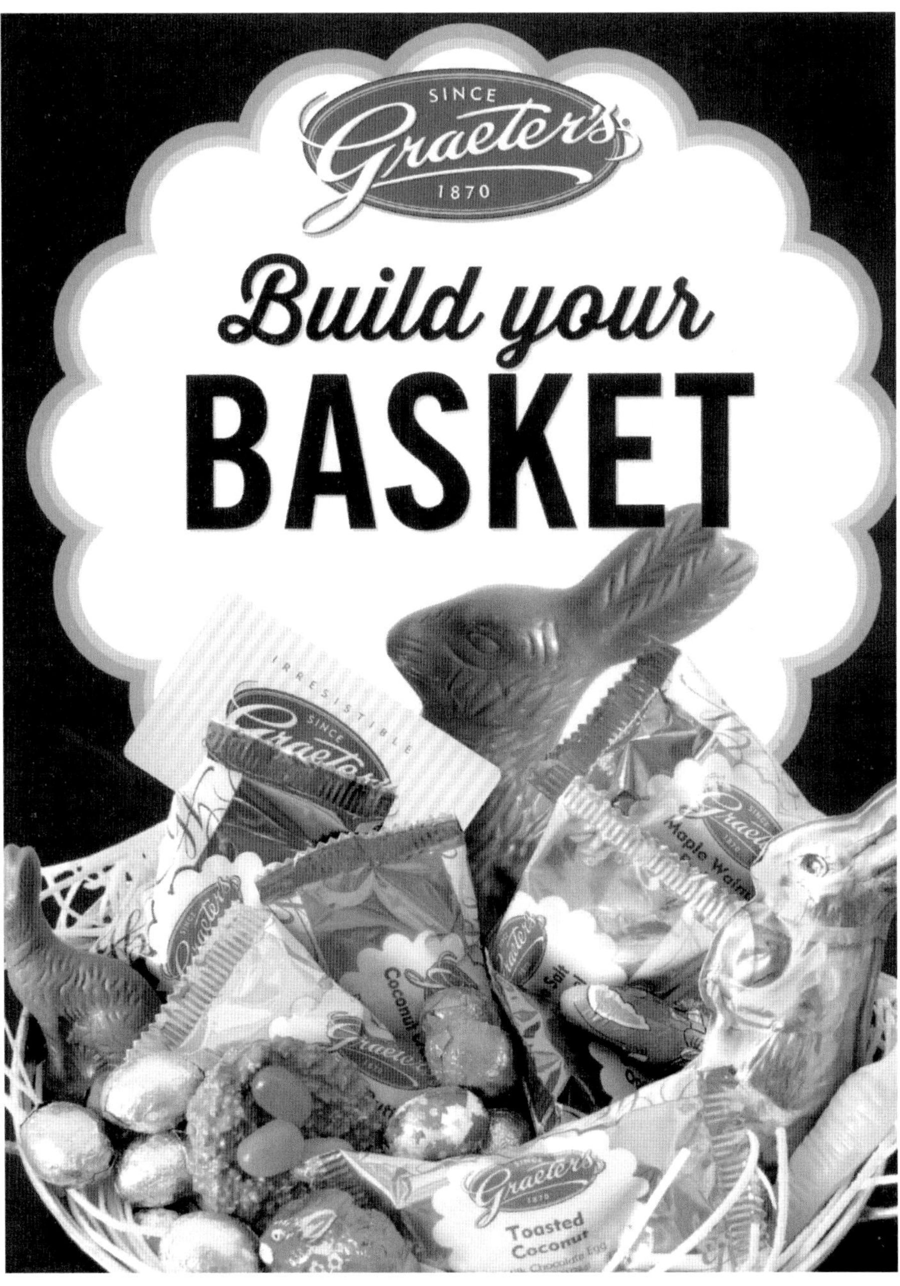

A Graeter's "Build your Basket" Easter candy ad. *Graeter's Corporation.*

sold them in the front room and lived in the apartment upstairs. They also opened a second store at 351 Vine Street, where they operated a confectionery and oyster parlor, making efficient use of the ice needed to refrigerate their ice cream.

The family made and oversaw their candy operations for many years. In about 2001, they hired Steve Hellmich as their chief confectioner to oversee candy production and product development at the Bond Hill Plant on Reading Road. He supervises the enrobing room, where confections receive their chocolate coatings under a waterfall of melted chocolate. In addition to keeping up to standards of consistency and quality, he also looks at variation on existing products, like a new Bavarian mint truffle.

A trained chef, food educator and candy maker, Steve Hellmich is known to most as Graeter's "Candyman." Steve is passionate about the culinary arts and enjoys sharing his knowledge of the properties of making confections. Prior to working at Graeter's, Steve was the executive chef and food service director at the Cincinnati Branch of the Federal Reserve Bank and is a graduate of the New England Culinary Institute.

At Easter, Graeter's advertises the ability to "Build Your Basket," supplying everything needed to create an amazing Easter basket. It can supply everything from chocolate bunnies to chocolate cream–filled eggs, jelly beans and even edible grass. Graeter's makes its own opera cream in milk, dark and white chocolate. It even makes the rare opera cream cross at Easter, each decorated with a colored lily in the center. For Easter, Graeter's also creates a variety of cream and fruit cream eggs.

One of its favorite signature confections at Easter is the Coconut Nest. The story of this confection goes back to pre-Christian times, when nests were used as signs of fertility and new life in spring rituals. Christians used the same familiar pagan symbols but repurposed them to remember the Resurrection and rebirth. To make these delectable treats, Graeter's uses a special blend of rice and toasted coconut and stirs in gourmet white or milk chocolate. It's then hand-scooped in palm-sized portions onto parchment paper with an ice cream scooper and flattened. Once the chocolate is set, they make a small dimple in the center that holds three jelly beans, representing the unborn eggs and new life.

The business today is run by fourth-generation Bob, Chip and Richard Graeter.

Witt's End Candy Emporium, Bellevue, Kentucky

Glass jars of chocolate and nut candies greet you behind the counter when walking into Witt's End Candy Emporium in Bellevue, Kentucky. Second-career owner Jack Witt chose an 1875 historic building in the Fairfield Avenue historic district for his old-fashioned candy shop. He opened on Memorial Day weekend of 2014. A bold move, as the decades-old Schneider's Sweet Shop is only a few blocks away.

But unlike Schneider's, which focuses on house-made chocolates and ice cream, Witt carries candy that will take any adult back to his or her childhood days. Wooden barrels of loose candy occupy the center of the store, waiting to be hand-bagged and weighed. Among the candies in this aisle are five flavors of Goetz bullseyes—the caramel chew wrapped around a cream center. A favorite of many is the black licorice bullseye or the rare green apple variety.

Witt also has Gold Medal brand popcorn and cotton candy machines, which he uses to make treats for children's parties and other events. He has a community meeting room in the back and a wedding area where brides can pick candies to fill candy bars at wedding receptions.

In all, Witt's carries more than three hundred varieties of candies to entice the adults and enough variety to make bug eyes in the kids. The oldest candy it has are wintergreen mints, but Witt's carries other old-time favorites like Bit-o-Honeys, Chick-O-Sticks, French Chews, Mary Janes and Squirrel Nut Zippers.

Jenco Brothers

Another recent candy store is Jenco Brothers, opened in February 2013 at 224 West McMillan Street in Clifton, near the University of Cincinnati campus. Brothers Chris and Joey Jenco made it a point growing up to visit any and every candy store that was near where their family vacationed. For the design of their store, they used these early years of market research to integrate all the aspects of each store they liked the most.

The store features more than four hundred different varieties of candies, from Sour Patch Kids to chocolate-covered peanuts. It also plays on the local favorites, like with its line of Grippo's seasoned popcorn, which has a very loyal following, especially the Grippo's BBQ Cheddar Popcorn. It also has a peppermint cookies and cream popcorn for the holidays. In addition to candy, it serves Graeter's Ice Cream and locally invented Slush Puppies.

Chamoda's Candy Café

Chamoda's is a candy store inspired by the life of a University of Cincinnati football player, Chamoda Kennedy-Palmore. Kennedy-Palmore was killed in 2014 in a motorcycle accident, but his dad wanted his winning spirit to be remembered. His father, Chamoda Palmore, started the business in 2015 in Sharonville at 11512 Chester Road with the moniker "The Greatest Candy in the World." The store is painted red, white and black in honor of the colors of Chamoda's Lakota and UC alma maters.

With a large selection of homemade gummy bears—seventeen flavors—the store carries on the tradition of Chamoda's favorite candy. It also sells a variety of handmade chocolates like cherry truffles, pretzel balls, coconut haystacks and toffee/almond bars. A portion of the sales from Chamoda's goes to the scholarship at UC in Chamoda's name.

OTR Candy Bar

A new urban confectionery opened in April 2015 at 1735 Elm Street near Findlay Market across from Maverick Chocolates. You might call it Findlay Market's new Candy Corridor.

The business is owned by family friends Pat Muck and his father, Jim Muck; Stephanie Recht; and Mike Petzelt. They are all very German-sounding names that could have been in Over-the-Rhine (OTR) more than 150 years ago. The store has a very sleek, modern feel, painted white with teal, with a candy-themed mural by local artist Alex Frank.

In addition to offering a large selection of local and national candies, fifty flavors of retro sodas, floats and gift baskets, the store offers birthday and event candy bar event services. A sleek bar with bottle cap–seat stools invites customers to sit, relax and have a drink and a sweet. And a fabulously dressed soda jerk will make you a float from your choice of sodas, garnished with a piece of old-fashioned stick candy.

The candy bar aims to have small-batch candies from around the country, like pecan fiddlesticks from Tennessee or Shurm's caramel apple candies from Michigan. And of course it sells Doscher's French Chew, made just around the way on Court Street.

SELECTED BIBLIOGRAPHY

Chapter 1

Broechel, Ray. "Land of the Candy Bar." *American Heritage* 37, no. 6 (October–November 1986).

Cincinnati Enquirer. March 19, 1903, 21.

———. March 12, 1900, 5.

Cincinnati Gazette. December 21, 1868, 1.

Cist, Charles. *The Cincinnati Miscellany, or, Antiquities of the West, and Pioneer History and General and Local Statistics/Compiled from the* Western General Advertiser. Cincinnati, OH: C. Clark, 1845.

Leonard, Lewis Alexander. *Greater Cincinnati and Its People*. New York: Lewis Historical Publishing Company, 1927.

Richardson, Anna Martin. *Homemade Candies and Other Good Things Sweet and Sour.* Cincinnati, OH: Robert Clarke & Company, 1890.

Solis-Cohen, Lita. "Savvy Buyers Snap up Rare Photographs." *Baltimore Sun*, May 31, 1992.

Chapter 2

Candy & Ice Cream 26 (1914).

Chicago Tribune. "Candy Trust Being Formed." March 29, 1899, 1.

Cincinnati Enquirer. April 9, 1940, 1.

———. August 16, 1967.

———. "Candy Trust." September 11, 1902, 5.
———. February 23, 1884, 8.
———. June 2, 1890, 1.
———. March 21, 1903, 5.
———. "Pioneer in Candy Manufacture." November 9, 1914, 12.
Confectioners Journal. February 1890.
——— 48 (December 1922): 53.
——— (1965).
Congressional Addition, vol. 5549, 60th Congress, Second Session. Tariff hearings, document no. 1505, 1908–9.
Der Deutsche Pioneer, vol. 11. January 1876.
Dunn, Jacob Piatt. *Indiana and Indianans* 5 (1919): 2,137.
Frank Leslie's Illustrated Newspaper. October 27, 1888.
International Confectioners 30 (1921).
——— 23 (March 1914): 9.
Kenny, D.J. *Illustrated Cincinnati: A Pictorial Handbook of the Queen City*. Cincinnati, OH: Robert Clarke & Company, 1975, 194.
Leading Manufacturers and Merchants of Cincinnati. Cincinnati, OH: International Publishing Company, 1886, 247.
Marquis, Albert N. *The Industries of Cincinnati*. Cincinnati, OH: A.N. Marquis & Company, 1883.
National Register of Historic Place NPS Form 10-900. "National Candy Company Factory," 7.
Notices of Judgment Under the Food and Drugs Act, issue 2501, part 2750. United States Department of Agriculture, 1913.
Report of the General Committee of the Cincinnati Industrial Exposition Held in Cincinnati September 21 to October 22, 1870. Cincinnati, OH: Published by the General Committee, 1870.
Scobey, F.E., and B.L. McElroy. *The Biographical Annals of Ohio, A Handbook of the Government and Institutions of the State of Ohio*. Springfield, OH: Springfield Publishing Company, State Printers, 1902, 1905.
Selbert v. Lancaster Chocolate and Caramel Co. No 4818. Circuit Court of Appeals, Sixth Circuit, January 8, 1928.
Townsend, Charles Berry. *The World's Biggest Puzzle Book*. New York: Sterling Publishing Company, 2002, 192.

Chapter 3

Cincinnati Enquirer. May 26, 1915, 1.

Confectioners Journal. "History of the NCA" (June 24, 1958): 19–31.

——— (1958).

Internal Revenue Hearings. "Revenue Act of 1921, May 9–27, 1921." Washington Government Printing Office, Washington, D.C.

Chapter 4

A&J Doscher Company, invoice no. 1888. From collection of the family of Marilyn Doscher Johnson.

Cincinnati Enquirer. "A&J Doescher, Candy Manufacturers Make an Assignment." February 17, 1892, 4.

———. February 17, 1979, 39.

———. May 11, 1921.

———. May 4, 1913.

———. May 19, 1926, 9.

———. October 5, 1985, 16.

———. October 1, 1916, 36.

Doscher, Cindy. Interview with the author, April 8, 2017.

Doscher Company website. http://doscherscandies.com.

Doscher, Harry. Phone interview with the author, March 2017.

Hamilton Evening Journal. October 22, 1923, 6.

Johnson, Marilyn Doscher. Interview with the author, April 8, 2017.

Kingery Manufacturing Company. Brochure. Cincinnati, OH: self-published, 1901.

National Association of Retail Druggists Journal 26 (1918): 208.

Tagliches Cincinnati Volksblatt. January 8, 1915.

Chapter 5

Case, Ron. Interview with the author, January 29, 2017.

Cincinnati Enquirer. June 25, 1956.

Herfurt, Alice Ruzic, and Molly Herfurt Imhoff. Interview with the author, February 18, 2017.

Mullane Book of Mullane's Candies, Made with Loving Care in Cincinnati Since 1848. Cincinnati, OH: John Mullane Company, 1918.

Mullane, John. *Mullane's Recipe Book.* Provided by Alice Ruzic Herfurt.
Mullane's Company. Brochure. Made available by Ron Case.
Recollections of George Case. Made available by Ron Case.

Chapter 6

The American Pure Food and Health Journal 2 (1910): 17.
Cincinnati Enquirer. April 1, 1920, 5.
———. April 12, 1913, 5.
———. December 29, 1913, 7.
———. February 4, 1900, 20.
———. October 16, 1903, 4.
———. September 12, 1926.
Confectioners Journal 47 (1921): 132.
Goss, Charles Frederic. *Cincinnati: The Queen City*. Cincinnati, OH: S.J. Clarke Publishing Company, 1912.

Chapter 7

Bearden-White, Christina. "Gustav Goelitz." Immigrant Entrepreneurship. University of Southern Indiana, March 5, 2013, updated October 4, 2013. https://www.immigrantentrepreneurship.org/entry.php?rec=142.
Cincinnati Enquirer. June 7, 1944, 15.
———. September 1, 1918, 14.
Collins, William H. *Past and Present of the City of Quincy and Adams County, Illinois*. Chicago: S.J. Clarke Publishing Company, 1905, 728.
Confectioner and Bakers' Gazette 30 (1908).
Pittsburgh Press. November 17, 1901, 12.
Sanders-Perry, Jana, Jelly Belly Corporation. Phone interview with the author, February 2017.

Chapter 8

Bang, Christian, Sr. Oral history related to Hope Hilton on April 9, 1959, published on July 4, 2013, on ancestry.com.
Cincinnati Enquirer. August 14, 2014.

———. March 27, 2002.
———. May 25, 1976, 14.
Evening Bulletin. February 12, 1898, 2.
Industrial Refrigeration 63 (1922): 228.
Kentucky Post. April 19, 2000, 10K.
———. April 3, 1993, 7B.
———. January 7, 1992, 10K.
———. May 26, 1986, 8k.
———. May 23, 1984, 1B.
Martin, Chuck. *Cincinnati Enquirer*. "Opera Cream: Candy's Dandy Diva." February 9, 1997.
Tenkotte, Paul A., and James C. Claypool, eds. *Encyclopedia of Northern Kentucky*. Lexington: University of Kentucky Press, 2009.

Chapter 9

Candy & Ice Cream 26 (1914).
Cincinnati Enquirer. April 12, 1929, 1.
———. August 9, 1929, 13.
———. December 11, 1937.
Pictorial and Industrial Review of Northern Kentucky. Newport: Published by the Northern Kentucky Review, 1923.
Pittsburg Press. April 5 1920, 5.
United States Circuit Courts of Appeals Reports, with Key-Number, vol. 158. St. Paul, MN: West Publishing Company, 1918.

Chapter 10

International Confectioners Journal 25, no. 1 (January 27, 1916).

Chapter 11

Carl Anthony Online. carlanthonyonline.com.
———. "Old School Wing-Tipped Peeps in the Black and White Era." March 30, 2013. carlanthonyonline.com.
Cincinnati Enquirer. April 21, 1907, 2.

———. December 16, 1905, 5.

Circuit Court of Appeals. *Selbert v. Lancaster Chocolate Company*. 25 F. 2d 233, 6th Circuit, 1928.

Dowie, Alexander. *Leaves of Healing*. Chicago: Zion Publishing House, 1900, 1903, 1987.

Gettysburg Pennsylvania Times. February 17, 1920, 7.

Scranton Tribune. May 17, 1901, 1.

Chapter 12

Cincinnati Enquirer. December 19, 1977, 25.

———. July 6, 1911.

———. July 6, 1961, 11.

———. May 8, 1950, 8.

———. November 29, 1927.

———. "Real Estate and Building." October 12, 1917, 15.

———. September 27, 1972, 16.

Department Reports of the State of Ohio: Containing the Decisions. Vol. 12. Columbus, OH: Nemar Publishing Company, 1920, 373.

Droganes, Sam. Interview with the author, February 12, 2017.

Hamilton Journal-News. July 14, 1999.

Hansen Roger C. "Pioneers in Nonviolent Action: The Congress of Racial Equality in Cincinnati 1946–1955." *Queen City Heritage* (Fall 1994): 25.

Hover, John C., ed. *Memoirs of the Miami Valley.* Chicago: R.O. Law Company, 1919.

Norwood Historical Society Website. http://www.rootsweb.ancestry.com/~ohnhs2.

Purcell High School. "Graduating Class of 1942." *The Cavalier*, 1942.

Queen City History, July 27, 2012. http://www.queencityhistory.com/index.htm.

Chapter 13

Confectioners Journal 28 (1922).

Goss, Charles Frederic. *Cincinnati: The Queen City*. Cincinnati, OH: S.J. Clarke Publishing Company, 1912.

Schimpff, Warren. Interview with the author, February 5, 2017.

Chapter 14

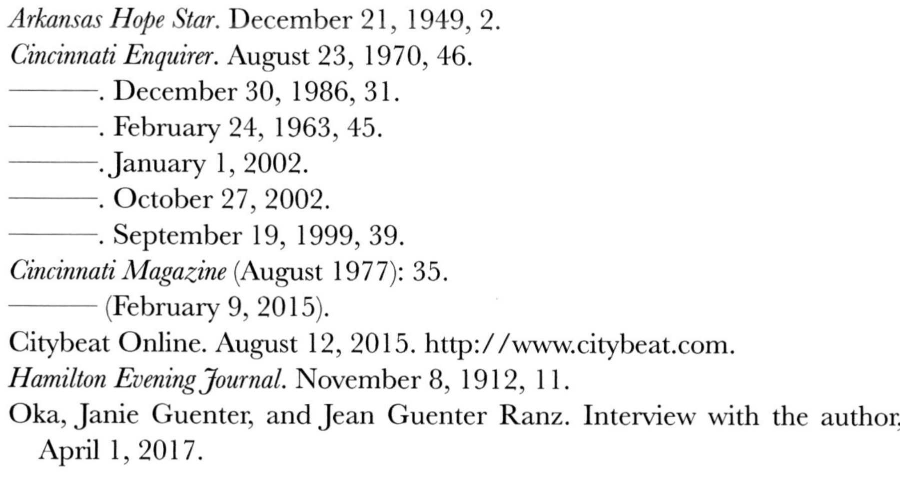

Arkansas Hope Star. December 21, 1949, 2.
Cincinnati Enquirer. August 23, 1970, 46.
———. December 30, 1986, 31.
———. February 24, 1963, 45.
———. January 1, 2002.
———. October 27, 2002.
———. September 19, 1999, 39.
Cincinnati Magazine (August 1977): 35.
——— (February 9, 2015).
Citybeat Online. August 12, 2015. http://www.citybeat.com.
Hamilton Evening Journal. November 8, 1912, 11.
Oka, Janie Guenter, and Jean Guenter Ranz. Interview with the author, April 1, 2017.

INDEX

F

G

H

J

K

L

M

N

O

P

R

S

T

W

Y

Z

ABOUT THE AUTHOR

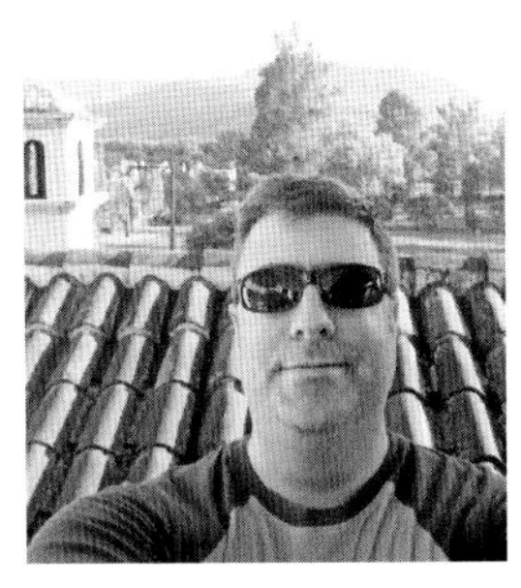

Dann Woellert has been in the product marketing world for more than a decade. The way to his heart is through Dutch black licorice and Green Tea Kit Kats. He writes the blog *Dann Woellert the Food Etymologist*, which discusses the origins of local and regional foods. Dann is affiliated with the Cincinnati Preservation Association, the German American Citizens League, the Over-the-Rhine Museum, the Brewery District and several local historical societies. He is a four-time recipient of the Ohioana Award for Literary and Artistic Achievement.

The author in Guatemala, the land of the Mayans and the birthplace of chocolate and chicle, used in gum manufacturing until the 1960s.